DRAWN TO SEA

Caitlin Press Inc.
8100 Alderwood Road
Halfmoon Bay, BC V0N 1Y1
www.caitlin-press.com

Edited by Barbara Pulling.
Text and cover design by Vici Johnstone.
Cover image copyright Yvonne Maximchuk.
Photo on page 10 by Debra Putman.
Printed in Canada

Caitlin Press Inc. acknowledges financial support from the Government of Canada through the Canada Book Fund and the Canada Council for the Arts, and from the Province of British Columbia through the British Columbia Arts Council and the Book Publisher's Tax Credit.

Library and Archives Canada Cataloguing in Publication

Maximchuk, Yvonne
Drawn to sea : paintbrush to chainsaw—carving out a life on BC's rugged Raincoast / Yvonne Maximchuk.

ISBN 978-1-927575-03-1

1. Maximchuk, Yvonne. 2. Frontier and pioneer life—British Columbia—Echo Bay. 3. Artists—British Columbia—Echo Bay—Biography. 4. Women fishers—British Columbia—Echo Bay—Biography. 5. Echo Bay (B.C.)—Biography. I. Title.

FC3849.E29Z49 2013   971.1'1   C2013-900597-8

DRAWN TO SEA

*Paintbrush to Chainsaw—Carving
Out a Life on BC's Rugged Raincoast*

YVONNE MAXIMCHUK

CAITLIN PRESS

This book is dedicated to my Hercules, my husband, Albert Munro, who helps to make my dreams come true and keeps me by his side by expediting my independence.

Contents

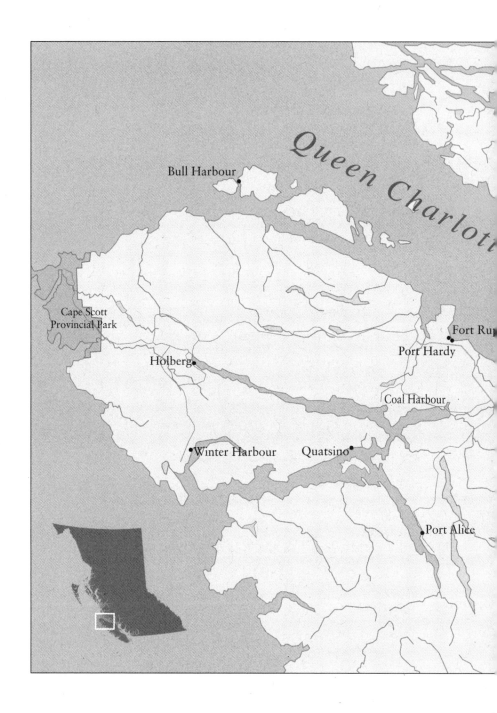

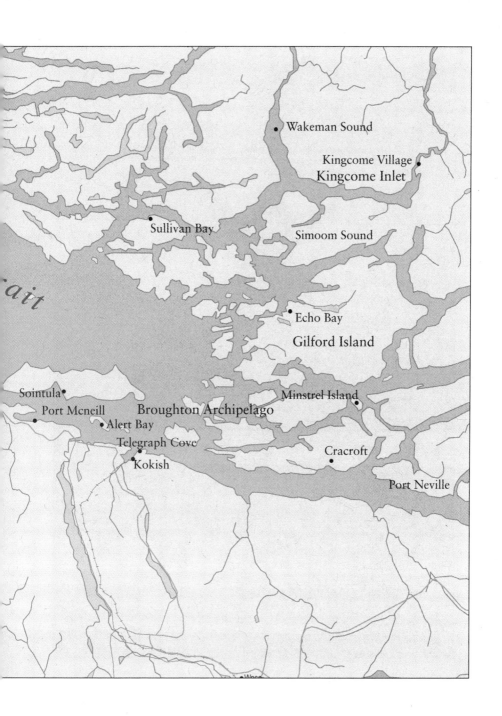

Wakeman Sound

Kingcome Village
Kingcome Inlet

Sullivan Bay

Simoom Sound

ait

Echo Bay

Gilford Island

Sointula
Port Mcneill

Minstrel Island

Broughton Archipelago

Alert Bay

Telegraph Cove

Cracroft

Kokish

Port Neville

Introduction

by Bill Proctor

THE BEAUTY OF THE BC COAST is like a magnet that draws you back, time after time. Once anyone with an eye for beauty has taken a trip along the BC coast, they are almost certain to want to return. So it was with Yvonne Maximchuk: once she had made a trip or two up the coast to visit her boyfriend, she was hooked. She wanted to see more, and explore some of the hidden wonders of this beautiful part of the world.

Being an artist makes it all the more interesting for her. Yvonne left the comforts of city life to make her home in the small community of Echo Bay. When one decides to make a home in such an out-of-the-way place, you have to wonder why.

It is a hard life that can sometimes be rather harsh, but when you open your door in the morning and smell the fresh, clean air and see the beauty all around you, you tend to forget the hardships. One morning you will see whales or dolphins playing, a raven looking for a handout, and a bald eagle searching for its breakfast. There is always something interesting to see if you are observant and take the time to look. Yvonne is such a person—always observing and eager to learn more about her surroundings—and this shows up in her artwork.

Yvonne married her boyfriend, Albert, and the two carved out a place with a nice big home and garden. From their deck, they can watch the sunrise turn the mountain pink and in the evening, enjoy the glorious

sunsets. They can listen to the wolves baying in the moonlight and watch the many seabird species engaging in their courtship antics. And from this magnificent setting, Yvonne creates her beautiful images of the surrounding islands and channels of the area.

Prologue

THIS STORY RELATING TO A CAVE near my home on Gilford Island, BC, was told to me by Ernie Scow Senior. It belongs to Ernie's people and is offered here with his kind permission. I met Ernie Senior through my friends Margaret Wilson and Ernie Scow Junior. Ernie Jr. brought Ernie Sr. by to visit while they were on a clam-digging trip in the Gilford Island area. The cave can be accessed by a short, steep climb from a rowboat tied to the shoreline rocks. I've always been interested in hearing the stories about this cave and asked Ernie Sr. what he might tell me. His story of the Animal Kingdom is centred on this cave.

"When the People used caves, they lived at Kumlah Island in Thompson Sound. One time a young man got ulcers all over his body. The People gave up trying to heal him and decided to leave him to die. They left him a canoe and went away. One day the young man saw a whale coming. The whale blow, what comes out of the back of the whale's head, was the colour of the rainbow, and some of it landed on the beach. The young man picked up some of that stuff and rubbed it all over his body. Within a few days the ulcers disappeared, so he took off in the canoe to find his people. He found them in Shoal Harbour.

"While the People were living here, another young man took off and went hunting in the woods and never returned. They got together all the people that were able to go look for the young man. After many

days searching, they decided they needed help. They asked all the people around to help search, but they could not find the young man. When they finally gave up the search, the sister of the young man decided she was going to look for her brother. She was drawn to a certain place when she heard the singing. She tried to see the ceremony. She tried again and again. She tried four times—everything was done four times, it was the custom—to see the ceremony. A Mouse came to her. The Mouse befriended the woman. He told her that the Master of the Ceremony, the Wolf, gave permission for the woman to watch the ceremony.

"Later on the young man was seen in different places. He was hairy. He may have been looking for something to eat. He became Bukwus, the Wild Man of the Woods.

"So now, the name of this that came from the cave, the tribal legend, was the Animal Kingdom. This name belongs to the Kwakwaka'wakw tribe, not one person. A similar story, 'The People of the Woods' story, came from Rivers Inlet."

This is my home now, the place marked "Receptacle of Supernatural Power" on old maps that include traditional First Nations place names. I feel this power in every breath I take and every drop of rain that cools my skin, in the cedar trees that sway in the sighing breeze and in the croaking talk of the ravens as they search for food. I draw on the power to guide me in my journey, to keep me heartfelt in my art, honest and kind in my dealings with others, to give me courage to stand up for those weaker than I am and to be true to my own being. I trust the power to provide the clean water that runs down the hill, the sun that warms the soil and coaxes out the blooms of flowers, the sea that births the fish whose flesh I honour and consume.

I offer my gratitude and the service of my being to the supernatural power. It is all I have.

The Call of the Wilderness

*What moves you, O man, to leave your shelters in
the city, to leave relatives and friends, and go into
the open country, up mountains and down valleys,
if not the natural beauty of the world?*

—Leonardo da Vinci *Advice to Artists*

As far back as I can remember I've loved the natural world, loved
rain on my face and wind in my hair, warm soil under my bare toes. I
was four years old when my parents moved our family of five from my
mountain birthplace, the gold mining town of Bralorne, British Columbia, to a small shack on the prairie outside Calgary, Alberta. Prairie life
was dramatic; once my dad burst into the house in a hailstorm of mythic
proportions. My older sister, Lola, almost six, my three-year-old brother
Peter, and I rolled the giant hailstones around in awed amazement. Our
second brother, Frank, was born shortly after we settled in. My dad really needed a good paying job to provide for this family and he found
it in British Columbia, where he became an ironworker and helped construct many of the bridges that completed BC's growing highway system.
We moved to Vancouver where the fifth child, my third brother, Anthony,
was born.

Our house had a hedge of roses on the street side, under which I created fairy houses with sticks, shells and petals. We had a fort in the plum
tree in the large backyard where my father hung a tire from a sturdy
branch. I'd pretend I was in a boat in a storm-tossed sea as I swung high.
From our sheltered front porch, I watched thrilling thunder and lightning storms, snuggled securely by my father. One of my favourite things

to do was to lie on the grass in the sunshine, squint my eyes closed, and observe the brilliant shards of light that formed on my eyelashes. When I shifted my head, the rainbow colours shimmered in overlapping prismatic circles. One hot summer day as I lay in a city park with my face in a field of clover, I was astonished to see the clover, too, broke into bits of rainbow light. It was the same with a piece of grass, a daisy and a dandelion; they all metamorphosed into the magical prisms. I had my first epiphany: everything was made of the same stuff.

City parks gave me a taste of something alluring, but family camping trips around Clearwater, where my mother's family had homesteaded, and summer weeks at Gun Lake near Bralorne fanned a flame that burned through the long city winters. My spirit hungered for wild places, for secret brushy hideouts away from the bustle and frenetic activity of urban streets.

Reading, I discovered, was another pathway to wilderness. I devoured book after book. Ernest Thompson Seton's *Wild Animals I Have Known* opened my eyes to the idea that everything in this world had a place, significance and function, whether humans understand it or not. I drew constantly, studying leaves, ferns, flowers and other natural elements. I never thought about becoming an artist, it was simply who I was and what I did. When I was old enough to go to college, I studied graphic arts and illustration. It wasn't exactly what I wanted to do but I learned to get the creative flow focussed and how to meet a deadline. When I got a job as an assistant animator at Canawest Film Productions in Vancouver, I was beyond thrilled. I loved to draw, and to be paid for it was heaven.

Already though, I was being drawn to the sea. I met my first husband, Byron, through a mutual friend. I fell hard in love with him and his beach-bronzed skin. Using only an axe, Byron had built a small log cabin from driftwood just off the open beach on the west coast of Vancouver Island, in under the wind-beaten spruce trees at Half Moon Bay. He'd lived there for six months until a government helicopter cruised low across the beach and a man inside the chopper pointed his finger right at Byron's cabin. Pacific Rim Park was born and Byron's time at the edge of the sea was over. We married, and with daughter, Theda, on the way, we joined the back-to-the-land movement in 1975, emulating the pioneer lifestyle with a group of others on a rugged property near Golden, BC. Two years later a second child, Logan, blessed our union. I was heart-broken when our marriage collapsed; I had not foreseen myself as an unpartnered parent with the responsibility for two vulnerable children.

I moved with Theda and Logan to the seaside town of White Rock, near my parents, and became a single mom. After a lot of soul-searching, I put everything I had into becoming a working artist. Through sales of my paintings and my pottery, a job in a framing/art supplies store, and another job teaching watercolour painting, I made a living from my art. I wasn't rolling in money but had enormous job satisfaction. There was enough to keep the three of us healthy and housed. We made a few good friends who lived on boats and we all loved the times we spent on the water.

Shortly after our move to White Rock in 1977, I met a friend of Byron's, a man named Albert Munro, who had long, red-gold hair and a dog named Wolfy. He was a mechanic, which was helpful when I had car troubles. We struck up a friendship in 1978. By then he'd bought a boat and taken up crab fishing, working out of Boundary Bay. He invited me to go fishing with him, and one Sunday I was able to. As we motored away from the dock, the bright sun bleached away all my troubles and the sea wind caressed my cheeks—perfect conditions for a new love to take root and sprout.

Over the next seven years, Albert fished new territory farther up the coast. He offered "no strings attached" voyages to sea with him whenever my children were with their father. I'd take my paints and head off to whichever harbour he'd arrived at in his travels. My first fishing trip was in Boundary Bay; a couple of years later he moved to the gorgeous Gulf Islands. He quit crab fishing and bought prawn traps, worked his way up the coastal passageways to Comox, through Seymour Narrows north and west to the Broughton Archipelago and Echo Bay area, and finally, beyond Cape Caution to the glacier-milk waters of Rivers Inlet. I loved all these beautiful, seagoing voyages and learned the ways of the boat and of the man who skippered it. When necessity demanded he come to the city, he'd stay with us in White Rock, always an occasion of great excitement for the kids and me—and our

Theda learning to fish.

friends, too, since invariably he would bring binsful of prawns for us to feast on. Although intermittent, his presence became a constant in our lives.

On a dismal February day in 1984, Albert phoned me from his boat in Turnbull Cove through radio-telephone and shocked me with his invitation, "Why don't you bring the kids out for the Easter holiday?"

"To the boat?" I said. Was he kidding? "You want me to bring *my* kids to *your* boat for a whole *week*? Are you sure?"

"Of course I'm sure. They'll have a great time," said Al. So on Good Friday the kids and I took a float plane ride to meet up with Al in Turnbull Cove. This wonderful week was a turning point in the long years of our relationship. Friction was minimal. Theda and Logan were comfortable in and excited by the boating life. We hung out with Al's fishing buddies, Chris McReady and Sharon Rogers and their son, Matt. They lived on a float house, a renovated double wide trailer perched on a raft of logs, in Turnbull Cove. The kids loved it when we let them row around in the dinghy with a seventy-foot line attached to the big boat, and one day we went to Craig and Deborah Murray's Nimmo Bay Easter party. It seemed possible we could blend into a family and a community. Albert wanted to show us where we could live, so we motored down Sutlej Channel to Echo Bay to fuel up the boat and meet some of the local people at Echo Bay Resort.

Up the long red government dock at the head of the bay, and across a park surrounded by forest, the one-room schoolhouse awaited its new students-to-be. A school in the middle of this maze of islands was a miracle to me, the single definitive factor that tipped the scales from "I might have to wait a while" to a definite "yes." Al thought the prawns were plentiful enough that he would not have to move in search of them and told me of the art galleries in Sointula and on Vancouver Island he was sure would want to sell my paintings. Like Chris and Sharon, we could live on a float house and boat around.

Once we got home, Theda, Logan, and I agreed we wanted to move to Echo Bay with my "holiday man," my fisherman, my love, Albert. It sounded like a good plan, if not quite real.

It took us two years to prepare to move and one way we did it was by playing with the kid's toys. We constructed float houses and toy boats with Lego blocks and used the Play People to act out activities we imagined we might do. After the kids went to bed, I played out imaginary scenarios of my own, trying to anticipate how my life would change. While I felt confident in the strength of my relationship with Albert—it had already been seven years, after all—periodic boating trips were a completely different proposition from full-time life in the coastal wilderness. Accustomed to total independence, I hadn't needed nor wanted to rely on anyone since my marriage ended. But the call of the

Theda and Logan took to the water like they were born for it.

Chris McReady and Sharon Rogers' float house, tied by ours in Greenway Sound, was a renovated double wide trailer perched on a raft of logs.

wilderness adventure was stronger than any of my fears. I would just learn to get along.

In late September 1986, Albert launched his newly completed gas-powered prawn fishing boat, *John*, at the Crescent Beach marina, and a few days later we loaded it up with my belongings. He departed with my brother Pete as crew for the long run up to Echo Bay. After my farewell in-home art show, I put most of my furniture in a storage locker. On October 3, I drove a rented truck full of boxes to Port McNeill. Albert and Pete met us there and the next day, a damp, grey but windless day, we loaded everything onto *John* and made the twenty-eight-mile run east across Queen Charlotte Strait to Echo Bay on Gilford Island.

A coastal fashion statement. Photo Peter Max.

Northwesterly Nightmare

Nor shall the sea belong to such faint hearts as scare
themselves, lest anything go wrong.

—Tanakawa Shuntaro

AND NOW IT'S REAL—WE'RE HERE. We rent a float house from Bobby
Halliday for three hundred dollars a month, but we need a place to tie
it to the shore. Al's friend John Brauer and his wife, Francine, and their
two pre-school-age children, Julie and Jason, live on a float house near
Echo Bay. John invites us to tie up beside them while we settle in. Al and
John set up a standing boom of logs to tie our house to and keep it away
from the shore as the tide rises and falls. Just north of Echo Bay, behind
a little point of land, the tie-up site is shadowed by a hill that blocks the
low autumn sun. But there's a good supply of water, enough for two
families. We're close enough to row to the Echo Bay Elementary School
and the store, fuel dock, and post office. We feel safe here, and right away
the kids like the one-room school with its playground encircled by forest.

A week or two after our arrival, I am kneading bread dough when
I hear a speedboat roar up to our dock. With floury hands I go out to
the front deck to greet my visitor. In a blue speedboat with a broken
windshield sits a grizzled-looking man in a dirty knitted toque. A day's
growth of whiskers covers his cheeks and thick-fingered, capable hands
grasp the steering wheel. In the bottom of the boat lies an axe, an odd-
looking hammer with backwards raised numbers, and a pile of coiled

ropes. Never once looking anywhere except at the dock in front of him, he introduces himself as Bill Proctor, says he lives around the corner with his wife, Yvonne, and daughter, Patty, and he'd like us to come along to his Hallowe'en party. When he starts to tell me about the community's salmon enhancement project in nearby Scott Cove, he becomes more animated. For the first time I see his eyes, bright with emotion.

"From September all the way to December sometimes, we've got coho running up the creeks to lay their eggs. Anytime you want to come over and see or help, just let me know. I'll pick you up."

"What do you do?" I ask.

"Well, we gotta get some of the coho into the tanks in the hatchery so we can take the eggs and look after them until they hatch, then plant the fry in the streams."

"Oh. Sounds complicated."

He laughs. "Not really," he says. "We're just trying to give nature a

Billy Proctor, a high-liner fisherman and dogged advocate of BC's wild salmon. Photo Deborah Putman.

hand repairing the damage that's been done." Clearly, salmon are a big deal around here and something my new neighbour cares about deeply.

The day after I meet Bill Proctor, a boatload of Native fishermen from Gwayasdums, Gilford Village, show up in a big old seine boat. The First Nations children from the village down Cramer Pass attend the school, and my children have already made friends with them. I hope to do the same with their parents since the school seems to be the place where the Native and non-native communities intersect. A dozen chum salmon are thrown off the boat onto our deck and John's.

Too much salmon! I'm overwhelmed with this unexpected bounty. Although I have lots of experience canning, I'm not ready for this. John and Albert solve the immediate problem by hammering together a second smoker to supplement the one John already has. They take turns keeping it going all night, feeding it with small sticks of green alder. Francine and I can like crazy. She introduces me to Yvonne Proctor, confident that she will lend us canning jars. Yvonne is abrupt, but not unfriendly. She hauls

Our new neighbour, Bill Proctor, dogging a log.

out boxes of half-pint and pint-size canning jars, and nods when we promise to replace them on the next shopping trip. She'll believe it when she sees it. She has done her canning already, jars of the sockeye Billy has brought home from his fishing trips. I have yet to appreciate the difference between sockeye and chum, only learning later that chum salmon's special gift is in the rich oily flavour resulting from the smoking process.

The pace of life in our first month rolls on briskly. I still have not got our little house arranged, nor have I had a moment to get painting. I like the row back and forth to the Echo Bay school dock each morning and afternoon. A feather falls from an eagle flying overhead one day, lands on the water nearby, and I sweep it up in a rush. A good omen. Every day is fraught with some new challenge, large or small, and, in equal measure, every day brings a great or small new joy. The Broughton Archipelago has lots in store for us, including a little lesson about the northwest wind.

One afternoon in late October, I row the little yellow dinghy to the school dock as usual to pick up my kids. Beating our way back home against the nasty slop is hard work. Intermittent and unpredictable gusts of wind push the boat around, like adolescent boys who don't know their own strength.

"Boy, that was freaky," I say to the kids after securing the boat and unloading their gear. "I wasn't sure we were gonna make it home in one piece."

"Too windy to fish," Albert says, coming in right behind us. "I'd've come looking for you."

After dinner and reading time, the kids finally in their beds, I run myself a bath. The cedar-stained water looks like tea sloshing around in the tub. I regard it dubiously but set a kerosene lamp on a chair by the tub and climb in with my book, determined to have a relaxing soak. The house is rocking up and down and the bathtub swells grow violent, sloshing from one end of the tub to the other. Eventually, feeling a little seasick, I give up trying to read just as Albert bursts into the bathroom.

"John's float's in trouble. Quick, I need the flashlight." Galvanized by his urgency, I leap out of the tub and find the flashlight, throw my clothes on, and then peek out the front door as he leaves.

In shocked silence I see flying white foam breaking off the tops of one black roll of water after another as the waves charge over the front deck of our new neighbours' home. Our float is simply rocking up and down from front to back. Brauer's float logs are oriented side on to the incoming waves, and with each rolling swell they heave up and plunge down again one after the other. The undulation is putting so much strain on the cables lashing the logs together that in some places they're tearing apart. Out on the treacherous deck of logs, I see two wildly bobbing flashlights as John and Al try to repair the damage. It's obvious they're going to die in this effort—slip down in between two logs and be squashed by the heaving mass of timber.

This is the end, I think. My bold new life is about to end in tragedy after less than a month. And what about Francine and her kids? I can't bear to watch, nor am I able to help. I go back in the house, shut the door, and move everything onto the floor that might fall there. What else can I do? I comfort my kids, who've gotten out of bed, doing my best to sound calm and confident.

"Albert will be fine. He's come through storms much worse than this," I reassure them, hugging them as much for my own comfort as theirs. After a terrifying two hours, with the wind screaming and the house bucking up and down, Al comes in the door, soaking wet and white with exhaustion. I make him a hot chocolate as he changes into dry clothes.

"We've done what we can," he tells me. "I think it will hold together for now, but we may have to move. John's float can't take any more of that."

"Our float faces the waves like this," he explains to the kids, waving his hand up and down from the wrist as if his fingers are pointing in to the swell. "Brauer's float is like this." He rocks his hand side to side as if the waves are coming against his thumb. "That's why their logs were going up and down and ours only made waves in your mom's bath."

"I don't like it," Theda says.

"Me neither," Al replies.

It isn't until the pale light of dawn glimmers in the east that the winds calm and we settle into a deep sleep.

The Rough and the Smooth

THE NEXT DAY WE'RE OFF TO HEAR what Bill, whom everyone calls Billy, Proctor can tell us about other tie-up sites. He says a good tie-up requires several specific conditions. The first is safety from the waves caused by the prevailing winds. The worst by far and least frequent of these winds is what we just experienced, a northwest blow. The more common winter wind comes out of the southeast with varying intensity. The summer wind is a warm, wet westerly, which can both carry mist and blow it all away. We need a cove or harbour that can provide protection from every direction all year round. Another essential requirement is a source of water, and this is not always easy to find. The shore must deepen quickly enough so the floats won't go dry at low tide, and if at all possible it's nice to have a sunny exposure. There are a lot of local bays that lie in the northern shadow of the tall trees cloaking the nearby slopes, but as we've already discovered, these shadowed bays can be depressing in the low light of winter. Extended darkness can cause odd or downright bizarre behaviour, turning a person "bush" or "bushed." After much discussion, the men agree that we'll move down Cramer Pass and attach ourselves to the shore at a little bay behind two islets in Blunden Pass. The bay there is deep enough, with shoreline enough for our two houses, and a chuckling creek emptying into the sea. It's protected from the prevailing winds by the islets, and it faces east. Perfect.

We spend the last day of October preparing for Bill and Yvonne's

Hallowe'en party. All day I feel a recurring sense of urgency, of things to do, preparations to make unrelated to the party. We're moving, again, and there must be something I need to do. The evening is great fun, though. It begins in Echo Bay, where Jack Scott arrives at the school dock in his big troller, *Soozee*. The costume-clad children climb onto Jack's boat with their empty candy bags. He motors to the Echo Bay store, then to the float houses just out of Echo Bay. Jack heads for the logging camp at Scott Cove, finally circling around to his own home in Shoal Harbour, and from there on to Bill and Yvonne's. When *Soozee* pulls up to our dock, Albert and I dispense Hallowe'en treats to the open pillow slips and bags, as do John and Francine, then we depart for the Proctors' place. We meet almost everyone who lives within twenty-five miles at the party and eat our fill of seafood and venison dishes. A bonfire roars in the field outside and we cheer, gasp, and applaud as fireworks bloom in the night sky.

I won't see a lot of these people again until Christmas time. The Proctors' "do" serves as a reliable annual event where community members can connect and restore social bonds worn thin from small frictions and magnified by isolation. I hear a lot of laughing as I stroll around the field in the dark. I am the third Yvonne in this community of thirty-six people. Yvonne and Jack Scott, the last of the old-time loggers, live in Shoal Harbour with their son, Alec, and Alec's wife, Josie, and sons, Billy and Byron. Yvonne Proctor, fine-boned with a cloud of white hair, presides over her pies. She calls the three Yvonnes, "the good, the bad and the ugly," but she won't say which is which. "One of us," she squints at me, "is ugly as homemade sin." I can only hope it's not me. There are three Bills, too, and two Glens, all at the Hallowe'en party.

The next morning Albert and John untie our floats and Jack Scott on *Soozee* tows us five miles down Cramer Pass to our new home site in Blunden Pass. A blissful move: no packing, no sorting, no cleaning. *This* is why I had nothing urgent to do yesterday. I sit on the deck with a glass of wine and watch the scenery roll by. A little breeze ruffles my hair as kingfishers chatter and dive for fish. I let go of anxiety and simply enjoy the passing scene. It's one long scroll painting and for the first time in a month the neglected painter in me sits up and takes notice.

Our new tie-up site is perfect, except for one thing. Echo Bay is five miles away, and I can't row the kids to school in the little yellow dinghy, or stop at the Echo Bay laundry building to throw in a wash on my way. Thanks to John and Francine, we have a place to tie up our float but being thrown into daily dependency on them is galling. I can't use up their resources, such as fuel to run the generator that powers their washing machine, but the alternative is to wash all our clothes by hand. Albert has to curtail his fishing hours to run Theda and Logan to school by nine and pick them up at three. Not only does this cost a lot in fuel; it reduces his income. I can never leave the float and go off by myself, because I *do not have a boat*. Albert and I argue a lot as we try to deal with the challenges of our new life together.

One grey December day as soapsud clouds scud across the sky, I row the little yellow dinghy out to the small island in front of our houses,

Two out of three Yvonnes, on Scott's boat *Soozee*. Yvonne Scott in the wheelhouse and me sitting on the side of *Soozee*. Photo Lola Miller.

taking with me Francine's five-year-old daughter, Julie. She sits facing me in the stern seat of the rowboat, big eyes regarding me over the too-large life jacket zipped to her small chin.

"My parents think you are strange," Julie announces solemnly.

I'm not surprised. I *am* strange. Or everything is strange to me, and I don't know the local protocols. I want people to let me know when they are coming to visit so I won't be hot in the creation of a wet painting and have to politely quit. Naturally, people are offended by this. Visits here take precious time out of a busy day. Often the visitor brings a gift: a freshly caught red snapper, a loaf of bread or a box of apples. People think I am unappreciative and snobbish when I don't want to stop working on a painting to visit. But now our house is somewhat orderly, I spend as much time as I can drawing or painting. My own income depends on maintaining my production of paintings. No one takes my work seriously since it has nothing to do with motors, logs, fish or boats.

The first visitor to come down Cramer Pass to welcome me to the neighbourhood is Joanie Hodinott, Billy and Yvonne Proctor's oldest daughter. She has smiling eyes and an easy, bubbling laugh. Joanie was born in Alert Bay, but raised in Echo Bay and attended the one-room elementary school there. Like all the teenagers living in these remote islands, she spent her high school years boarding at the school dormitory in Port McNeill. For five years, her father ran his fishing boat twenty-eight miles through the mainland inlets and across Queen Charlotte Strait every Friday afternoon to pick up Joanie and all the kids whose parents lived at the Scott Cove logging camp. Every Sunday afternoon he returned them to Port McNeill. Now she lives near her parents' home with her husband, Phil, and sons, Glen and baby Derek, in a house she and Phil built with an Alaska chainsaw mill. I envy her independence and admire her competence, particularly when I see her monkey-wrenching a chainsaw. And she does appreciate my work, asking me to do a small painting of Billy's boat *Twilight Rock* as a Christmas gift for him.

In this environment, food acquisition, storage and preparation, cleaning up our rented float house and dock, and caring for the needs of my partner and children are a lot more demanding than I'd ever imagined.

Our Play People scenarios didn't take into account most of my daily activities. Hardest of all is making the adjustment from having a lover I could leave when I felt like it to living with a "husband" whose needs, habits and rhythms are completely out of sync with mine and drive me crazy. Our float house is isolated, I have no friends, I can't make a move on my own, money is pouring out much faster than it is coming in, and Albert's fishing boat keeps breaking down.

I go out on the deck one freezing December day to wash some clothes in the wringer washer John kindly rigged up for me. Although I enjoy looking around as I work, at the mergansers and the Barrow's golden-eyes nibbling on the mussel-clad boomsticks at the back of the float and the peaceful view of islands out to the front of the bay, my hands burn from the cold. My eyes burn with salt tears that stream down my cheeks. I am not crying just from the pain in my hands. Some things clearly need to be done differently, and I am furious and frustrated. I surprise the Steller's jays hanging about with an outburst: "This will not do. It will just not do."

John suggests it might be better for Albert and the kids and me to move down to Echo Bay. Billy says we should contact Bobby Lamont, owner of the lot next to his, for permission to tie up our float house on Bobby's foreshore next to Echo Bay Resort. So in January 1987 we move again. Being situated right in the bay makes a huge difference to the physical demands on me, and developing friendly relationships is much simpler. Everyone comes to the bay to take their kids to school or to get their mail and fuel. From here it is easy to get on Billy's fishing boat, *Twilight Rock*, twice a month to go grocery shopping in Port McNeill. It will be easy, as well, to put up a sign in the summer and attract boaters to look at my paintings.

One of my new neighbours, Alexandra Morton, lives with her four-year-old son, Jarret, in a west-facing house high on a hill at Echo Bay. Billy Proctor yarded her house off its float and up onto the land in 1985. Alex is making a name for herself as a killer whale researcher. Albert and I had met her husband, Robin, on the dock in Echo Bay in August 1986, three months before we moved here, but by the time we arrived, he had

31

drowned in a diving accident. Alex stoically plods through the days one at a time, and continues the work she loves that she and Robin once did together. She likes to have a companion when she sets off to observe the orcas frequently cruising up Cramer Pass. We have enough in common to make companionship enjoyable; we're close in age, have a similar level of education, share intellectual curiosity and artistic talent, and are both parents of young children. Our families often eat dinner together, and as Alex and Jarret row away home, we fill the evening air with our version of howling wolves.

When Alex spots the misty blows from her home up on the knob at the top of Cramer Pass and radios me, I am ready to jump in her boat and follow the whales. I'm ecstatic to have encounters with killer whales from the safety of her Hurston speedboat, and my kids and I rapidly learn a lot about them. Alex explains the different characteristics of the "resident" and "transient" killer whales. Resident orca pods are larger than transient pods. Residents eat salmon, have curved, more rounded dorsal fins and create a great variety of underwater sounds. Transients are the so-called "wolves of the sea" because they prey on marine mammals. Transient family groups can be as small as three or even two; their dorsal fins are more triangular and pointed, and they cruise silently along the shore. As Alex shares her knowledge of the two species, I learn to anticipate the rhythms of their breathing and the clues that will reveal their next appearance.

One day we have a close encounter with a three-member family group of transients marine biologists have named Y pod. They are being uncharacteristically friendly as we putt down Cramer Pass, making sure not to crowd them. Because the small group is cruising slowly and milling about, Alex stops the boat and turns off the motor. She hangs her hydrophone over the side, hoping to hear some rare transient vocalizing. Jarret, Logan, Theda and I along with Alex's dog, Kelsey, hang over the sides of the boat waiting and watching for the whales. Kelsey has lots of experience at this and knows not to bark. One female surfaces and blows, then heads towards us. She rises through the water beside the boat, rolls on her side and, from three feet away, looks directly at us with her big eye. As we regard her, she regards us. I've never felt so thoroughly scrutinized, and I wonder what she thinks—*if* she thinks—as she looks at the boat, the humans and the dog all looking back at her. Her beautiful black-and-white patterning is clearly discernible, and her large eye conveys benign curiosity. After a long few seconds, she dives without a splash, and comes up a moment later by the side of the big bull with his huge triangular fin. The third whale joins them, then the whales dive deep and never reappear.

Another day Alex radios with news of a seven-member pod with a newborn. We putter out towards the Burdwood Group, giving the family lots of room. The whales pause in the calm centre of the islands while the mother nurses the baby. We are quiet, breathless, motor off and cameras clicking. Once again the whales depart, then blow half a mile away towards the north shore of Tribune Channel. We follow. The whup-whup-whup of helicopter blades comes to us on the wind, nearer and louder then fading again. The whales are heading directly for the helilog boom tied close to the shore beneath the steep slope. What are they doing? We watch in horror as the killer whales cruise right up beside the boom. Every three minutes, a giant Sikorsky helicopter swings over the crest of the hill with a cluster of hundred-foot logs dangling off the end of a long cable. Right over the boom the logs are released, and they plummet, straight down into the targeted area, the circle of boomsticks. A man riding his boom boat like a cowboy rides his cutting horse rips out to the centre of the boom and herds the new logs to the edges after they pop to the surface. Seven times we watch the helicopter drop the heavy logs into the ocean. Seven times it retreats over the hill, then returns exactly three minutes later to drop another load. The whales wait beside the boom, the baby lolling close to its mother, the others not much farther apart, until after the seventh drop, decisively, as one creature, they breathe and dive and come up on the far side of the boom. Why would they do that? Is it to teach the baby timing? Is it fun? Do they like risk-taking?

It's apparent the whales understand something was falling directly into their world. The deliberateness of their approach and their wait beside the boom for the twenty-one minutes while logs were dropped into the water and the impeccable timing of their dive under the boom were intentional acts. They must have had a reason; we just don't know what it was. Mysteries like this more than make up for the frustration and

I spent hours watching and photographing the whales. Their sleek profiles and majestic movement make them wonderful subjects for my paintings. Photo Albert Munro.

difficulty of my new life. I take hundreds of photographs, close up and more distant, and then use the photos to draw and paint the whales.

My first few months in Echo Bay are a lot like attending a new school; every day I'm introduced to a new topic, new instruction or a new instructor. I'm ready for anything, because flexibility brings great rewards. Most days, if I start with a plan, by 9:00 am my plan is out the window. Partly due to my boating experience with Albert and partly from paying attention while on excursions with Alex, I quickly learn my way around the islands and inlets. I'm ready to run my own boat. I long to go where I please. As for drop-in neighbours, I work to change my attitude to one of open acceptance. No one in a small community is ever invisible, and being new puts us in the spotlight. People come to check us out and see what we are like, and I'm grateful for the friendship offered. I've learned a lot more about weather and winds. The north wind, while rare, is unfailingly ferocious and must never be underestimated. One of the best things I've learned is that Billy and Yvonne Proctor can be relied upon to help anyone who helps themselves.

It All Breaks Down

DESPITE HOW MUCH I'M COMING TO LOVE THIS PLACE, learning to live with Albert turns out to be far more demanding than I anticipated. We're very dissimilar, polar opposites in many ways, with different daily routines, and it takes hard work to get in sync. He likes to stay up late, and I need to get to bed early to be up with the children and accomplish my daily to-do list. He's never hungry when we are and isn't used to a family routine.

Al takes on being a stepfather with willing love, but it is a long time before everyone is comfortable with it. My children travel back and forth, spending holidays at their father's home in White Rock. I don't think they mind. However, travel plans are subject to sudden change, due to weather, Al's fishing requirements and boat breakdowns. The one-room school at Echo Bay is a good place to learn, but there are problems to sort out with the different teachers who come and go. I put a lot of effort into finding several galleries on Vancouver Island and one in Sointula to represent me. My income improves as my work is seen by a larger audience, but I don't own a car, so framing the paintings and moving them around requires enormous planning effort and co-operative weather. Financial problems plague us continually, and Albert spends almost as much time monkey-wrenching his boat as he does fishing.

I promise myself I will not leave before at least one year is up. One

DRAWN TO SEA

year passes, then two, then three. Gradually, I realize our relationship is
not getting better, or more satisfying; in fact, it's deteriorating at a great
rate, and nothing I do improves matters. Almost every day Albert and
I end up in an argument. When he comes home one day after a trip to
Vancouver, with a giant St. Bernard puppy, I know for sure things aren't
going to work. We both cry the day he packs his belongings and the dog
he names Buddy onto his fishing boat. Knowing that parting ways is
necessary doesn't make it any less painful.

By August, not quite four years after our move to Echo Bay, I'm living
as a single parent again, faced with the decision of whether to move back
to the familiar life I left behind in the Lower Mainland or to stay here.
Theda, almost fifteen, will spend the school year in White Rock with her
father so she can attend grade ten there. Logan, going on thirteen, is doing his grade eight schooling by correspondence. Leaving might be the
simplest answer or the best choice, but I'm in love with the coast life now
and I find I cannot tear myself away.

Logan learned a lot about firewood working with Al.

My atunement to the sea and the environment, the combination of purification, exaltation and liberation I feel here, have become as essential as oxygen. I love the sweet breath of the westerly wind and the stone taste of the cold, clean, drinkable water running down to the shore. I love the small flower-carpeted islets, the mutable silver light on the water and the holiness of the moss-draped spruce forest. I sit in the old tin skiff Joanie gave me and expand my listening for miles, hearing the kingfisher chatter before it dives for a fish or the faint, far-off whoosh of a humpback's blow. I even love feeling like I have taken on more than I can handle. Dammit, I *am* going to handle it. All my senses are more alive here, and I can't give that up. The confinement and protective desensitization of city life seems intolerable: my stomach heaves when I think about it.

I love to jump in my skiff and run out to the islands, tie up to a streamer of bull kelp and joyously paint the scene before me. Painting plein air like this gives my work a freshness and immediacy it never had before. I want to keep growing in that direction. I made a commitment to move here with a man I loved. It's turned into a commitment to place. Here in these mainland inlets is where I want to grow into my best self.

Logan and I have a new roof over our heads, a renovated bunkhouse trailer. Billy had yarded it onto a new float Albert had built, and we'd torn out some walls and painted others and installed a wood heater. Logan makes a major contribution to the firewood supply and other household chores. I believe I've had enough experience of the weather on the water not to make stupid decisions. I know I can learn whatever else I need to survive. I make enough money from my paintings to provide for myself and my children. I can supplement my income by teaching watercolour workshops. Logan is okay with staying, for now, although he wants to go to high school in White Rock eventually. So we stay.

The first thing on my new agenda is to acquire a speedboat. I've learned from going about with Alex and Billy that my boat of choice is a sixteen-foot speedboat powered by a fifty or sixty horse outboard motor. I need a boat I can beach and climb in and out of easily. I want it to be powerful enough to tow home a firewood log and fast enough to make a fine-weather run to Port McNeill in an hour and change. And that is just what I get.

In November I make a trip to Campbell River and see my dream boat near Courtenay, at Nautech Marine: a sixteen-foot speedboat with a six-and-a-half-foot beam, a canvas canopy, nice seats, wheel steering forward and a fifty horse Mercury outboard motor. The asking price is $3500. I offer the owner $2500 cash. He accepts and the deal is done. I'm euphoric but my practical friend, Mike, who spotted the boat and took me to see it, says I must get a mechanic to check the outboard. Thirty-five dollars and an hour later, the mechanic says it's a great old motor and running fine. I am the proud new owner of *Sea Rose*, a wonderfully sporty yet sturdy boat—my birthday gift to myself.

Look out Broughton Archipelago!

Getting Landed

Sunk is the moon and the Pleaides soon will sink in the sky. The hours go past, midnight at last but alone I lie.

—Sappho

SPRING IS GALLOPING AT US on thundering hooves. In spite of the fact it is only February, the air pulses with a southeast sweetness that sets a'swaying the swelling pink buds on the flowering currant. Lime green leaves unfurling complement the rosy stems of the red osier dogwood. I love February for its brevity, its unpredictability and its tender-to-tempestuous weather. I'm used to a freeze-up in February but this year it's warmer than usual. One cloudy night I listen to a chorus of wolves for an hour. I'm in bed when I hear the first call, and I open the window wide and snuggle down under the covers. A multitude of scents waft in and I lie in clouds of fragrance until the last bell-like notes of the wilderness lullaby fade.

Getting through Christmas was a challenge without Al. I wanted only to wallow in misery. My kids were sad, too. I checked around with family to see who was planning what, and my brother Frank in Terrace said he'd love to have us come for Christmas. Bless him, a couple of weeks later a cheque to cover the ferry fare had arrived in the mail, the most beneficent surprise I'd ever received.

The scenery up the coast to Prince Rupert was magnificent although much of the voyage was through the night. Theda and Logan were hugely excited by the adventure. I felt the old thrill of embarking on a long

I loved my little red chainsaw. I knew it was an essential survival tool. Photo Theda Miller.

journey by sea. Frank took us out sightseeing around Prince Rupert and Terrace, and the deep snow everywhere was a dramatic contrast to the rainy greys of home. It was a fast week and it set the grief at bay for a while.

My February to-do list is long, and it keeps me fully occupied from early until late. A chainsaw and a paintbrush are my daily tools.

Just after he moved out last summer, Albert towed the float house around the corner out of Echo Bay, to the eastern side of the entrance to Shoal Harbour. It's now tied up to a standing boom in front of the fore-shore of a property soon to be subdivided into lots. Billy Proctor owns over a hundred acres of land here. A year earlier he'd taken Al and me on a two-hour tour of the property. A relentless rain had made the land slick, especially near the small creek bubbling merrily down the slope.

"Well, what do you think?" Billy had asked us after we'd admired the creek, the view, the thick stands of hemlock, fir and cedar and the solitary pine tree.

"It's very nice," we'd said. "Terrific. Beautiful."

"No, I mean, do you want to buy it?" said Billy. I couldn't believe our luck in hearing this. A simple yes was all it took, and the entire shape of our future had changed. And now it had changed again.

Billy plans to subdivide his property in order to help people who want to stay here get settled on land. I don't know what will happen now that Al's moved out, but I still want to build a house and live here. All my energies are bent towards this end. The subdivision process unfolds excruciatingly slowly; wading through the bureaucracy is like wading through low-tide "loon shit."

The truth infusing my every moment is this: the man I love has packed up and moved down the pass. I anesthetize myself from pain with a gruelling routine of land-clearing work in the morning and painting in the afternoon. This keeps me so fatigued I can't stay awake long enough at night to dwell on my life's gaping losses. In the long working hours, whether clearing land or painting, I find peace of a kind, a detachment from the painful absence gnawing at my consciousness. It's a little like how after a tooth has been pulled you keep exploring the tender space with your tongue. No, it's more like a painfully infected tooth that you can't get any drugs for. Hmm, it's exactly like having a broken heart. I can't decide if it's more painful that Al's still in the neighbourhood and I must see him from time to time than it would be if he just disappeared completely. Once in a while he comes over to discuss boat business with me, since I am co-owner, or does a bit of clearing two hundred feet down the foreshore, planning to build his own house a distance away from mine. Trying to untangle the ties that bind us and yet creating new ones with our desire to own this land and live on it is fraught with conflict and complications. Can two houses really work?

In any case, I'm in the groove, twenty-two paintings destined for an exhibition in April at a gallery called East of Java in Port McNeill and the land clearing moving right along. I've cleared about a hundred feet of shoreline back in to thirty feet. Billy comes over a couple of times a week and fells four or five trees for me. After the crashing and shaking is over he throws down his saw, gleefully rubs his hands together and cries,

"What a mess!" Then he leaves me to it. I bought a wonderful new tool, a red Shindaiwa chainsaw with a twenty-two-inch bar, just right for me. I buck the branches off the felled trees, the way Billy showed me, and make a big burn pile. The flames roar up quickly as I build on the coals from the previous day's fire. With my shiny red Shindaiwa I buck the trunks into firewood rounds. I split the rounds into pieces of firewood and stack them in a lean-to I built. If the tide is high, Logan and I load the firewood into the boat and take it over to the float. I am like Pacman, eating up the debris, chomp, chomp, chomp. If I hurt myself twice in one day I quit.

There's a particular style of bruise you get when working around a lot of branches: a red bull's-eye puncture wound with a purplish yellow aura. I've got plenty of those, mostly on my thighs and forearms. Besides the array of bruises decorating my flesh, I've noticed my body changing from the physical labour. My lower back feels much stronger from chainsawing and lying flat on my back in bed I feel a more substantial muscularity in my shoulders, biceps and pectoral muscles. I'm burned out at the end of each long day but refreshed in the morning and eager to get back at it.

It's a sunny March Sunday, and the vivid magenta salmonberry flowers are swelling early into vermilion berries. Little salmon fry are exiting the rivers and schooling under the float. I take the day off from working the land and spend a long time painting. I've done three paintings this week, but my show date is looming and many are yet to be framed. Logan is bored with his correspondence schoolwork and the sun is bright, so we head out to the Burdwoods in beautiful *Sea Rose.*

The Broughton blesses us with another gift. Each time I go out something wonderful and noteworthy happens. This time it's a group of Pacific white-sided dolphins, about thirty of them, and they want to play. They surge towards us in long soaring arcs, circle the boat as we head for the islands, swim fast below the bow, leap the wake swell behind us, cavorting to the left of us, flipping to the right of us, two and three at once.

I stop the boat and climb over the windshield onto the bow while Logan takes over the wheel. The dolphins love it when we go as fast as we can, making giant circles and figure eights. They're clearly annoyed whenever the boat slows: they circle around and flip water on us with their tails. Each time we rev up the motor and take off, I'm sure I hear a "yippee!" as the dolphins burst into action.

From the bow of the boat I have a close-up view of the dolphins. Their movements look oddly mechanical from this vantage point. They undulate in fast jerky bends rather than fluid curves, appearing hinged and jointed. Their timing is impeccable as they stay just ahead of the swiftly moving boat. It's evident they can go a whole lot faster, because they take turns at the bow, one zooming off and another immediately taking its place. I lie above them, cushioned by my life jacket, hanging on tight with one hand, dangling the other down in hopes of touching the fin held so tantalizingly close.

My speedboat *Sea Rose* gave me infinite freedom to explore. Photo Deborah Putman.

As the water rushes past an arm's length away, the dolphin pumps its sleek body rapidly, humps its back and slaps its fin into my reaching hand. An electric rush of joy courses through my body, a flood of awe and amazement at the deliberateness of the dolphin's action. I shriek, "Touched by a dolphin!" and the dolphin sheers off and leaps straight out of the water as if to exclaim, "Touched by a human!" I give up my place on the bow so my son can have his turn. We rip around like this for an hour until the dolphins tire of us as sport and, as one mind, change direction, popcorning into the distance as swiftly as they arrived.

Back at home, after lunch, I cogitate on the plumbing. It appears most men naturally understand things mechanical. I don't, and I'd prefer not to know. However, since I am going to stay here, and it looks like it'll be without a man, I've vowed to learn what I need to know. After Billy's lessons and some practice, I feel comfortable with the chainsaw, and I love the feeling of power it gives me. Of course, it has nothing to do with

Pacific white-sided dolphins seemed to love flirting with us and often approached my boat to play. Photo Ingrid Rebar.

the length of the bar. Now I must tackle plumbing—again—not quite as much fun as chainsawing.

Packing jugs of water home is tiresome. My stream is small, but the water runs sweet and clear, unlike the cedar-stained water elsewhere. About eighty feet up the steep creek bed is an angled granite slope, down which water continually runs as it seeps out of the sidehill. The base of the slope levels out into a natural dish, the perfect site for a small dam with a hose poking out of it. Billy gives me two large plastic barrels to serve as holding tanks. I set these up a little way below the dam. I join the two barrels together with a short hose and run a line from the dam to the barrels. Next, I insert a half-inch waterline into the base of one barrel, secure it with a hose clamp and run that line down the creek bed and across the water to the float. The last step is to clamp the end of the water line to the hose at the back of the house. The process takes a ridiculously long time but finally it's done. I saunter into the kitchen, turn on the tap and water pours forth: sweet, cold, clear water. I drink that glass of water, thinking about how easy this was compared to what I went through to plumb in the new hot water tank when I still lived in Echo Bay.

The old tank had packed it in, so I bought a new one. It sat in the bathroom for weeks, mainly because I didn't know how to make the little flare on the end of the copper tube to connect the tube with the fittings. I didn't have a flaring tool. Didn't have any solder to install the tap on the top of the tank. Didn't have a tap for it, either. And I didn't know how to solder. Too many other things to do, too, but the time finally came for it to be tackled.

I needed to construct a short connecting ramp from the porch to the back of the float, where the propane tank sits. I carefully placed a piece of cedar two-by-four to prop up the copper fuel line that runs from the tank along the outer wall of the house, and into the kitchen through a hole in the wall by the door. The propane line goes to the fridge and then along the back of the living-room wall to the bathroom where it connects to the hot water tank. I turned off the propane line at this point until I got the new tank installed. There was a board that needed to be cut away before I could install the ramp, so I powered up the saw and began the

cut. The vibration caused the two-by-four supporting the propane line to fall over, the copper tubing dropped onto the running chainsaw and the teeth snicked a small hole in the tube. So fast!

My heart jerked in my chest as I saw the quick spark flash. I flicked the off switch, threw down the saw, leapt the gap I was planning to bridge with the ramp and cranked closed the tap on the top of the propane tank. When my heart rate slowed and I could breathe again, I laboriously (no leaping this time) climbed over the slippery float logs to get back to the doorstep. I not only had no hot water, but I also had no refrigeration. But it could have been worse. I could have blown myself up.

Over to Joanie's to borrow flaring tools and find out how it is done. She rooted around in their shed and found a tap for the top of my hot water tank as well. Back home I discovered I didn't have enough copper tubing to replace the length I'd put a hole in. Jack and Yvonne Scott came by to see how I was doing and the next day they brought me a twenty-five-foot coil of copper tubing from town. At first I was clumsy, but after a couple of practice runs I managed to flare the new tubing and connect up the line to the fridge. The next step, getting the fridge going, is a ridiculous procedure. I lie on the floor in an awkward position with my hand squeezed through a small opening to press down a knob, while holding a lighter to the gas port. The lighter gets damn hot before the port finally lights, but the knob must be held down for five more minutes. If I let go too soon, the pilot light goes out and I have to start over. Finally the fridge was fired up—and I knew how to use the flaring tools.

My next task was to solder the tap Joanie gave me to the cold water intake at the top of the tank. I needed the generator to run the soldering iron, but the generator needed fuel and I was out of gas. So off to Echo Bay store I went to get some. Finally I sat down with all the bits and pieces at hand and soldered the tap to the copper tube as nice as you please. What a relief. My confidence was pumped, anticipation of the coming hot bath thrumming in my blood.

But it wasn't over yet. I had everything all lined up, hooked up, soldered up, I turned on the cold water tap to fill the tank and—no water. The water had quit, and in order to get it running again, I faced a gruelling slog in the swiftly falling dark, looking for the break in the hose. The water line in Echo Bay ran through the creek for 150 feet and then travelled 600 feet up into the bush. I jumped in the little yellow dinghy and rowed up the creek, watching for the telltale clue of a floating section of hose. I landed over on the backside of Billy and Yvonne's property and found the problem there.

In order to build pressure, the diameter of the hose is stepped down over the length of the water line. At this break, the smaller hose had slipped out from inside the larger one. Sometimes bears chew on the hoses and I wasn't up to tackling that right then so was glad I didn't have to go up into the woods. Mending this kind of a break isn't difficult if you have a screwdriver and three hands. Water gushed out of the hose, drenching me with a cold shower while I shoved the small hose into the big hose. Holding the two hoses together against the water pressure, the hose clamp must then be screwed tight. Nothing to it.

I was holding the hoses down, one knee on each side of the break, trying to tighten the hose clamp, when Bill came ambling over the hill. He wrestled the thing into submission in no time. I climbed into the dinghy, rowed home, laid down flat on the floor, stuck my hand in the small opening at the bottom of the water heater, pressed down another stupid button while I held a lighter to the pilot light.... When the ring of holes for the gas lit up with a whoosh, I dropped my head to the floor and sobbed. What a long, luxurious, delicious, hard-earned bath I revelled in after the water was up to temperature.

Not Approved

OFTEN I THINK I MUST BE NUTS TO STAY HERE and go through one ordeal after another, when I could live elsewhere and just turn on a tap and have hot water come out of it. Flick a switch and have a light come on. But my encounters with dolphins and other wildlife more than make up for the traumas. A lot of people were sure I was going to leave, and it feels good to be capable of living here alone. Alone with wonderful neighbours, of course. It took four of them—five counting moral support, lunch and a rough pep talk from Yvonne Proctor—to get me through the hot water tank episode. When I went over to Yvonne's, crying the blues, she told me I had a face like seven miles of unpaved highway. Every time I'm bogged down in misery, I think of her saying that and cry tears of laughter instead.

April is a busy month full of small wild pleasures. Every morning there are birds, birds on the land, birds on the sea. Before I arise I hear the sweet long trill of the varied thrush. Out the bathroom window of the float house, while I'm brushing my teeth, I might see a pair of red-throated loons or hooded mergansers. A common loon puddled along the foreshore, and I suspect they are uncommon here, as I've only ever seen one. Logan spotted a strange creature swimming behind the house, a mystery until it got directly between us and the land and we saw its long paddle-like tail. It's novel to see a beaver in the salt chuck, although there are plenty of dams and beaver houses on the streams and lakes in Gilford Island's interior.

Harley Snowdon, a hand-logger friend, and his son, Steven, arrive to begin the work of felling and yarding the larger timbers off the hillside with their tough old tug, *Ocean Planet*. After they fall several trees, Steven-of-the-very-long-legs climbs rapidly up the hill, packing a big saw and bucks off all the branches in the crisscross. There's a long cable wrapped around a towing post on the stern of the old tug and Steven drags the other end up the hill and hooks it onto the felled timber. Harley fires up the rumbling motor of the *Ocean Planet* and takes off hard, away from the shore. The trees shoot down the hill and into the chuck with a generally smooth slide and a massive swoosh as they hit the water.

Logan and I are often lured from our work of the day to watch. Harley is careful to leave no debris in the water as they boom up the logs. I've asked them to set apart any trees less than eight inches in diameter, for me to buck up for firewood. The pile is growing. Logan is having a good time practising running along the floating logs like Steven does, though he lacks the requisite gear: caulk (cork) boots to give him a good grip.

Logan cautiously navigating the logs without caulk boots. Harley is in the background crossing logs to the *Ocean Planet*.

Steve (front) and Harley Snowdon booming up the hand-logged timber by my foreshore.

I'm certain he is going swimming with every step.

The projected completion date for the clearing of the land has moved forward considerably with the arrival of Harley and Steven. I've enjoyed "pacmanning" my way across the front of the property, beavering away at the trees Billy fells each week, but using that method it would take me five years to create a clearing. The process has been therapeutic, but my need for therapy is not as great now. I'm eager to get to the part where I build a house.

Clearing the land has made me feel satisfyingly strong, and that strength has poured into the paintings. My painting of a logger friend, Brent Wehner, was published on the cover of *West Coast Logger* magazine, and the show at East of Java was a wonderful success, eight paintings sold. You never know when you present an exhibit of paintings what the results will be. Striking loggers, poor fishing, a burp in the stock market or plain old bad weather can all negatively affect attendance and sales. I'm lucky *I* made it to this show. I missed the opening night of the last one I had in Sointula due to storm-force winds, humbled by the power of the elemental forces. Watching the red dots get neatly placed beside the sold paintings caps my joy at painting them.

One painting was of a stunning display of northern lights I'd seen on a cold March night. I was in the bathtub—can't get enough of that hot water—when my neighbour, Ingrid Rebar, called on the VHF radio. The volume was low, so I could barely hear her tiny voice calling my boat name, "*Sea Rose, Sea Rose, Northern Dream.*" Briefly I debated whether to bother climbing out of the tub to answer, but the social rule of the coast is strong. I'd never forgive myself if she needed help and I was too selfish to answer.

"Look outside," Ingrid said, when I responded. Dripping and sudsy under a towel, I peered out the door. The entire northern sky undulated with ruby brilliance. I stumbled into my clothes, barely wiping off the bubbles, woke Logan up and watched until the magnificent light faded to black. This must be painted immediately, I knew, and I worked half the night in a blaze of inspiration.

When I hear comments at the show such as, "It's like I saw it myself,"

and "I didn't even see it, but I feel like I was right there," it makes me feel like I really *am* an artist.

Home from the intense emotion of a successful show, I crash into the backwash that always follows the high. My mood is not elevated when Billy comes by to tell me my lot has not been approved for the subdivision due to a lack of "good water access." This is just plain stupid in view of the obvious: 600 feet of waterfront. I eat some of the soup Logan made, have a nap and try not to think about it.

Coastal Communications

I'VE BEEN BUSY BOPPING ALL OVER THE MAP, including down to Victoria to the Leafhill Gallery, the first gallery I approached with my work years ago. I'm ecstatic to be accepted instead of being told to go home and paint some more, as I was advised in 1973. Good advice at the time, and I followed it. This time I'll be participating in a group exhibit in the gallery and hope to establish a new market.

We're deep into summer now, and in the warm, dry weather, my creek runs dry a couple of times, but a little splash of rain refreshes it. Billy helps me pile rocks to make a new dam farther up the granite slope, and we set up the water hose and a filter. I need a larger holding tank for water storage. I've added it to my must-get list.

The piece of property next to mine is spoken for by prawn fishers Glen and Marg Neidrauer. Glen is also a Fisheries officer and a diver. He offers to put some barrels under my float. He and Marg, who watches from above when he dives, arrive with his compressor, and he places twenty-five barrels under my float. It rises about sixteen inches, and within twenty-four hours the dying mussels and other marine life are emanating a nauseating miasma. The stench makes me gag, but I must endure it since I have nowhere else to go.

Theda is here for the summer and my niece, Heather, is visiting for a week. To get away from the smell for a while and offer the children an

adventure, we set out with our friends, Thea and Ted, on their lovely old boat, *Cresthaven*, to help move their belongings out of Hopetown. We leave Echo Bay towing *Sea Rose*. Ted offers gas as a thank you for our efforts at boxing and packing, so I fill the tank in my boat from some jerry cans.

In the evening we head for Turnbull Cove in *Sea Rose* to spend the night with our old friends Sharon and Chris and their son, Matthew. I feel a rush of warmth when I see them standing on their flower-boxed deck as we motor in—tall, lanky Chris flanked by the shorter, rounder forms of Sharon and Matt. I *need* to see them, because we had a disturbing miscommunication a couple of months ago. Feelings got hurt, and I want the fences mended. There are too few people out here to let slights fester until relations are strained beyond repair. Chris and Sharon have been Albert's fishing buddies on *Miss Centennial* since 1979. Chris and

My friend Sharon and her partner, Chris, fished with Albert in the '80s.

Albert travelled together, explored new territory, helped each other out with boat breakdowns and prawn survival problems, fished and sold prawns together. I've known them since my first float plane flight to visit Albert in Smith Inlet in 1981: Once they'd settled in their float house in Turnbull Cove and Albert and I were twenty-five miles away in Echo Bay, our get-togethers became infrequent.

They're glad to see us, especially Sharon. Her smile is a warm benediction, and over her good cooking, we offer explanations and apologies and harmony is restored. Matthew is bouncing with the excitement of three visiting kids. Being with Sharon and Chris brings back good memories of previous visits, and I miss Albert deeply. But I go to bed feeling okay about my first journey to visit someone without him, in charge and in my own boat.

In the morning *Sea Rose* fires up nicely and we hug everyone goodbye, but a hundred yards from the dock, the motor stalls out. I can't get it going again. All my pleasure in feeling in charge, in my own boat evaporates instantly. I have no clue where to begin. Chris putts out in his skiff, tows us back to the float and helps me clean the carburetor. It turns out the fuel from the jerry can at Hopetown had sludgy water in it, and even though I'd poured it through my filter, some of it got through the fuel line into the carburetor.

"You need an on-line filter," says Chris. Add it to the list.

Turnbull Cove is the farthest I've been from home in my speedboat since I got it last November. I had to pump up my courage to make the decision to go the twenty-five miles back home on our own.

The kids offer their fearless, blissfully ignorant encouragement, but the run home is worse than I imagined. At the bottom of Kingcome Inlet an outflowing wind presses against the tidal push, setting up an ugly pointy sea, like a miniature erupting mountain range. It isn't a hard wind, but the sky is black and low, and the rough sea whacks hard against the hull. Stinging spray slashes over the canopy. The windshield bangs with every slapping wave. Water splashes in my lap.

"Mom! The windshield is coming loose!" Logan cries.

"What? Why?" I scream over the roar of the old Merc.

The screws that fix the windshield to the fibreglass curve of the dashboard have loosened from the repeated banging. The boat's canopy is fastened to the top of the windshield with snaps, which creates a tension that pulls on the screws with every thudding wave. The screws are popping off, the canopy snaps are tearing loose, and the boat is bucking and banging in the turbulent sea. Logan finger-tightens the screws as best he can (something else for the list, a tool kit for the boat), since it takes all my attention to steer. He holds the windshield down from Stackhouse Island the rest of the way home, two-and-a-half gruelling hours.

My legs are shaky when I try to get out of the boat, and I climb out onto our dock on my hands and knees, grateful the motor ran okay after its encounter with the contaminated gas. I'm proud of my good brave sailors who stayed calm, quiet and helpful.

No more adventures, the kids tell me. I find the right kind of screwdriver and wrench (another complicated problem, it can't be just any old wrench), and Logan and I tighten all the nuts. We pour all the fuel out of the tank and filter it again. On a nice calm day we run Heather to Port McNeill to catch the bus and I buy an on-line fuel filter. Billy helps me put it in place before he heads out on a fishing trip. Logan goes with him, so Theda and I have a few days alone before she returns to White Rock. After she leaves, I enjoy a restorative week of solitude.

My artist buddy, Deborah Putman, is my next visitor. Two days before she's due to arrive, a screaming norther tears off a section of the roof and generally wreaks havoc in the neighbourhood. I gather up some 1 x 4 strapping and other materials to repair it but don't get around to it right away, due to dealing with water lines, firewood, gardening: the list goes from here to the moon. When Deb arrives on Orca Air's float plane, I'm repairing a break in the water line to the house, the result of an extreme low tide and the line getting hung up on the boomstick. I hustle her into the guest room, and tell her to get changed into her camp clothes and come give me a hand. No time to sit with a glass of wine and update each other. She is game, and we ding to the shore in the little yellow dinghy with the hose rings and screwdriver (a different kind) at the ready.

"Likely we'll end up wet from this little project," I warn her. By the time we are finished repairing the hose, we are beyond wet. Water drops sparkle on the curly ends of her short hair, spike her eyelashes, and drip off the end of her nose. Her sopping shirt sticks to her body. She's laughing so hard she can hardly speak as she dumps water out of her boot and tells me about an art show opening she attended the night before, wearing strappy heels and a pencil slim-dress. I'm grateful for her help that day and over the next two when we fix up the roof. Finally, we get to do a bit of running around in the boat taking pictures, painting, picnicking and generally having fun.

It's been a good summer, except for the hole in my heart. No sign of Albert and yet he is always with me. I pray for the day I wake up and think of something other than him first.

Harley had some boat problems, but *Ocean Planet* is running again and he is back, with Don Cameron, a clam-digger neighbour. They are

Painting on location can be hard on the derriere. Rain and wind and bugs can make it uncomfortable but it is inspiring and lots of fun. Photo Deborah Putman.

yarding the felled logs off the property. The last bit of falling awaits: the giant cedars at the top of the bluff above the house site.

It's still early on in this project, but I'm already designing house plans, sketching ideas for an hour or two before bed. I've always loved designing houses. When I was little I created floor plans using any element the seasons brought. In the fall I'd rake out a floor plan with narrow piles of fallen leaves. After a snowfall it wasn't a snowman I wanted to build but a floor plan. Indoors, my Barbie dolls got lovely apartments the perfect size for them, which I made by standing two *Little Golden Encyclopedia* books vertically on their ends and opening the covers at right angles. The endpapers were beautiful colours, magenta, teal and azure blue, and I'd carefully choose two colours for the walls of each room.

In my last year of high school I'd chosen drafting to complete my course load, with the idea of going into architectural design. "Drafting isn't for girls," the principal said, at first. Shop, which included wood and metalwork, automotives and drafting, was for boys only. Girls were required to take cooking and sewing. I talked my way into being the first girl allowed to take the drafting class. The following year, all restrictions by gender were dropped.

Good thing girls can run chainsaws or I'd never survive here.

This delicious September morning I'm in a marvellous state of well-being. Shortly I'll ding over to the land and commence my morning hours of clearing. Now, in the early dawn glow, I'm feeling the ache of no daughter here again. I love having Theda with me and always cry when she leaves to spend the school year with her dad. I miss her lovely and loving presence so much, although she can get into a huffy little snit at times. I don't know whether to laugh or cry when the other Theda (Albert calls her Theatra) shows up and flounces dramatically about with her haughty nose in the air. It's always over quickly though. I'll be meeting with her school counsellor next time I go to White Rock to see her perform in the school play, *Les Miserables*.

Logan wanted to go to White Rock to live with his father and sister for grade nine, but his dad said no. Staying home with me doing another year of correspondence isn't high on his list of preferred options. He needs to be around kids his own age, have access to drafting, wood and metalwork classes, or even home economics. I haven't been the happiest of companions this last year, I admit, and he, too, misses Albert. So we're all set for him to do grade nine in Port McNeill. I've registered him at the dormitory for outlying high school students, where Billy's daughter, Joanie, and other Echo Bay kids all stayed when they were in high school.

One week before school begins, we find out that the dorm is closed due to declining numbers. Instead, we find room and board for Logan with Craig and Shelley Dmetrechuk at the Sundown Market in Port McNeill. He'll have his own space and take his meals with their family. I'm grateful we have a safe place for him to stay, and the school board will pay some of the accommodation and travel expenses.

Each Friday afternoon Logan comes home, and on Sunday evening or Monday morning he returns to Port McNeill. To run him the twenty-eight miles across Queen Charlotte Strait to Port McNeill in *Sea Rose*, it absolutely must not be blowing over twenty knots southeast or northwest. If one of my neighbours is going to town, Logan catches a ride. I need a full-time secretary to take care of all the organizing. I go to bed dreaming of chauffeurs, wood splitters, secretaries but only I show up for work in the morning.

Despite the stress, it's been fun running across the strait so far. On my first trip to pick up Logan for the weekend it's flat calm, so I go out Arrow Pass instead of the usual route by Retreat Passage. The strait opens out before me, wide and silver blue, and half a dozen dolphins soar in perfect shining arcs. They approach me directly as I steer into the azure band of bright ocean, turn into my boat wake and escort me halfway across the strait. Foolish, I know, but I read it as a good omen. They make me feel welcome and secure.

Making arrangements with Logan is never simple. Telephone service is through VHF radio. I can call Coast Guard Radio to put through a call or use a telephone channel, 24 out of Port Hardy or 86 out of Alert Bay. First I key the mike (press down the "talk" lever) for three seconds. When an operator answers I give my radio call numbers, which are

Victor Delta 3893. VD when spoken in letters only: lovely. The operator puts me through. As the phone rings in Shelley's house, I know there are people all over the coast listening in. Everyone waiting to make a call or monitoring the station to hear the gossip or awaiting a call themselves will hear my conversation. Even though I can ask for "privacy," a beeping noise that masks the speech transmission, it only covers my side of the conversation.

On the Port McNeill end, someone has to be in the apartment to answer the phone. One day I call to tell Logan that Jack and Yvonne Scott are in Port McNeill on *Soozee* and he should get down to the dock and catch a ride home. Three-and-a-half hours later, when the Scotts arrive home, he isn't with them. I phone again.

"Oh," he says. "I didn't know you meant right away." Due to the avidly listening ears, I had to wait to yell at him.

Other people's telephone calls are entertaining for sure on long solitary evenings on a boat in the middle of nowhere. One evening I was on *Silverwing* with Al when he was waiting his turn to speak with his prawn buyer. We heard a fellow from a logging camp call his sweetie, who answered the phone with a squeal.

"Babycakes!" she cried. "When are you coming home? I am soooo, so, so lonesome I might have to find a new boyfriend!" The two ended up in a fight. Gripping drama.

Another time, after I'd returned from my two-month painting trip to France, I made a call to Albert's boat. That evening we provided the entertainment.

"I have a present for you," I said coyly.

"What is it?" he asked.

"French lingerie!" I gushed.

A pause and then, "Do you think it will fit me?"

Found and Lost

The choice of brushes is a personal affair to be
determined by experience.

—Robert Henri *The Art Spirit*

As we move into autumn, I feel overwhelmed, undone by the sheer
volume of work that faces me. I burned slash for six hours yesterday,
three hours today, and am exhausted beyond proportion by the work I
did. I ache all over. I wish I was younger. A few hours chainsawing and
dragging rotten chunks to a fire and my legs and back are burning with
pain. Bruises decorate my thighs due to a hard fall. Today, back at the
float house, tears burn my eyes, then spill over and run down my nose. I
let them flow for a few minutes, then wipe my eyes, blow my nose, make
a cup of tea and dig out Emily Carr's journal, *Hundreds and Thousands*.
Reading that, or about the tormented life of Van Gogh, always makes me
count my blessings.

On a happier note, I spent several days in late August with fellow
artist, Kayak Bill. Bill Davidson is a real man of the wilderness. He was
living in a little shack at Echo Bay Resort and doing maintenance work
for the owners when we moved here. What he really wanted was to jump
in his kayak and paddle away, but he needed a bit of cash first. Bill lived
in an orphanage near the Rocky Mountain foothills as a child. From an
early age, the challenge of climbing the nearby peaks had been his solace
and his strength. In the climbing community, Kayak Bill is renowned for
his fearless search for new routes up ever-higher peaks, mountain walls
and cliff faces.

Bill Davidson (aka Kayak Bill) enjoying an uncharacteristic glass of wine.

Once Bill put on a fabulous slide show in the Echo Bay Community Hall of memorable images of soaring granite spires, blue crevasses and bottomless abysses. He's not only an excellent photographer; he also paints watercolours and makes music on an electronic synthesizer he built. Even as a kid he had great techno-mechanical skills, and he built a robot in high school. Logan likes this kind of stuff, and he went over to visit him a few times in his Echo Bay shack. I've never seen Bill's synthesizer but from time to time I heard the weird and wonderful sounds he created with it.

For years Bill has lived mostly from a sturdy fibreglass kayak, travelling to a series of camps situated on various little islands. I think he leaves a bit of his spirit wherever he has stayed; he often comes to mind when I'm painting on some secluded island. In the 1980s he lived in a little shack under the trees by the double-backed beach in the Burdwood Group, alone for a while and then with Lori, his love. They moved onto a float house when she was pregnant with their child, Westerly. The Burdwood camp was exquisite, a perfect campsite, but possibly a little too well-known for someone as reclusive as he. Slowly Kayak Bill worked his way up the coast, creating a string of new campsites, plenty of places to stop or run for cover if the weather turns bad. He is camped for a while at the Spiller Pass site now and came up to Echo Bay to get some rolling papers and tobacco. I run into him at the store in late August and invite him to dinner.

Kayak Bill is a brown person. Brown clothing over brown skin, weathered from years of exposure to sun and salt. Brown eyes twinkle above a strong nose, a bushy moustache and beard, and a warm, shy smile.

He is pleased to have a dinner invitation, says his own meals are getting tiresome. Dinner is in the oven by the time he arrives in his kayak. My kids and I examine the kayak with curious interest and shower Bill with questions about his lifestyle. Every answer inspires more questions.

Theda asks him skeptically, "Do you *never* live in a house?"

"Not if I can help it," says Kayak Bill. "Catching or foraging for food takes up most of my time, also repairing the kayak or my fishing gear. I paint when I have enough to eat."

Logan asks, "What do you catch to eat?"

"Clams, cod, halibut, crabs, seals and oolichon for oil, salmon sometimes," says Kayak Bill.

"And what do you forage to eat?" is my question.

"Different kinds of kelp, salal berries, huckleberries, blackberries, goose tongue, which tastes like string beans, wild peas and their spring sprouts, and sea asparagus. Of course, wild onion to flavour everything."

One of Kayak Bill's camps showing the tarp frame.

I nod. I harvest and eat that myself. As we sit down at the table, Kayak Bill gives us more details about what it takes to live wild. His campsites are simple, he says, consisting of a ridgepole, a tarp, a fire pit, a little stash of dry firewood and a lighter.

"I mark each place with a Z, the Zig-Zag rolling papers Z. That's my mark."

After the roast chicken disappears, Kayak Bill sets up his bedroll on my deck, and a couple of hours pass in conversation about painting and our differing styles. He has a small portable kit and a 4 x 6 inch box he keeps his brushes in. They are acrylic fibres, not the sable or acrylic/sable mix I use. He cuts the handles of the brushes down to four inches or less so everything packs easily into a small kit. He almost never mixes colours but uses the pigment straight from the tube. I show him my palette. It includes rich, dark blues, particularly indigo, which he doesn't have. It's a wonderful, saturated midnight blue, excellent for night scenes. I give him my tube; I can easily get more.

Bill's paintings are coastal images composed of small, clearly defined curving shapes built up in bands of colour. They're not "realistic" but convey the spirit and magic of the coast through the colours he uses and the curved forms. Many of his paintings contain an elemental image of a craggy visage embedded in a rock face, expressive of the spirit of earth, maybe, or of wind, sea or sky.

Except for my once- or twice-yearly visits with my artist buddy, Deb, I haven't spent much time with other artists since I moved to Echo Bay. I miss having art conversations in detailed, specific language like the coastal lingo of come-along, crank shaft and gurdy wires. Words and terms like quinacridone, colour surprise, picture plane and focal distance lie in my mind begging to be used. Even a taciturn, solitary artist knows the language of paint, of image and concept. Being able to "artspeak" with Bill gives me the same relief speaking English with someone did when I was in France.

Kayak Bill stays for a couple of days and helps us burn a huge slash pile. The "logging" of the land is over. Harley, Steve and Don corralled all the logs they yarded off into a big boom and towed them away, leaving giant piles of debris all over the hillside. After a dirty day spent feeding the fire, I offer Bill the use of my bathtub.

"I might lose my protective cover if I wash the grit off," he jokes. "Haven't had a bath in two years."

On his last night with us we sit outside late, talking into the dimming evening light. I say goodnight, then notice the sky to the north is suffused with an odd light. We watch, wondering, as the star-filled sky suddenly shimmers with other-worldly radiance: the aurora. Instead of the evening ending, the final act has just begun! I wake up Theda and Logan, get our sleeping bags. We lie on the deck in the sweet-scented night watching a fabulous performance of northern lights. Luminous white beams glow on the northern horizon, backlighting the silhouetted trees on the hill towards Echo Bay. These beams start low, then billow straight up, widening and undulating as they rise. I imagine a stage manager, setting in motion one light after another. Like visible music, the light ascends in slow, upwelling beams. As one swell of light rolls up to fade high in the sky, more light up at the horizon's edge. We cheer and clap when the lights fade to dim.

Our whole visit with Kayak Bill is illuminated by fantastic weather phenomena. The morning he leaves, a horizontal double rainbow lies over the sea surface out towards Baker Island and circles around to end near the entrance to Shoal Harbour. We watch Bill kayak away into that rainbow and know we've had a special time with a unique individual.

Something terrible has happened... the unthinkable, the thing that could happen to anyone. My dear friend Sharon Rogers and her young son, Matthew, have died in a plane crash on a never-to-be-forgotten date. September 30, 1991. I'm in White Rock with Deb when Logan phones around midnight to tell me the devastating news. He's crying so hard he can hardly speak. After our visit with them in July, Sharon and Matt were in Echo Bay for a few days in August and we had a good, warm visit. I never, ever thought it would be the last time I would see her.

Sharon, with Matt, had been flying to Port McNeill on the way to

White Rock for her daughter Miranda's high school graduation. It was an afternoon "sched" flight, misty with a thickening fog. They never made it to Port McNeill. Sharon and Matt, and the pilot, Syl, all disappeared with the plane. There were search parties out in Drury Inlet for days following. A few bits and pieces were found floating in the area: a paddle, a first aid kit, part of a pontoon. It was surmised that Syl tried to turn around to go back to Turnbull Cove but he may have misjudged the distance between the plane and the surface of the water. In a thick fog, you can't see where the air ends and the water begins. A float plane tilts when turning, and if a wingtip hits the water, that is most certainly going to bring down the plane.

Sharon is on my mind every second. I think about her motherless children from her previous marriage, Miranda and Dustin, about Chris, who is insane with grief from the loss. That is, when I am not thinking about Albert and Logan and Theda. I work harder than ever to exhaust myself into sleep. My mother's words of wisdom often resonate in my mind, "This too, shall pass."

The days grow shorter, and on weekends, when he is home from school, Logan helps me burn the slash pile. In the late afternoon, we "tuck in" the fire for the night. Sparks fly as he rolls in the larger pieces of punky root and wrestles some of the chunkier pieces of rotting debris into the flaming heart. We tidy up the burning debris around the edges and the pile smoulders until morning.

I go home in the dark after one long day's work holding in my mind's eye the image of a column of golden sparks arcing and dancing against the evening sky. All day I've felt the painting gestating inside me. As soon as I'm in the door, I strip off my dirty clothes, wash face and hands, slip into clean pants and a t-shirt and head for my studio. With a break to make us toasted cheese sandwiches, I'm at it until 2:00 am in the morning, long past my bedtime.

I sleep deeply until grey dawn, when the storm warnings broadcast last evening as I painted become a reality of hard gusts buffeting the house. Lying snug in my bed I listen to thudding and thumping, the hard percussion of raindrops and the creaking of the house with each swell.

This wind began as a southeasterly, sneaking in the back door cracks, but during the early morning hours, it veered crazily around to the northwest. This is the wind of nightmares and lost roofs. My float house faces directly into the long stretch of open water to the northwest, towards Mt. Stevens. From any other direction I am well protected, but here the pounding swells billow up on my foreshore.

On go the gumboots and a raincoat over my flowered flannel nightie. Grabbing the flashlight, out I head into the frantic wind. The boats are still securely tied, bumpers suitably bumping. The boomsticks around the last of Harley's logs look okay. The flashlight beam reveals our roof is still there. All seems well, and if it isn't, it can wait until full daylight. For the first time since I've lived here without Albert, I feel no anxiety. I return to my still warm bed and, in spite of the thrashing rain, the arrhythmic shuddering of the house and the howling wind, I immediately fall into a deep sleep.

Total silence reigns when I awake, except for a deep chuffing noise. What the heck is that, I wonder, as I peek out the door. Thick fog has rolled in behind the rain and wind, and eight river otters are playing on my deck, running and sliding. As I watch, seven of them array themselves in a circle, with their tails inwards and heads pointed out. Companionably, they all defecate on an old blanket sitting there, then proceed to roll in the mess. I've had enough of their charm! I shut the door with a decisive thump and the river otters dive as one.

I paint every afternoon after my daily land-clearing stint, working towards an exhibition at my Sointula gallery. I love the contrast of hard physical labour in the morning and painting in the afternoon. Life is somewhat more tolerable these days, good even, with intermittent moments of bliss. The approach of a new year gives me strength, hope and energy. I accept that my life with Albert is over, and I'm actively shaping a new one. Staying healthy, envisioning a house to build, painting into new and challenging territory, and providing emotional stability for Logan are my goals. My perception is honed by the sudden death of my dear friend Sharon. Just being alive is good. Wonderful.

Lovers and Salmon

IT IS AMAZING WHAT LIFE OFFERS when you least expect it, when you've given up all hope of realizing your dreams. Or maybe it's only when you reject compromising what is best for yourself, stop trying to make sure things are good for everybody and ask, "What is it that *I* need?" that the energies shift from a stalled pattern. I don't know.

After more than a year of living in an agony of hopes raised and hopes dashed, I am done trying to get things to work out with Al. I awake one day with "I am an idiot" ringing in my ears: fantasizing that we could own this land jointly as friends, build two houses on it and live happily ever after, side by side. Nope. I'm certain that eventually some other be-sotted female will move in with him; I'll murder them both in a jealous rage and spend the rest of my life in a jail cell. I cannot pretend a func-tional friendship when my heart burns with love and loss.

What I need is to have Albert completely gone from my life. I know I can live a good life without him. In a firm letter, I request that he accept my proposal for him to let me buy Billy's property myself. I ask him to remove me from any involvement in ownership of the fishing boat, or I'll have to sell my interest. He blows his stack and is all set to find a lawyer for a big fight. But, as I learn later, he goes to see a friend of his who asked Al how he feels about me. His answer surprises both of them.

"I love her," he blurts.

"Okay, then, maybe you should go see her before you see a lawyer," says his buddy. On November 13, Theda's birthday, Albert pulls up at my float after dark.

"What do you want?" I demand as I hold his boat off my dock.

"I just want to talk to you," he says. "There're things we need to talk about."

"It's too late for talking," I reply.

"Please let me come in," he says. Wordlessly, I tie his bowline to the cleat. We sit in silence at the kitchen table, for what feels like hours. Staring at the flame of the kerosene lamp, I sit with crossed arms saying nothing—not my usual procedure. If he thinks we need to talk, perhaps he has something to say. If I wait long enough, perhaps he will say it.

Finally he speaks, and looks aghast at the words that press out of his mouth.

"You are so beautiful."

All this does is infuriate me. If he thinks this is what I want to hear, maybe I *should* have filled in the silence with chatter. I give him my best Medusa glare. Perhaps he will turn to stone and I can use him as an anchor rock.

"What I mean is—I'm sorry. I love you. I hate this. I had everything I wanted to say all planned out, and now I can't remember any of it. I just love you so much, and I can't stand this anymore." Now he is crying, and so am I. I can't help it. The dam breaks and I am flooded, awash in the power of his surrender to such deeply felt emotion. How can I resist such a heart-to-heart entreaty, a soul-to-soul plea?

Turns out there is a lot to talk about, and we talk the entire night through, thirteen hours of talking before we reach out to embrace each other.

Albert leaves for Vancouver to take care of the boat business, and when he returns he'll move back in with me, along with Buddy the St. Bernard and Huey the cat. We've renewed our commitment. We'll work together to shape a new life and build a new home. I'm still reeling from

When Albert returned from Vancouver to start our new life together, our family grew to include Buddy the St. Bernard and Huey the cat. Photo Bill Munro.

the shock of this turn of events and sincerely hope I'm not making a terrible mistake. I can't let myself believe it yet. I'm disassociated from the Yvonne that had an all-night conversation with Albert and plans to let him come back. If that Yvonne is right, we've had an enormous breakthrough in the state of our feelings for each other. The skeptical Yvonne is certain the bubble will pop any second. My new-found equilibrium has been shot to hell, and I teeter be-tween intense anticipation and terrible fear. This is a momen-tous turning point in my life, a hair-raising breath-stealing venture in which each step I take down the jungle path might reveal a man-eating tiger. My mind is consumed with all the things we said to each other, and I can barely bring my attention to bear on anything else. It takes an enormous effort to get through each day until he returns and proves it's not a dream. Is it crazy ridiculous to give this a second chance and hope things will be different, better?

It isn't a dream. Al returns from the big smoke, as Billy calls it, and when I hear his warm voice on the radio, full of love, gooseflesh bumps rise on my arms.

"*Sea Rose, Sea Rose, John.*" The tone of his voice conveys the joy and triumph of a mission accomplished. The weary voyager has returned to claim his bride. Or something. I won't know for sure until his boat pulls up at my dock.

Finally Albert is here, in the flesh, in spirit and heart. We touch, we laugh our way around the kitchen, dinner, dishes and bed. He looks at me, heart in his eyes, trust and fear in equal measure.

"Will you marry me?" he asks.

"Yes. Yes, I will."

I phone Logan to tell him, and it's an easy decision to move him back home. Our reunion has far-reaching impacts, and the family that was exploded by our break-up coalesces rapidly, like a film of the Big Bang run backwards, all the planets rushing towards each other. My mother and Theda are shocked when I phone to tell them the news. Theda rallies quickly, saying "Congratulations, Mommy. I'm so glad. Tell Albert I love him." My mother, out of fear of more pain for me, I'm sure, is reticent, and I, not truly certain of the gamble, cannot defend my choice.

Logan uses hog ring pliers to close the holding traps, which keep the prawns alive in the water until they are shipped to the buyer by float plane.

December 6 we move Logan home, and he resumes schoolwork by correspondence. Theda is coming up for Christmas. Al and I are going crazy working on the land and designing the future together. Our friends and neighbours shake their heads, but I know we're providing welcome drama for the community. The euphoria won't last, but we are the current episode of the local soap opera. Our wedding date is set for September 19, 1992. Boy, is that a leap of faith.

Joanie tells me that when her five-year-old son, Derek, hears "Yvonne's getting married," he exclaims, "What the hell is she going to do about Albert?" Looks down, scuffs one boot, shakes his head, cursing just like Grandpa Bill.

In spite of the bliss of our recent reunion, the daily grind grinds on. When not grubbing out the house site or doing schoolwork, Logan, Albert and I help Bill and other neighbours capture adult coho returning

Theda, deckhanding on *John*, takes on handling the 300-hp boat. The kids became adept at everything coastal, including running the boats.

to Scott Cove Creek. Every autumn we participate in the brood stock capture, but this year there are more returning coho than usual. We're over at Scott Cove two or three times a week right into December. These hundreds of coho should result in a quarter of a million eggs for our hatchery manager to take care of through the winter. Almost everyone in the neighbourhood turns up at one time or another to lend a hand, and a party atmosphere prevails in the hatchery building and along the stream-side trail. Returning salmon, like reuniting lovers, engender happiness.

Outfitted in hip waders and toting a couple of dip nets, Billy climbs down into the rocky gully where the stream boils along. Leaping from boulder to boulder, he crosses to the other side. He uses a long-handled dip net to scoop up salmon, and Albert or another of the men climbs down there with him to assist. Their job is to place the salmon head-first into water-filled vinyl plumbing tubes for their journey to the hatchery.

It's not easy to capture the coho. Nature compels them to surmount a boulder-filled watercourse, and working upstream against the rushing flow takes every iota of their focus and energy. They're fully aware of the threat posed by large, bear-like figures. Plenty of dark pools offer hiding places before they make the next leap. To net the fish, Bill must be quick and sure. Powerful side-to-side sweeps of the tail propel the coho. With mighty thrusts they arc over the boiling current to slam again and again against the granite, fall back to recoup and gather strength for the next attempt. Their leaps against the current are dazzling. It's breathtaking to watch and we cheer when one makes it to the next level.

Bill swirls the net in the foamy brown boil, reaching far under the rock on which he balances, feeling for the bump of contact with a salmon. When he feels it he pulls up the net. Maintaining steady lift, no sudden moves, he drags the netted salmon to the rock by his feet. Carefully and quickly he extricates it from the tangle of netting and slips it into one of the tubes the helper has ready.

The helper crosses the rocks in four quick steps and snaps the tube to a clothesline strung above the creek. Another volunteer mans the clothesline pulley on the higher bank. It takes a lot of energy to yard the fish up and across the creek. It's hard on the stomach and back muscles to

hand-over-hand the line through the pulley, and people take turns at this job. When the fish-filled tube arrives at the hatchery side of the creek, the pulley person unsnaps the tube from the line and hands it to the person waiting, who begins the relay run to the oxygen-filled waters of the hatchery tanks. Twenty or thirty yards down the trail another volunteer awaits delivery of the fish. Joggling along upside down in a narrow black tube for four to seven minutes can't be too comfortable for the fish, I think, consoling myself that our efforts and the fish's discomfort will result in a net increase of coho in the Scott Cove system and many other streams in the Broughton Archipelago.

Our hatchery organization, Mainland Enhancement of Salmonoid Species Society, began in 1984 with a donation from a sport fisherman named Pete Tageres. Billy told me when Pete asked how much it would take to build a hatchery and heard ten thousand dollars, he got out his chequebook, wrote out a cheque, tore it off the book and handed it over. Pete didn't want to be named but he has since passed away, so it's time to acknowledge his contribution. Ours is not the only hatchery Pete supported in this most practical way, either. From a low of fewer than fifty fish in the 1970s, the runs of returning coho have increased to an average of four thousand spawners. The return this year is extraordinary, and everyone is excited about it, especially fish-lovin' Billy.

In the hatchery, large tanks filled with a continually fresh supply of Scott Cove Creek water are waiting for the brood stock we bring in. If there are ten volunteers to relay the fish to the hatchery tanks, all goes quickly with a minimum of strain. If there are fewer than five volunteers, and plenty of salmon coming in, it's a tiring three or four hours running back and forth from the site of the pulley on the creek bank to the hatchery.

The eggs of the female salmon in the water-filled tanks will ripen up until they are ready to be fertilized. This might be right away or three weeks from the moment of capture. Billy is gentle yet firm as he caresses the bellies of the female fish, checking for ripeness. The males have been ready for this moment for weeks, and there is a lot of ribald joking as Billy cradles and strokes them to stimulate the ejaculation of sperm. Someone holds a bowl below the male to capture the milt, which is mixed into the eggs. The fertilized eggs are placed in stacks of trays.

When Claudia Maas was hatchery manager, she once showed me the eyed eggs in the trays. As she passed her hand over the tray full of round pink eggs, all the small black pinpoint eyes moved in unison, following the movement. The first thing a tiny salmon egg without a body does is watch its surroundings. Amazing.

Yvonne P. says the hatchery is nothing but trouble, with people squabbling all the time. Undoubtedly that's true, but rebuilding the coho runs in the Broughton Archipelago makes up for it. Little baby salmon are being planted in the Scott Cove system, Loose Lake,

The hatchery was a lot of work, but rebuilding the coho stocks made it worth the effort. Deborah Putman, Billy and me in front of the hatchery.

Viner River, Shoal Harbour and Gilford Creek. Peter Barratt comes in the spring with his helicopter, and we load buckets of wriggling fry into a "Bambi Bucket" hanging from the helicopter on the end of a long line. Peter flies off and drops these fish into faraway systems such as Whakana and Cockatrice Bay. The net result, in the best of all possible worlds, will be thousands more salmon returning to their natal rivers, where their flesh brings nutrients from the sea to build river estuaries, grow more trees, enrich the soil and feed countless other species. Including us. And maybe, as people's motives, ideas, working styles and pecking order needs jostle against each other, the friction provides an opportunity for insight and growth, both into ourselves and others.

House as Idea

Every wise woman buildeth her house.

Proverbs 14:1

AS USUAL, BILLY'S BEEN OVER WORKING with us on the land. He loves to give a hand with a project, especially if it involves falling trees or burning anything. His own home site is well managed, cleared of cover all around to prevent wolves, bears and cougars from getting close. His dock is always in good repair, safe to walk on or tie a boat to. His income-earning work is fishing in the summer and log salvaging in the winter, and he has the necessary tools for every task ever done out here.

Billy, way ahead of Al and me, says we'll need some bolt holes for the U-bolts that will hold our future dock in place. These bolts are u-shaped pieces of iron, ten or twelve inches long with pointy ends. He brings over a rock-drill and drills holes into the granite on the foreshore. I've never seen, let alone heard, a rock drill and the second the horrendous, pain-inducing, grinding noise begins, I run away fast. I grab my earplugs out of my work coat pocket, then return to watch and take pictures. Billy never wears hearing protection and tells me he has a constant roaring in his ears, like the sound of rushing water. I am adamant that Logan and Albert wear earplugs no matter what noisy job they are doing.

Once the U-bolts are inserted into the drilled holes, they will be secured with sulphur, which creates a chemical bond between iron and stone. A chain from each corner of the dock will be secured to the U-bolts on the land. A ramp will link the land and the dock.

"I've got my eye on two big fir for your ramp," Billy says. "I'll get 'em up on the boat ways, and you and Al can throw some decking on and we'll tow it in here." It'll sure be nice to have this ramp. We are still "dinging" over to the shore in the little yellow dinghy or the larger tin skiff we use for firewood loads. If the tide is high, we paddle across twenty feet of water; if it is low, there's only about four feet to cross. It's a real pain at the end of a day to slide down the foreshore rock to get to the boat, after we've been on the land for six hours and the tide has fallen eight feet. It's especially annoying if the boat has half-filled with water from the returning tide. We've gotten smarter, though, so this doesn't happen as often.

On December 22, during the highest tide of the last six months, Billy drives his old "Cat" off a flat rock by the shore at his place onto a barge, tows the barge over here with his speedboat, and drives the Cat off the barge onto our land. Disaster looms while Billy guffaws. I don't even know I am holding my breath until I suddenly suck in air with a gasp. Albert and Logan stand by to help however they can. I take pictures and try not to flinch as the old treads 'slip on the granite, then finally grip, and the Cat lumbers up the slope. Bill works every day for the next three weeks pulling out stumps, piling up debris and rearranging the hillside for our proposed house site.

He uses the winch on the Cat to raise a pole—a tall tree trunk stripped of branches—and secures it with three stay lines cabled to stumps. On the top he hangs a block, a big pulley. The winch cable runs from the winch on the Cat up through the block. The free end hangs loose on the land. Logan and Al drag the cable across the slope and wrap it around stumps. The old Cat shudders and the winch drum groans as Billy winds it in. Slowly, slowly, the big stumps we haven't been able to dig out release their hold on the earth and are dragged over one at a time to the growing pile underneath the pole. The stump pile swells to twenty feet high and the hillside is pocked with stump holes.

Finally the job is done and Bill reverses the process, and drives the Cat off the land onto the barge. I watch him towing the Cat-laden barge away and wonder what we would do if Billy wasn't here or didn't have a Cat or wasn't willing to help us or wanted $5000 for the job. He even

Billy used his old Cat to raise a spar pole, yard stumps out of our hillside clearing, and push rocks and dirt around. The fence encloses my first cellular garden.

acts as peacemaker when Albert and I squabble. A few rip-roaring fights about things that are ridiculous help us sort through to the real issues, and working so hard to build our house reminds us of the need to use our energy wisely. Sometimes we are like a match to tinder, though, and we had better get used to it.

One day, Albert felled a couple of big trees left over from the hand-logging Harley did and one fell right on the woodshed I'd built and filled with split pieces and small rounds. The woodshed split open like a ripe melon spitting seeds. I fell about laughing so hard I had to go behind the bushes. For reasons unknown, Al got upset at my laughter. Then we had a big fight about the height of the windows from the floor. What floor, one might ask? Indeed. As yet there is no floor, no windows, no house, no foundation. We saw the foolishness, thank goodness, in fighting about something that exists only in our minds and in a few sketches on paper.

The house, as idea, gets bigger and grander every day. Holy smokes. Albert's vision certainly exceeds mine in what can be accomplished. The small house I'd designed has grown, in theory, to a forty-four by forty-four square foot, three-storey, hillside-climbing behemoth that should provide space for everything we could possibly want over three lifetimes. My dream of an art retreat and studio home has become more tangible every day but I'm apprehensive about how long it might take to complete.

It's wonderful to have Albert's energies allied with mine. We have different working styles, though, and this can be a double-edged sword. I like to juggle several activities. That keeps me fresh, prevents me from hurting myself by spending too long doing something difficult. I get a lot done in my well-rounded daily life. Albert likes to do one thing only, until it is done, and not think about anything else. He has enormous endurance and can work twelve hours a day for three weeks or seven, whatever it takes. That can be a problem when I need to enlist his help with some smaller project. The friction generated from working through our differences is simply rubbing off the dross to get something smooth... or so I tell myself! And mostly we're able to meld our working styles into something functional. I'm content.

Community Rituals

And the food of islanders is reaped from the sea's harvest.

—Frank Collymore

ALBERT AND I SET THE PRAWN GEAR TOGETHER on the first day of fishing, April 1, and host his annual opening-day prawn party, which hasn't been held for a couple of years. Once we've set all three hundred traps where Al wants them, we pull one string of fifty, and take home whatever we've caught and invite everyone over. This was our community ritual when we first lived together. It was sorely missed over the past two years, and not just by me. The whole neighbourhood comes over, happy to "prawn out" and celebrate. People are practised at how to help, so they form an assembly line of choppers and cutters. When a couple of dozen garlic bulbs have been chopped into tiny pieces, the prawns are cut in half down the belly, split open and piled on platters. Three frying pans wait hot on the stove. Albert cooks with panache and lots of butter. He fries the prawns belly down, splashes the smoking prawns with soy sauce, and a final grind of pepper, et voila: a bowlful of hot butterflied prawns to be accompanied by belches, groans and moans of gustatory ecstasy.

Initially people brought potluck dishes, too, but there was always food left over. Nobody eats anything else when there is a table loaded with prawns. We simply devour forty or fifty pounds of them and loll around in the spring dusk, stuffed. I love starting the fishing season this way. Albert gives a bagful to all the neighbours and I like this about him.

Alex Morton, Eric Nelson and their daughter, Clio, feasting on prawns.

He never counts up the cost of these prawns. It is something he has that he can share, and he does, generously and quietly.

Nothing in the world is so delicious as a sunny Easter morning in Echo Bay and this one, April 19, 1992, is no exception. It's my sixth Easter Sunday in this island community. Today and every day I give thanks for the blessings flowing into my life. I'm not sure how many years the Proctors' Easter ritual has been going on. I'd guess since their daughters were small, but it's a time-honoured ritual in this neighbourhood. The excitement begins with days of advance preparation. Moms and kids dye hens' eggs with the colouring kits that have been available since I was a kid. On Easter Sunday we converge on the Proctors just before noon, each with a potluck dish. I bring a big Greek salad to go with a bowl of prawns and garlic butter. This is always a pleasant gathering—unless there is some festering neighbourhood wound, which we do our best to

ignore or rise above, possibly even mend. After lunch the kids are corralled in the house and the "bigs" go outside to hide both homemade and candy eggs for every "little." We place some along the plank walkway outside the back door so the little ones can find them and we hide eggs for the older kids in stump holes, hummocks and tree crotches way up the water tank hill. Before the kids are even let loose, bursting out of the house with baskets and bags ready, the ravens are hovering. There's always at least one spotted flying off with a wide-open, shiny black beak stretched around a bright pink Easter egg.

The first year we participated in this Easter egg hunt, 1987, I carried Bill's one-year-old grandson, Derek, around so that Joanie could assist her other son, Glen. Now Derek attends Echo Bay School and is fleet-footed in the race to find the hidden eggs. My own son is tall, not a child and not yet a man. He doesn't want to hang out with the adults, so he

Easter at the Proctors'. Russell Knierim (right) helps Cullen pick up her spilled Easter eggs. Photo Theda Miller.

finds a kid who needs a little help and guides him around the terrain. I'm proud of Logan when I see how kind he is. Living like this in an all-ages community has a profound effect on a kid's psyche. There are no barriers between age groups here. People in the middle, not yet big and no longer small, can help someone smaller and be appreciated for it. Surely this is a better way for character to develop than the "avoiding everyone not in your peer group" style of interaction I see in larger communities.

My joy in this Easter event is multiplied by the arrival of Theda. I acknowledge her right to choose to live with her father, though I always have a hard time letting her go. Easter for her is mainly about connecting with friends who, like her, have moved away and only return on holidays. She takes a terrific photo of one child helping another to pick up her eggs after a spill. Great material for a genre painting.

The Easter event at Billy and Yvonne's loops us from year to year and functions, as does their Hallowe'en party, as a seasonal measuring guide. We gather in an outdoor milieu under a bright sky, and I see how people have changed and grown, whether they are stressed or ill, joyful, desperately unhappy or simply overwhelmed by monumental tasks. Young mothers discuss when the community health nurse will be flying in; men clump together and smoke. When Billy saunters over, they talk about the best site for someone's new float, or who needs a couple of boomsticks, or when the next good high tide will be to put a boat up on Billy's ways. His paternal manner and obvious care for his neighbours radiate in this setting. I see his optimism and cheerful irreverence reflected in the lightened mood of someone worrying about dragging their house off the land onto a float.

"If I can't do it, nobody can," Billy claims and walks off laughing. You gotta believe him. There is always a new coastal performance to anticipate and I'll be there to watch, the next time he yards a house onto or off of the land.

The Easter egg hunt probably won't survive beyond Bill and Yvonne, assuming there are even any children left here in twenty-five years. At Easter and Hallowe'en, a bonfire in Billy and Yvonne's field draws everyone around it. Since ancient times, fire has brought us together, made us

part of the fabric of a greater whole. These annual events offer us a sense of security and continuity in this vulnerable community.

Before we leave, stuffed again with too much seafood, I make a date for tea with Billy's Yvonne, lend a hand with the dishes, agree to clean the school for Yvonne Scott when she and Jack go on their trip to Scotland, and hug several people I probably won't see for up to another year. By 3:00 pm, the crowd is thinning. Albert and I walk hand in hand down the ramp to the boat, call the kids, and go home to fire up a big burn pile until well after dark. It's a joyful contrast to the stress of last year's Easter party, when he and I were bitterly estranged.

Our current grunt activity is the production on Billy's mill of building lumber for our house. After many evenings and crumpled pieces of paper, Albert and I work out our floor plan and building specifications, then give the list to Bill so he can cut the lumber. He cranks up the old Cat and winches the logs up the chute below the mill, then "peevees" them onto the deck and from there onto the mill carriage. The mill motor is even louder than the rock drill, and Billy actually wears hearing protection. My ears, as usual, are firmly stuffed with little orange squishies. Even so, I can't think for the noise and simply work like an automaton. As one cut plank after another comes off the mill, I manhandle them down the ramp and pile them neatly with small boards set crossways in between each layer: "strip-piling" to ensure even drying and prevent warping. This is gruelling business, milling day after day all through the month of May. There is a brief change of pace when Billy puts the *Twilight Rock* on the ways to get her ready to go fishing. The boat is sitting on the cradle when a stiff gust of wind hits and the blocking gives way and she falls over. Albert pulls Billy's boat off the cradle with his prawn boat, *John*. The same day Billy has to yard Albert's old fishing boat off the beach, because it broke free from its moorings and drifted up on the high tide. Some excitement there alright. I was just happy not to have to mill.

More whale adventures make the week exciting. In Cramer Pass in my boat, Alex Morton and I are approached by a single bull orca. We hear echo-locating sounds pinging through the hull of the boat, getting louder and louder as the animal approaches us underwater. When the big bull blows explosively and surfaces near enough the side of the boat for me to touch it, Alex and I scream, grab each other's hands and fall down on the floor of the boat. Her son, Jarret, said later he heard us from the dock. The whale does this three more times, surfacing and blowing within two feet of my little speedboat, off the bow, at the stern, alongside. Once we get over the shock, Alex theorizes that a salmon may have been seeking shelter around my boat. No other idea seems to make as much sense.

And soon I get to go fishing! I'm to be Billy's deckhand on *Twilight Rock* this summer, making a voyage to the magical Queen Charlotte Islands. I can't wait.

Being Billy's Deckhand

*He has a power and influence, both direct and
indirect, which may be the means of much good or
much evil.*

—Frank Shay "The Captain," *A Sailor's Treasury*

THE PLAN TO GO FISHING WITH BILLY unfolds quickly. I know he has no
deckhand so I talk it over first with Albert and then with Billy's Yvonne.
When Al was just my holiday man and not my fiancé, I travelled the coast
a lot with him. Now that we're getting married and building a house, I've
been like a barnacle on a rock, glued to Echo Bay. I no longer make long
sea voyages to new vistas, but going to the Charlottes—to fish chinook
salmon—will be a first-time destination for Bill and I want to be on that
boat. In the end, it's simple: I ask and he hires me on. I don't doubt I'll be
an alright deckhand since I've had plenty of sea time with Al. My deeper
excitement is rooted in the opportunity to paint the Charlottes.

We depart Wednesday, June 24, with a big bag of Albert's prawns and
several loaves of bread from Yvonne P. We're well supplied with love
in the form of food. Spend a night at Port Hardy at the Seafoods dock,
where we load up with fuel, water and ice. The second day begins with
a long, hot walk uphill to downtown Port Hardy for groceries and last-
minute necessities.

"Get whatever you want to cook and lots of chocolate bars," says Bill
as he hands me a blank cheque. After groceries, it's over to the gear store
at the dock, where I find a terrific pair of gumboots, the last Italian pair

they have in stock. Men's size six, too small for most guys: I guess that's why they're still there. Lucky for me. Bill loads up on new hoochies and other fishing gear.

All over the docks an air of intense excitement shimmers like a heat wave, a pulsating energy barely held in check. People don't walk, they bustle purposefully. Skippers huddle in little knots, muttering in low voices—talking fishing secrets or the price of salmon, I guess. Deckhands brag about how many seasons they've been out and what terrible weather or skippers they've endured. Such electric energy is completely different from the prawn-fishing scene.

In spite of the obvious competitiveness, the nature of salmon necessitates that fishermen, and women, fish very near each other. Fish school together, fishers follow them. It's in everyone's best interests to selectively share information. In the prawn-fishing scene, each boat fishes alone; the prawners' guard their "set" locations fiercely and ship individually to the buyer. In both fisheries, I notice, it's often difficult to distinguish fact from fiction.

A ten-minute walk from the Seafoods dock is all it takes, after lunch, to deliver my paintings to Holly Clayton, a young woman who commissioned two watercolours of her family's waterfront property, one of the oldest homesteads on Hardy Bay. I love to paint old gardens, and this one truly qualifies. Surrounding the dignified old house, blue with white trim, are meandering paths of bluebells and columbine, and a lichen-covered gate opens to the beach. I'd visited earlier in the spring to shoot two rolls of film of the old house. Holly's mother promised to send me seeds from the pink columbine dancing all over the garden. Its crinoline-like layers of petals look like ballroom gowns for fairies. They're so frilly compared to their natural parent, the simple orange and yellow columbine found wild on the islands. Holly loves the paintings as much as I loved painting them and I return happily to the dock with my cheque in my hip pocket.

Back on *Twilight Rock*, preparations are complete. Our food is stowed away in the cupboards and storage bins under the seats in the cabin and the meat is on ice in the hold. I try out the telephone Billy recently installed, but there is no answer at home. Billy has one last conference with his fishing buddies: Alec Scott, our Echo Bay neighbour, with sons Billy and Byron on *Canadian Mist*, Ron Dawson on *Kelly-O*, Dave Gark on *Tropic Isle* and John Gibson on *Severn Mist*. Rigging clanks in the stiff breeze and my heart races as (at last!) we untie the mooring lines and Port Hardy recedes in the midday glare. After we pass Scarlett Point Lighthouse the sea heaves mightily, flinging white water up at the wheel-house windows. *Twilight Rock* lifts and falls, shudders and bucks under us. It's a long time since I last felt the dance of a boat with the sea. For hours I absorb the endless shades of blue, turquoise and sea green, running water and colour together in my mind. Bill breaks the long silence.

"Are you scared?"

"Should I be?" I gasp.

"Well, some deckhands are pretty scared," he says, laughing.

"I'm elated, enthralled, thrilled to bits. Are *you* scared?"

"Of course not," replies Bill.

"Well, if you're not scared, I'm not scared," and I turn back to the flying spray.

In my sea-going experience, if something goes wrong, I'm usually too busy to be afraid until after it's all over. And I have total faith in Bill, as I do in Albert. From time to time I've caught a ride with someone other than those two and realized quickly there are only a few to whom I'd entrust my life on a long sea voyage. So, trusting, I simply enjoy.

My stomach grumbles. Time to get busy boiling eggs for potato salad. Billy stops me when I go to throw the shells over the side of the boat.

"You gotta crush the shells before you throw 'em over," he calls out.

"Why?" I shout, suspended in mid-action as a wave leaps over the gunnel.

"Witches will ride out to sea in them and create winds."

I file this with something I learned from Albert: that it's bad luck to open a can upside down on a boat and if you do it must be thrown away.

"What else?" I ask Bill. "Got any more crazy fishermen superstitions?"

Billy thinks for a minute, then says, "Never leave a bucket of water on deck overnight. And no whistling in the wheelhouse, or you'll whistle up the wind." Some superstitions make good safety sense: you could trip over a bucket of water on the deck.

We pass Pine Island Lighthouse almost an hour after Scarlett Point. Seas rolling, spray flying, sun sparkling on blue and white water, the hull of the boat plunging eagerly through the swells; I'm electrified with joy. I stand between the skipper's seat and the deckhand's chair on the starboard side and let the lift and fall of the boat move me in a balance dance. My camera hangs around my neck, and I shoot two rolls of film of lighthouses, including Addenbroke Light. Around the Storm Islands we hear Prince Rupert Coast Guard Radio instead of the familiar voices of Alert Bay Coast Guard Radio. In the dusky blue hour, the sea calms and we set the hook in Kwakume Inlet after a successful crossing of Queen Charlotte Sound. Billy's fishing buddies motor in one by one and anchor up together, mast lights gleaming bright in the gathering violet twilight. In my mind I choose the colours and begin the painting.

At 4:30 am on the third day from home, Billy fires up the engine, and twenty minutes later we are on our way. Wind blows southeast at ten knots through a thousand shades of grey. We run all morning and are in narrow Finlayson Channel before the mist dissipates and the cloud cover lifts. I sunbathe for a while, dozing on the warm deck, protected from the breeze. Eventually I stir enough to get out the watercolours. Two paintings: the first, from memory, of the view out of Kwakume Inlet as we left and the second, the view as we motor up Tolmie Channel in the afternoon sun. The paintings go well, conveying the moisture-laden numinous light. We are in a dreamy bubble the whole timeless voyage through the endless inlets. It's lovely to have such lengthy painting periods, interspersed only by food preparation.

Three more lighthouses appear in the distance, grow closer and then are left behind: Dryad Point, Ivory Island and Boat Bluff. I photograph them all, hoping I can remember which is which. The skipper is happy plotting his course to the Charlottes. We make good time.

Boat Bluff, cemented to the rock in 1931, is the *most* scenic of lighthouses. All of them, in my books, can be called scenic. We pass very close

to it as we make the turn into Tolmie Channel. The neatly painted buildings cling like limpets to the steep rock, completely secure. Our ninety-degree turn gives me an excellent panoramic viewpoint of the red and white lighthouse buildings. I force myself to stop shooting after half a roll of film. I wave at someone up on the stairs; he waves back. I wonder if many visitors stop in to visit. It could be strange living in a lighthouse, solitary yet seeing dozens of boats pass closely by. We pass the gleaming white BC Ferry in the narrows, also a couple of colossal cruise ships. Coughlin Anchorage on Promise Island offers safe harbour. Tonight the regular thump of the oil pump delivering diesel to the stove does not keep me awake. Nor does Billy's snoring.

The fourth day dawns a flat silver calm with a sliver of crescent moon fading as the day brightens: a perfect day for running. The water temperature is a little warmer than yesterday; I'd expected it to get cooler as we travel northward. Billy says salmon like cold water.

Today we pick up Ketchikan Coast Guard Radio. Billy and I exchange a glance; we're a long way from home. Grenville Channel is the last long narrow waterway before we reach Prince Rupert. By the time we get to the northerly end of it, the water flows an opaque milky-green from glacial silt. Past the mouth of the Skeena River the water runs greeny-brown.

As long as I've known Billy I've learned something new every minute from him. Now at last I'm able to balance the scales a bit. We while away some of the long hours with language and math skills for him. He's been doing a bit of writing over the last few years and has some questions about grammar. He writes a piece, something about his fishing experiences, for example, or a creature he knows a lot about. Then I X with red every misspelled word, and he looks them up in the dictionary he keeps on the boat. He rewrites the piece with those corrections. I'm teaching him the multiplication tables as well, and long division with flash cards. I used to love to play teacher, and it's still fun. Billy is a dedicated learner. He sits at the wheelhouse table, scowling at the paper full of long division and times table drills, then hands his answers over to me to check.

Billy tells me he had no formal education. When his mother brought in the correspondence books, he said, "I ain't doin' that," and ran off into the woods. He taught himself to read as an adult, an admirable achievement. Until now, I've wondered why he got me to fill out cheques when we bought fuel or groceries.

Although Billy hates to play card games, he has a crib board sitting on the windowsill. When we get tired of writing and math drills, I teach him how to play. It doesn't take him long to get the hang of counting fifteens and pegging points.

The morning of the day we arrive in Prince Rupert, Billy notices the sounder is working badly.

"Doody butt pee stink pee, toddy oddy," he mutters.

"Is that a curse?" I ask.

"Yup," he says, laughing. "That's how we'd swear when I was a kid. It's a pisser, though, got to find a repairman when we get to Rupert. We're going to need that to see fish under the boat as well as know how far down the bottom is."

On the last long leg of the voyage to Rupert, I contact my brother Frank in Terrace by Coast Guard radio-telephone. He drives up to Rupert to have dinner with me. It's good to see his familiar face and hard to say goodbye when Billy and I depart Prince Rupert and head west. It's rough, with a big long sea running towards us so we don't bang around too much.

"Feels like the inside of a rubber ducky," I say as we buck into another green one.

Billy laughs. "Nothing like a west coast troller."

I've never been in seas this big, but we are ploughing into the waves, rising up, breaking through and sliding down the hollows. We are both high on it, making stupid jokes and laughing. Maybe the action of the foaming seas releases a lot of oxygen. Or laughing gas?

Two days left before opening day; plenty of opportunity for exploring and painting. The sea calms as we approach the north coast, and our first stop is at Cape Naden for a bit of beachcombing. Ranks of deer-pruned,

wind-stunted spruce trees hold on for dear life, and I do a detailed drawing. We walk Yatah Bay Camp and Halibut Beach. I'm breathless as we
ride the rough swells through the breakers to Halibut Beach, but Billy's
rowing skills are flawless. Tucked safely in behind the rocks we come
upon a group of juvenile harlequin ducks in eclipse, just changing into
their distinctive adult colouring.

Halibut Beach is where I finally find a glass Japanese fishing float all
by myself. I just don't have Bill's practised eye and I'm practically standing on top of a "rolling pin" style float before I see it. Finally we anchor
at Jorey Point, behind Mazarredo Islands in Virago Sound. Another day
of beachcombing brings us to a safe anchorage on the west side of Pillar
Bay, named after a great obelisk of rock soaring ninety-five feet straight
up with trees growing out of the top. In the wee hours the wind rises and
sets the boat to rocking gently, one way… then the other, each shift accompanied by a rattling thunk. We get up three or four times to search
out the source. It takes three tries before Billy finally secures the forty-
and fifty-pound cannonballs that are stowed under the floorboard by the
bunks. How irritating is an arrhythmic thunk… thunk… thunkthunk
when you are doing your best to fall sleep.

Although we're not yet fishing, we get up about 4:00 am, and even
that is late for Mr. Early-Riser Captain Billy. He clatters around the cabin
until I give in and get up. I never mind getting up early, though, because
the first breath of daylight always tingles my senses. Every morning on
Twilight Rock I feel a profound sense of anticipation. What will happen
today? Poking around shore just after sunrise, we discover the carcass of
a seven-foot-long squid. I wonder how long it lived and what caused its
death. After our cup of tea Billy pulls the anchor, and we head out to sea
so he can teach me how to work the fishing gear.

To work the gear, we stand in the cockpit, or well, at the stern of the
boat. I feel cozy and secure in there with the boat rail high up against
my midsection and not much room to flop about if it's rough. Directly
behind the cockpit is a deck-height space covered with a fitted board.
Underneath the board is a storage area where the flashers, snaps, leader
lines, lures and hooks are neatly coiled when not in use.

"This," says Billy, "is the 'bucket.' You got to keep it neat at all times, or it'll be a hell of a mess with all the hooks and fishing line tangled up."

Each leader line is attached to a snap. Billy shows me how to clip the snap to the wire stretched across the inside of the bucket. Fishing line, lure and hook are attached to the snap; sometimes a flasher is added. This arrangement is an exact number of inches long and one of my responsibilities as deckhand is to never reveal exact secrets like that. We coil up the leader as it is pulled in and then tuck the hook into a foam strip attached all the way around the back curve of the bucket.

Billy puts me on the port side, although I'll also work the starboard side from time to time. From the cockpit I face the bow. Directly in front of me sits a row of three hard, round, vinyl rests. Each cradles a fifty-pound cannonball attached to a slim cable. Beside each cannonball is a big brass lever, which I push forward to put the hydraulics in gear. A smaller, shiny brass lever activates the hydraulic power that raises and lowers the cannonballs. Move the lever to the right, and the cannonball comes up. Move it to the left, and down it goes. I raise a cannonball just enough to free it from the vinyl rest, swing it over the side of the boat, then press the lever to the left so the cannonball sinks into the water. Small brass markers attached to the cable mark two fathoms (twelve feet), and I snap the assembled leader to the cable every second fathom as the cannonball sinks.

We'll be using a variety of lures. We tied hoochies while running. We don't know which ones will attract the fish, so we've got dozens to choose from, all beautifully iridescent. Hoochies are tied about three feet behind a flasher to make them wiggle. Pink hoochies are for pink salmon. We won't be using those since we are after the mighty chinook. Several brass and chrome spoons together simulate a flashing school of fish.

Four or five times, I lower the cannonball, snap six or eight hooks on it at two-fathom intervals, and count the fathom markers as they descend so I know how deep the cannonball sits. The main line goes straight down over the side of the boat, but the other two lines are spread away and back from the boat through the action of a Styrofoam rectangle called a pig. Billy shows me how to clip the pig onto the line, and I

practise this move several times as well. After all three lines are set and dragging behind, I bring them in one by one, unclip the leader lines and coil them neatly in the bucket. Billy makes sure the hydraulics are working smoothly. He's excited about fishing tomorrow, as am I.

After working the gear for a couple of hours, I write and Billy alternately studies charts and confers with various fishing buddies on the radio. They have the radio tuned to a special channel only they can monitor. Rather naively, I'm amused by this, not yet fully comprehending the cutthroat nature of the business. Not everybody is honourable and respectful like Billy, it appears. He points out a couple of boats that are heading for Masset and tells me they're going to deliver on opening day.

"How can that be?" I exclaim in disbelief. There's so little patrolling and enforcement by the Department of Fisheries and Oceans (DFO) that some boats have already been fishing for a week, he tells me. I'm disillusioned.

Sprawling on the beach later in hot afternoon sunshine soothes my sense of outrage. I pinch myself to make sure I'm not dreaming. Am I truly here on the beach at Pillar Bay at the top end of the Queen Charlotte Islands? We probably travelled about 600 miles, and we're roughly 450 crow miles from home, but the distance feels immeasurable. The rocks here are like cookie dough full of raisins and fruit, great splats of hardened lumps. I paint a watercolour sketch of Pillar Rock through the steamy afternoon while Billy walks head-down looking for glass balls. He found a few earlier today and I did as well, although I mostly leave that job to him.

I'm in bliss, alone and painting. My gaze lingers on the impossibly blue sea, the monumental stone spire. Sandpipers run forth and back, playing tag with the rolling edge of surf. Warm wind plays a soft tune in the spruce trees cradling the beach. I hug myself with the thrill of it all and squeeze out a bit of Prussian green.

"Let's go row through the swell." Billy's voice breaks into my painting dream a long while later. I'm as good as done anyway, and stiff. "Just leave your stuff there, it'll be fine." I guess it will; there's not a living soul on the beach but us. I pick up my camera and climb into the rowboat. Bill shoves it out into the surf and jumps in.

Billy is a total maniac in a small boat, but when he says "Let's go for a row," I can never say no. I take pictures from the bow as the little dinghy sashays through the swells. Big green rollers lift us up... up... we hang high on the wave tip for a long second and then whoosh, down we plummet towards the flat rocks, the round rocks, the sharp and pointy rocks. I'm sure we're going to hit wrong or slide and end up ass over tea kettle, but we never do. Billy has an unerring instinct for pulling the oar a little left or a little right at the absolute *last* moment. I scream a lot for the fun of it and use up a roll of film. I don't get a photo op like this every day, and the roller-coaster thrills just keep coming.

Billy reminds me the small halibut we hooked this morning is slow-cooking in the oven, and I've plans for a pineapple-upside down cake. A good dinner to end a good day. He expertly extricates us from the maze of rock and surf and stops at the beach for me to get my painting gear. The baking halibut sends a beam of fragrance that draws us homeward.

After dinner we investigate the interesting things our beachcombing has

Monumental Pillar Rock on Haida Gwai'i. *Twilight Rock* is in the distance.

netted to date. Our collection consists of one sea lion shoulder blade, which I'll take home to my garden; one deck bucket; one black Japanese survey-or's stake; five round glass fishing floats; and one rolling pin style float.

One of the glass fishing floats has Japanese symbols on it, raised from the surface. The colours of the glass range from the palest sea green to a deep rich teal. Only one, my solo find from today, is a completely differ-ent colour, a greenish golden-brown exactly like bull kelp. Some of the floats are as small as two inches in diameter, and the largest is about five inches across. I know Bill has some at home that are much larger, includ-ing a double-bubbled one called a "Dolly Parton." One of the floats has netting woven around it, and the glass is roughened and worn in the spaces in between. I imagine the float trapped high in the intertidal zone and rolling round and round for a long time as the surf swirls it against the rocks. We reflect a while on just how long some of these things have been floating across the sea from Japan, and how many glass balls there may still be bobbing around out there. They're so much more appealing than the North American Styrofoam or plastic corks that can be found all over the beaches. Old-fashioned carved cedar corks are considerably more appealing than the plastic ones but nothing beats the beauty and mystery of a glass ball.

I make notes as Billy lists the wildlife we've seen. Today was our first sighting of whales, two of them, humpback whales blowing offshore while we worked the gear. A delicate spotted fawn walked the beach with us just past Wiah Point, and five adult deer the next day. Besides the harlequin ducks on Halibut Beach, we've seen hundreds of rhinoceros auklets, a dozen sooty shearwaters, four oyster-catchers and one north-ern fulmar. Sounds like a Christmas song.

It's been a day rich with stimulating activities, compared to the days we spent running sixteen to eighteen hours, watching an endless parade of islands roll by. Time to say good night and climb into my rocking bunk, listen to a few amazing fishing tales in the dark before Bill begins to snore, send a good night to my Albert, and sleep deeply until 3:30 am. Tomorrow we fish.

Fishing the Mighty Chinook

iron bound / *edged with rocks or cliffs; rugged; as,*
an ironbound coast

Webster's Dictionary, Unabridged 1979

The first day of the opening, July 1, we bring in twenty-one smileys—spring salmon weighing thirty pounds or more—by 8:30 am. I'm astounded and exhausted, and we've barely begun. I'm already counting my chickens and figure I've made close to seven hundred dollars. The bite slows down, but we pick up another seven fish throughout the day. I'm in a state of vibrating alertness during these adrenaline-charged hours. At the end of the day I declare in the fishing log "I love to fish!"

Once a big spring hooks on the gear and is brought close to the boat, Billy shows me how to heave it in. He leans confidently over the side, whacks the hook of the gaff under the fish's gill plate with practised accuracy and deadly speed, and in one smooth, powerful arc flings the salmon onto the deck. My delivery of the salmon onto the deck is less wonderful. I make numerous attempts to even begin to be accurate in the initial swing of the gaff. Once I do get the gaff hook under the gills, I lean way over the side, and hand over hand, pull the gaff and then the salmon up into my arms. If the fish is smaller, less than twenty-five pounds, I can fling it onto the checkers, the working area in front of the cockpit. If it is larger, I wrap my arms tightly around the muscular creature, turn and slither it bodily onto the deck.

Billy says I cuddle them in while the poor things are fighting hard to get free. I have the same set of feelings that I experience with prawn fishing. It's

My first smiley. Getting it into the boat was a huge effort and nearly brought me to tears.
Photo Bill Proctor.

powerful and exciting to wrestle a large creature into submission, it will make me a lot of money if we get a couple of hundred of them, yet it feels terrible to kill these shining bronze fish we bring up from the deep. Billy takes pains to kill them as quickly and respectfully as possible, and we clean the bodies thoroughly and pack them well in the ice in the hold.

The salmon caught on our second day of fishing are distinctly different from the first day's catch. They're all slightly smaller and narrower, because they are schools from different natal streams. Some of the big chinook have a great number of large dark freckles on their tails and heads. Spring salmon have a distinctive smell, brassy and metallic, not "fishy" at all. More like hot metal.

Unfortunately, catch volumes deteriorate quickly. On our second and third days fishing the top end of the Charlottes, we catch fewer than ten salmon each day. I lose a big one trying to wrestle it into the boat, but Billy doesn't get upset. He just goes into the cabin and leaves me to it. He

Billy's technique for hawking in spring salmon.

99

awards me a smile if the fish is there lying on the deck and says nothing if it isn't. This is a marked contrast to many skippers who verbally abuse their crews and blame them for everything that goes wrong. A couple of young fellows told me their skipper wouldn't let them out of the cockpit even to eat meals. Some skippers are tight-fisted with the groceries and dole out skimpy portions to their deckhands. I'm horrified to hear some of the things said on the radio about wives and/or crew. Billy doesn't say one word about me, except for raving about the chocolate chip cookies I bake for us. For this I am thankful.

Billy's fishing buddies Ron, Dave and John, decide they will head for Vancouver Island through the Inside Passage, but on *Twilight Rock* we vote (all two of us) to work our way down the outside coast. Alec, with Billy and Byron, on *Canadian Mist*, says if we don't leave him behind, they'll come too. Billy agrees to run a bit slower so Alec can stay with us.

After the vote to tackle the western coast, we deliver the salmon we have on board to Masset. En route Billy has a little panic attack when the bilge pump won't shut off. The boat appears to have sprung a leak; however, it's only a small stick lodged in the pump. Billy wires in a spare pump pretty quickly and we carry on. The weather has been grey and gloomy ever since fishing opened. It continues to darken when we leave Masset and approach Langara, a sea-swept terrain of glistening shards of black rock and sharp spires. Billy wants to take a little "look see" at the fabled Langara Lighthouse, which is still manned, so we plough our way through a wicked coal-dark sea under a bleak sky and fish for a couple of hours.

Retracing our route around Langara Island, we turn west through Parry Pass. Sport fishing heaven here, and the pass is studded with large floating fishing camps and vessels. Numerous small boats full of orange-suited people bob along in a sluggish swell, dragging half a dozen fishing lines. Out of Parry Pass and into Mother Ocean again, smooth and velvet grey with a barely perceptible edge between sea and sky. At Cape Knox we make a clean ninety-degree turn and commence the southward expedition.

We've been using Kathleen Dalzell's book, *The Queen Charlotte Islands*,

Volume 2, as our companion guide to the inlets and bays of these islands. Her information helps us decide where to explore and what to look for on our land excursions. Billy gets the idea one day that he could write the same kind of book about the history, lore and natural details of the Broughton Archipelago.

"What do you think?" he asks. "Is my writing good enough to do a book?"

"It could be. You just need practice."

"Well, maybe you'll help me put something together," says Billy. Sounds like he means it.

"Sure, be fun," I say.

"You can do drawings and pictures, too," he says. I like the idea and he's eager to begin. Now when he writes, he focuses on his home territory and draws rough charts with short notes on them like "goat farm here." It's a start.

The good ship *Twilight Rock*, sturdy and intrepid, makes her way down the western coast of Graham Island, enwrapped by thick fog, buffeted by the unceasing lift and fall of heavy swells. We're followed by the beamy *Canadian Mist*, a fitting name for a boat in these fog-bound waters. Both crews troll steadily as we motor along. From time to time someone heaves a smiley over the stern. Can't really *see* the Charlottes in these conditions, and I'm glad when the fog thins and the sun peeks through late in the afternoon.

Tian Village is a welcome anchorage. We amble around in the misty forest searching for the old village site and the Welcome Figure. In that moody, haunting place, wraithlike tendrils of fog conjure up the spirits of long-dead people unwilling to depart their home site. Later we head out, fish the evening bite for a grand total of two, return to the old village and drop the hook for the night.

The next two days turn out to be major wildlife sighting days. I get that smile on my face as I hook onto a couple of big ones, but I lose one right beside the boat when Bill has to speed up over shallows. The extra speed rips the hook out. We come upon a group of dolphins, leaping a hundred strong. In the evening, as we put the gear in the bucket, a pod of killer whales blows by. The following day, orcas again. One large bull rises majestically off the bow. At the entrance to Tasu, a humpback whale blows and leaps, and nearing Gowgaia Bay, a pod of Dall's porpoise zips along beside us for several miles. These fellows are very natty dressers, their colouring resembling a tuxedo in distinguished black and white, much like the orca. The wildlife sightings are rejuvenating; I never tire of marine mammals. All creatures great and small are bright spots in an infinite landscape of sea and sky. Another night, another anchorage; this time Goski Bay, where we savour baked sockeye for dinner. There's time enough to complete a detailed drawing of an interesting configuration of rocks and trees.

A Canadian song I hear on the CBC goes like this "Rocks and trees, trees and rocks, rocks and trees and trees and rocks and rocks and trees...." A catchy rhythm and memorable lyrics that sum up Canada from the mountains to the sea. This landscape is basically trees, rocks, water and sky, yet each place has a fifth element, which is its essence. An ineffable something that cannot be defined with words but can be alluded to through the painted image. Every little bay and nook has its own special mood and character and hopefully, the unique essence can be expressed and perceived in a painting.

As a wonderful finale to our Queen Charlotte Islands fishing/exploring adventure, we are escorted around the southern tip of Anthony Island (Sgan Gwai'i) by an energetic group of Pacific white-sided dolphins. We approach Ninstints (Nan Sdins) Village at 7:30 am. A pale sun dissolves the pearly morning fog, drop by shimmering drop.

This village is situated in a jewel box of a bay, sheltered from the westerly winds by verdant forest. A tidewater inlet and small island lie to the east of the curving white beach. Once Billy drops the hook, we put the dinghy over the side and enter through a narrow channel bounded by Anthony Island to the south and the small island to the north. High on the grass above the beach stand several sombre time-worn totems. Several more are tilted or have fallen to the spongy ground, inevitably being reabsorbed into the forest. Animal and human figures are stacked one upon the other on mortuary poles and house frontal poles. Sea Grizzly is here and Wolf too; Killer Whale, Eagle, Beaver and Frog. Human Watchman figures and Grizzly Bear, with human legs protruding from his mouth, show how vulnerable thin-skinned humans must have felt. Long ago seventeen houses stood here facing the curved shore.

Only the wind sighs now. It whispers to a doe as she wanders out of the spruce forest nonchalantly nibbling, large brown eyes gazing at me as her ears flick. Slowly I circle the fallen mortuary boxes, pacing out the depression in the soil where once a cedar dwelling stood. I imagine how it once was: an active village full of purposeful people. I'd expected to find it enchanting and magical, but I am not fully prepared for the way the silent old totems and the stillness of the site generate a sense of eternity. The wind tenderly draws faint music from the needles of the venerable spruce; raven kroks and the heat of the rising sun stirs up a salty fragrance from the kelpy sea-wrack on the beach. I remove my coat and let the sun lie golden on my closed eyelids, feeling the weight of the world turning and generations of human lives passing.

A memory of another time surfaces. In August 1985, I was in southern France on a painting trip. As I ascended the deeply indented stone stairs in the two-thousand-year-old coliseum in Arles, I trailed my fingers along on the stone wall beside me, thinking: how many people over thousands of years have walked these steps and slowly worn them down? I felt a change in the texture of the rock under my hand, looked as a shiver rushed over me. My fingers had sensed a fossil in the stone wall, a fossil of a shell. These stones had been quarried more than two thousand years ago from a nearby mountaintop five hundred feet higher than this old town. I fell spinning through time, catapulted back two million years, to when ocean covered this mountainous land and the shell was a living being in an ancient sea.

Ninstints creates the same response in me of time immemorial, my own consciousness just one small flash in the vast proceedings of the unfolding universe. We live, we make our mark. We die. The ancient cedar trees outlive us. The granite mantle of the earth, the sweeping escarpment of stone outlasts the trees and is ground down through slow millennia.

Ninstints is a special place, no doubt about it, a place I've longed to visit. It begs to be painted; no painter can ignore its call. I only hope I can do justice to the powerful feeling evoked in me by the place. It's a cultural treasure, entirely worthy of its designation as a UNESCO World Heritage Site.

And once more we are off into the great blue sea. With a pang in my heart I write, "We are leaving the Queen Charlotte Islands, magical Haida Gwai'i." I've got to stop for a minute and wipe my eyes. I'm surprised I feel this sad. Cape St. James fades into the darkness behind us as dawn breaks, a lemonade spill across an ink-blue sky. It's blowing thirty-three knots southeast. Billy snores in the bunk. I'm on morning watch, and the first thing I see is a shark fin! I don't see it for long, but it's definitely a shark fin and goosebumps rush for my scalp.

We're headed for Cape Sutil, an eighteen-hour run, the course is set for 105 degrees. Billy gave me a lesson in using the parallel rulers for navigation before he crashed. "I hope we won't be too far off course when I get up," he muttered as he headed for the bunk. Nice.

Not much to look at out here today. Six hours running before Cape St. James disappears completely, then six hours of only the lonely grey sea before finally the faintest smudge, Cape Sutil, on Vancouver Island, appears.

A multitude of images flash in front of me as I sit here gazing at the empty horizon. My notebook sits open upon my knee, and memories wash through my mind. I'm replete, almost fat with a treasure house of new visual sensations, enriched by the experiences of the last ten days. Once in a while in my life I'm aware I'm in the midst of events that will mark and shape my future. Often, like now, those moments have been at sea.

I remember the first time I went crab fishing with Albert, out from the White Rock pier into the shallow waters of Boundary Bay, in the summer of 1979. As his little double-ender *Ruby* pulled away from the dock, I had a strange, slipping feeling, as if I was time-travelling. Everything that seemed important or stressful simply melted away, receded and diminished along with the dock, the houses, the town, and the land mass upon which they all sat. I wanted, no, knew I must have more of that feeling. That trip presaged the entire future shape of my life. It's taken thirteen years for me to get here to these fabled mystical islands. I've put in a lot of sea time in the interim, and I'm a long way now from Boundary Bay.

It's with a sense of fulfillment that I take my leave of these misty isles. I'll probably never know them intimately, but I'm grateful to have gotten this close. Two humpback whales appear in the grey gloom ahead, breaching and smashing their tremendous tails again and again. Geysers erupt from their massive cavorting. Ten marvellous minutes of fabulous entertainment as we drone along. Here comes the skipper out of the bunk, up the short ladder, ready for a cup of tea.

"How 'bout I beat you at a game of crib," Billy offers.

"Fat chance," I say, getting the cards and the board from the windowsill.

"We gotta tie some leaders after that so we're all ready for Cache Creek."

Billy wins two out of five crib games. I guess I'm going to have to sharpen my game.

Fishing the Gully

AFTER EIGHTEEN ENDLESS HOURS OF RUNNING we finally make it to Cape Sutil, set the hook with great relief and topple into bed.

"I sure love my little bunk," says Billy, every single night when he gets into it. The bunks are narrow with a high side to keep you in when the boat rolls. I do not yet love mine—I'm used to a much bigger bed—but they are soft enough with bright striped blankets knitted by Billy's mom.

Cape Sutil's contrasting sides give it a split personality. On the east towards Port Hardy, the beach curves in a gentle white arc; the surf softly tumbles in, and it's safe and protected. An arm of rugged rock stretches out to separate the eastern face of the cape from the western. Behind that barrier, from the northwest, the sea explodes in thunderous billows. The roar of the surf provides constant background noise as I prepare tea on the oil stove. It takes a psychological commitment, real determination on the part of the skipper, to up the anchor and poke the nose of the boat out from behind the rocks and around the corner to fish. *Twilight Rock* heels over as we round the end, then straightens up when Billy turns the bow into the heaving swell. Perhaps it's a trick of how the light lies on the water that makes it appear dark and foreboding. A dozen eagles perch on the rocks; there must be something of interest to them. Maybe the same thing that interests us. Fish. The low tide slack offers up twelve spring salmon, but once the tide turns to flood, things slow down considerably.

Into the bucket goes the gear, and we head for the calm side of the cape to anchor.

Cache Creek cannot be found on the chart, only the name "Shuttleworth Bight." At the turn of the century, halibut schooners that fished this area stashed gear and spare dories in the bush here—hence the name Cache Creek.

It's only 4:00 in the afternoon, and Billy thinks we can make it through the bush to walk the beach on the west side. We pull the dinghy off the wheelhouse roof, lower it over the side, climb in and row for shore.

"There's a good trail over from here," he tells me. "You can get a piece of the whale skeleton that's on the beach. There's a face carved in the rock I'll show you." Billy pokes around the bush for a few minutes, then impatiently dives in. I follow him and soon the trail brings us to our knees. I'm certain this isn't the easy path he has in mind but rather a bear trail. Billy leads and I crawl behind him. If we're going to meet a bear I'm selfishly glad it'll be him nose to nose! An incendiary glow through the tangled thicket reveals the northwest-facing beach. The sky burns gold, and the surf lies calm in lambent, incandescent sheets. We find the killer whale skeleton and the face-like petroglyph, still in good condition, pecked into a flat stone. I gather up one of the vertebrae, another addition to my collection of natural wonders. Luckily Billy finds the proper trail for our return and we hurry along it through the gathering dusk.

With our catch from the Charlottes and the twelve from Cache Creek, we have a good load of spring salmon iced down in the hatch. Billy is encouraged by our one day of fishing here and decides we'll deliver to Seafoods in Port Hardy, then fish Cache Creek for the next few days. As we head for Nawhitti Bar, I hose down the decks and the cockpit. When the telephone rings in the cabin, it's such a shock, I jump and run for it. I'm sure it's Albert. While running I slip and fall hard, ramming my knee into the edge of the stabilizer, but I scramble up and make it to the phone.

"He's coming!" I yell out the door to Billy, after I hang up. "Al's coming to Port Hardy! He's bringing bread from Yvonne!"

"Take the wheel and stay close to the starboard shore," says Billy,

climbing out of the cockpit. He's all business running the boat over the Bar. Still, we are entertained by grey whales playing near the beach and one lone minke whale. Billy heats up water and shaves, puts on clean clothes. Right. We are heading for civilization. Following his lead, I take a bowl of hot water down to the bunk, wash, dry and change into the clothes I tucked away in the drawer under the bunk the day I came on board. They smell musty but faintly perfumed; no dried blood, salt or fish slime. No way to wash my hair, though, kept in a braid under my Seafoods baseball cap for almost a month.

It's the best end to a good trip. After the boat sidles up to the Seafoods dock, there, coming down the boardwalk, is a hairy, slobbery St. Bernard. Following the dog, two legs are visible below a gigantic bouquet of roses. It's Albert, my husband-to-be, with Buddy, my dog-to-be, come to Port Hardy for my twenty-four-hour shore leave. Two dozen fragrant roses billow from his arms: 'Fantin Latour', 'Double Delight', 'Chrysler Red'. He packs a big bag of mail as well, and my smile cannot spread wide enough to express my joy. Albert gets us a room at the Port Hardy Inn, which, in spite of its comparative luxuriousness, allows Buddy in. I spend so long in the tub Al teases me about making love to a raisin.

Off to sea again the following day, July 13. Iced up, fuelled up, grubbed up, all ready for another trip. Our first fishing day is amazing; we circle around and around in the same spot for twenty-six good spring salmon. I lose three and Bill loses one or we would have had thirty. It's disappointing to lose one but thrilling to bring in a double header.

My knee starts throbbing. It's infected from the fall I took on the deck. I do all I can to fight it. Never, never, *ever* run on a wet deck, or on a boat, period. I've learned my lesson.

When the fish quit biting on the ebb tide, we reward ourselves for the endless hours doing the "circle jerk" with shore excursions. In goes the dinghy and it's off to shore we row, hey ho. Painting imagery everywhere here, abstract natural sculpture. Four rocks lodged immovably between two smooth driftwood logs show the force of the sea that hurled them there. Dried seaweed in red, orange and golden browns add calligraphic decoration to the sculptural flow of the weathered driftwood. "Rocks and trees, trees and rocks…" I think, as I make a quick sketch and shoot a photo. A small deer looks at me curiously as I limp from behind some large rocks. The beach is difficult to navigate with a swollen hot knee.

I spend most of the next day in the bunk, sweating with fever. Billy is worried enough that he brings me a bowl of soup, and finally we decide I need medical care. It sure feels like blood poisoning to me. I'm not much use as a deckhand since I can barely roll out of the bunk to use the head. Billy hates like hell to turn back, especially when the fishing is good, and I hate to be the cause of it, but he pulls in all the gear and heads for the Bar. I'm in Port Hardy hospital with an IV injection of drugs for a couple hours while Billy picks up a prescription for me. My knee improves steadily, and within twenty-four hours I'm back in the cockpit, "hawking" in smileys.

The day after the drugs take effect on my knee, I break out in spots. What now? Billy has a bad sore throat. We're both fed up with the unceasing swell here, too; it never lets up. Billy feels queasy, whether from seasickness or some virus, he can't say. I think it's seasickness. We got spoiled with the stimulation of a new landscape daily in the Charlottes. Here at the top end of Vancouver Island, every day is the same: the grey sky; the heaving grey sea; the monotonous, unarticulated shoreline; fishing the gully around and around, hour after droning hour. In the afternoon I snooze in the bunk. Billy lies down on the wheelhouse floor to catch a few winks between rounds.

To relieve the boredom, we try innovative gear-setting techniques to see how fast we can get the hooks in the water in the morning. Most days we are up at 3:30 am. Here at Cache Creek the anchorage is close to the fishing ground, so the time lapse between when we get up and when we begin to set is short. Up to now, we each have been setting the gear on our own sides of the boat, me on the port side, Billy on the starboard. Naturally, Billy is much faster than I, though every day I've become a little more efficient and now it only takes me a few minutes longer than

him to snap on the hooks. When he has all three lines out, he comes over to my side to hand me snaps, and I hook them on to the line for the back pig, the last line to be set. Billy suggests we try taking turns handing the snaps to each other for all three lines on each side. The next day we begin with me slapping snaps into Billy's outstretched hand while he hooks them onto the line as fast as he can. He does the same for me while I set my gear. With this method we get the gear in the water more than twice as fast.

There are a lot of hours to fill between 3:30 am and 10:00 pm, when we fall into the bunks. Having mini-competitions or devising methods of doing things faster perks us up a bit. When not working the gear, cleaning fish or dishes, or snoozing, Billy writes in his notebook, dredging

Billy and I fell into a good rhythm of working together. It was satisfying to see the checkers fill with spring salmon.

up memories and thinking about what to put in his book. I doodle in my sketchbook, sometimes drawing him or the stove or what's out the wheelhouse window, sometimes just constructing imaginary drawings that develop into whales and swans and fanciful figures. Billy looks over my drawing and says, "I couldn't draw a straight line."

"You don't really have to for imaginary drawings," I tell him. I give him a short lesson and he tries his hand at it but he is not comfortable with the idea of drawing imaginary shapes. I love this way because I can easily pick up where I left off when interrupted by the need to bring in a salmon.

I stretch and shake my drawing hand loose; fingers and brain need a change of pace. Time to check the gear so I pull on the black Marigold gloves, the yellow "wristers" or sleeve protectors and the Helly Hansen rain pants, cross the deck to the stern, and grab onto the short rope Billy hung from the end of the boom to ease the swing down into the cockpit. I scan the poles—could be a spring salmon hooked on. I scan the sea wide and far as I flip the gurdy lever to bring up the cannonball. In the distance a grey whale blows. The breeze off the land carries the scent of conifers. The gurdy wire hums.

The end of the fishing trip draws near. We put the gear in the bucket for the last time and run down Goletas Channel under a cloud-tossed sky. The moon flirts with veils of mist, now you see me, now you don't.

"What're you smiling about?" asks Bill.

"I'm just so happy," I say. "I love this. I love being at sea and fishing and shore parties, drawing and taking pictures and seeing the whales and everything. Don't you?"

"Yep. Except for drawing. It's not my thing." Out the window, a moon-spattered sea. In my mind, a wedding dress. Oh! I can't think about that right now, with my mind full of fishing.

Wedding in the Park

We're in a chaotic flurry of activity, digging out foundation holes for the house, preparing for our wedding, canning sockeye. But today is a sunny Sunday, the kind of day I'm compelled to do as little as possible.

I'm out in the Burdwood Group, poking around a small island beside a narrow surge channel that goes dry at low tide. Several large squarish boulders sit here, arrayed as if by some unseen hand, on a pristine shell beach. Dappled with the lacy shade of an ancient twisted fir tree, the setting is monochromatic, running the full value scale from earthy black through warm ochre to bright white. It seems perfectly designed, with the principles of simplicity, austerity and restraint that characterize the formal Japanese garden. A friend modelled here for a painting once, nude, seen from the back, seated on the edge of the rock, knees up in a contemplative pose, gazing into the dazzling sunsparkle of the tide running the surge channel. The figure in the painting is part of the scene, vulnerable, with only the thinnest skin to protect her from the elements. This is what it is to be human in wilderness, reliant on your wits and will to create a safe place. I sit in the same place, notebook on my knee, warm in the September sun.

The tide gently burbles and chuckles its way higher up the white shell beach. As the celadon-green water rises, tiny fish poke around, searching for food scraps. Crabs barely the size of my thumbnail erupt from under the layers of shell, scrabbling out as the sea water moistens their hiding places. Attracted by the flurry of activity, I squat down by the edge of the rapidly advancing sea. A small crab clutches a limpet shell with both claws. The unfortunate limpet looks exactly like a tiny white roast on a platter. But the crab has a problem.

He can't let go of the limpet to eat his catch because small fish and other crabs are grappling to capture the tasty treasure. A mighty battle is playing out like a silent movie in the three inches of water below my feet. The crab fights hard to keep his catch. When a sculpin butts at him, he lets go of the limpet to snap his claw at the fish's nose. The sculpin jerks straight backward, but in a flash another crab snatches the limpet and scrambles away, victorious. The crab that has lost its dinner waves its claws around in a fury. I swear I hear a scream of rage and loss. High drama; miniature characters.

Echo Bay Park is the perfect place for a wedding. The long government dock provides parking for boats, the grassy sward an open space for the gathering. There is room under the old cedar trees and the giant maple for tables laden with the beautiful food our neighbours bring: smoked salmon, crab dishes, halibut and prawns, seafood supreme. My high school friend Liz (Millar) McEwan is the officiating marriage commissioner. Her mom was a Landsdowne from Kingcome Inlet, but Liz has never been there. Liz's mom was the first person outside my own family who urged me to pursue an art career. I hope she knows somehow that I did. My parents come and my brother Frank, joining the guests that Billy picks up in Port McNeill the day before the wedding. Best man Dave Dabor, Al's brother Bill, maid of honour Deb Putman. Jacob from Victoria with his son Josh, our musician friend John Douglas with his guitar. Ted Emmonds, our friend who moved away from Echo Bay for a few years, and his family come from Lund by speedboat. Everyone is being taken care of by one neighbour or another.

The evening before the big day Albert butterflies fifty pounds of prawns for a family dinner. My mom perches by the platter and eats with

gusto. Prawn juice runs down her chin; her fingers glisten with butter. I watch her enjoying what we have to offer and file this good family moment in my memory. Logan chops garlic valiantly, Theda keeps up with the cut prawns, Albert keeps a'cooking.

"Play the guitar, Daddy, okay?" He obliges and we sing "Blue Eyes Crying in the Rain" and our old familiar train songs. My best memories from childhood revolve around the comfort and joy of singing with my dad. We have spent many evenings singing together like this but never in my own home. I look around the room, feeling unmitigated love and gratitude that they came to my wedding and that we are in this room singing, eating and laughing together.

The bridal party disembarks from *Twilight Rock* at Echo Bay dock just as the rain begins. Deborah and Theda are behind me, and Logan is just behind Billy. Photo Alex Morton.

Later, we try on our dresses to make sure we have the necessary accessories. I shopped for my dress in Vancouver with Deb and Theda. The one I drooled over was a star-shot midnight blue, full-length, beaded Oleg Cassini creation. However, I couldn't bring myself to break the bonds of tradition and my own practicality. I settled on a white, floaty satin skirt with lace panels and a lacy top with a deep V-neck and full pleated sleeves. Yeah, way more practical. Theda's dress is perfect, icy blue satin with lace and bows at the shoulders: a Snow White gown. She looks so beautiful in it I burst into tears.

Everything that can go wrong during the wedding weekend does. While we're doing a clean-up the day before the ceremony, Logan goes out to burn some garbage in the burn barrel and slips on the rain-wet deck. Instinctively he flings out his hands to grab something to break his fall. In mid-reach, he realizes he'll burn his hands if he grabs the hot barrel, and instead, he clasps it with his arms. He sustains bad burns on both forearms, and Joanie runs him the twenty-eight miles to Port McNeill Hospital. The morning of our wedding day, the generator quits working so we can't iron out wrinkles from the wedding clothes. The water in the dam runs dry so we have to dump-flush the toilet with buckets of sea water and go to the Proctors' for baths.

When Albert and I chose Echo Bay Park for the wedding, we were counting on lingering September sunshine to provide a bright day. Around noon, Joanie organized the potluck dishes on two long tables on the grassy mound outside the hall on the ancient midden. We've had eighteen days of sunshine in a row but the sky clouds over on the afternoon of the nineteenth. Half an hour before my bridal party and I are due to arrive at 2:00 pm, rain spills from the clouds. Later, I learn Joanie marshalled the wedding guests, who moved all the tables, chairs and food inside the community hall just before the deluge.

Albert goes on ahead to the park with Bill and Dave. Billy comes to our float house in *Twilight Rock* to transport the bridal party to the park. Logan, the ring bearer, Theda, the flower girl, and Deborah and I board the fishing boat, and voyage in fine style to the Echo Bay dock. Through the increasing rain, Alex Morton takes pictures of us from the top of the

ramp. Not what I envisioned, but there it is. My bridal party and I are draped in the shawls that usually hang over the back of our couch. My hair is already dripping strings. Logan's blue silk shirt is soaking wet and transparent, the bandages from his recent burns clearly visible.

"What a crew," says Billy as he gallantly hands me off the boat. In spite of the rain, the photos Alex shot will be wonderful, the light soft and blue and everyone's skin moist and glowing. John sings "I Can't Help Falling in Love With You" as we enter the hall. For the second time in my life, I walk down the aisle—though this isn't an aisle exactly. I do prefer things to be less formal and the Echo Bay community hall is that, with basketball hoops hanging askew from the end walls.

Weddings are such a blur, my own no exception. Tears overflow, my nose drips. I turn to Theda, who *always* has a kleenex tucked away somewhere. She looks startled, pokes around in her Snow White dress and somehow comes up with a thick wad of paper towel. I snort a laugh in a distinctly unladylike fashion, but the laughter enables me to utter my vows without croaking. Liz stifles a grin, keeps a straight face and carries on with the ceremony. I float through the event, do as I am directed, say I do, kiss, hug, sign here, look up, smile. Now we are married. Let the party begin.

Back to normal, if there is any such thing. Ted has offered to be our framing carpenter for the house construction.

"How much?" says Al.

"Room and board plus ten dollars an hour, if that's okay," says Ted. Our eyes meet, thrilled. We can probably afford that when Al starts prawn fishing. Ted can have Theda's room while she's in White Rock. There's some foundation work left to do before we can begin construction and Ted has some jobs he has to finish in Lund. We'll begin in the new year, 1993, January or February.

January is the month for stalking the wild swan. Billy has told me the trumpeter swans winter in Viner Sound, and he'll take me in to see them. They descend from the higher altitudes as the inland lakes freeze up in December. I'm all fired up about painting them. It's about five miles into Viner, and cold in the inlet where freezing air slides down the slopes of Mount Reid and is funnelled straight onto the water. Running in the open speedboat, my eyes tear up from the burning cold. I'm thankful for the orange survival suit Albert gave me for Christmas.

A long mud flat in the estuary goes dry on low tides, so we arrive an hour before the high tide. A quarter mile ahead I spot the creamy white swans: elegant, glowing pearls against the dark forest, guddling about in the icy waters where the river meets the sea, digging at the roots of the sea grasses. Billy pulls up to the shore on the left side of the estuary.

"We can walk a ways from here," he says, "but in a bit you have to get down and crawl." I'm thinking, *How am I going to crawl with my camera shoved down this bulky survival suit?* I don't say it though. I know I'll do it.

It's as taxing as I'd imagined. I slither along on my belly through snow a couple of feet deep, with the camera and telephoto lens stuffed inside my shirt, trying to be quiet so the swans will not hear me. Two hundred yards later I'm in position, sweating profusely. The lens fogs up when I bring it into the cold air. It needs several wipes before I can see through the viewfinder. My eyes burn from sweat dripping off my forehead. I rest, cool down, then focus on the swans and shoot, then again and again. The swans hear the strange clicking sound and get restive. Heads come up out of the water, lift and turn, graceful necks poised, listening. I wait, barely breathing, then focus and shoot four times more. They sidle away towards the evergreen darkness of the far side of the estuary, but I'm ecstatic. I have seven shots, some good shots, excellent references all my own of trumpeter swans, and I have not caused an explosion into flight.

Too happy to move, I lie in the snow for a few minutes, inhaling the cold sweetness of the resinous air, looking up through the lacy tangle of cedar branch and bough, noting how the snow is grainy, a textured manganese blue, some parts of the cedar bark an alizarin crimson but mostly burnt sienna, thinking about the paintings to come from this day's efforts.

Swans aren't the only wildlife thrill. We've heard reports of cougar

 Drawn to Sea

sightings, and several times we've listened, entranced, to the song of the wolves. My days are a wonderful balance of painting and physical effort on the house project. We've devised a list of the actual sizes and numbers of pieces we'll need for the house. It's going to be a lot of wood.

Like big rising bubbles, ideas for paintings, and for the house, burst up throughout the day and in my dreams.

The Salvage Expedition

Sweet smells are running up and down the earth kissing every nose.

—Emily Carr

ALBERT, LOGAN AND I PREPARE THE HOUSE site for Ted's arrival. The guys dig post holes and I spend gruelling days pulling lumber off Billy's mill and strip-piling each piece. The bright spot of each day is Yvonne's calls to lunch. Billy tells us about a pile of concrete blocks up in Thompson Sound that might work as foundation blocks for our house. One snowy day he takes Albert, Logan and me in *Twilight Rock* to have a look-see.

Several dozen concrete blocks are strewn around the site of an old logging camp, overgrown and obscured by young alders. If we can get them out, they'll be perfect post foundations for our house. The problem is that each block is two feet square or larger and weighs three hundred pounds or more. We'll need twenty or twenty-five of them, depending on how many post holes won't accommodate a block and will need concrete poured instead.

The manager of Weldwood Logging turns down my request for permission to take some of the blocks. I write an angry response, then tear it up and write a nice polite one, explaining in detail my need for the blocks. A few weeks later I receive a lovely letter from a company engineer, informing me we may have exactly 25 (twenty-five). I could just picture the engineer saying to the boss, "For Christ's sake, let her have the damn blocks; they've been sitting there forever!"

I radio Billy. "Weldwood says we can have the blocks! Can you move them?"

He spouts his trademark claim: "If I can't do it, nobody can." And, of course, he can. A week after the swan excursion, we embark on the concrete block salvage expedition.

Billy's old Cat is over at Echo Bay Resort because he'd yarded Bob and Nancy Richter's store buildings off the old floats up onto the giant concrete bridge section they'd recently acquired. He tows neighbour Glen's small barge over to Echo Bay and ties it up beside the bridge barge. The Marine Link freight boat pulls alongside and lowers their loading ramp onto the deck of the concrete structure. Billy drives the Cat onto the ramp. This is his idea of a real good time, and he's sitting on the Cat laughing while the engineer swings the boat sideways to lower the ramp to Glen's baby barge, where Billy backs the Cat off the ramp and settles it dead centre.

Off to Thompson Sound we go, towing the Cat on the barge under a

Billy having some fun dragging the concrete foundation blocks to the shore.

warm grey sky. At the head of the sound Billy ties it up to the rickety old dock and drives the Cat off and up the road. Albert and Logan wrap drag chains around each of the selected blocks, and Billy drags them down to the foreshore with the Cat, placing each one neatly along the water's edge. After all the blocks are arrayed on the shore, he drives the Cat back down the dock onto the centre of the barge and then settles the barge against the shoreline. This grinds into an all-day job, as Billy predicted. As dusk falls, we eat the stew I made and climb into the bunks on *Twilight Rock* for the night.

The second day dawns calm and grey, and we complete the job. With the winch on the front of the Cat, Billy yards each of the blocks up onto the barge, placing one row of blocks on each side of the Cat, and two rows in front and back. There's barely room to manoeuvre the machine, but Billy sure knows how to run that old rig.

With his old Cat, Billy loaded the concrete blocks onto a barge and then we towed them home.

Albert and Ted mixing concrete for the post footings where blocks would not work.

Mission completed, we motor victoriously homeward with our booty in tow. Over the next two days we unload the blocks and move them up onto the land. From his perch on the Cat, Billy is Master of Ceremonies. Albert wraps the winch cable around a stump and brings the end back to wrap around a block. Billy puts power to the winch and slowly reels in the cable. The block inches off the barge in short jerks, bounces onto the land: bump, scrape and drag, the thing slowly moves up the slope to settle near a post hole.

Logan's job is to run the "haulback line" with the tin skiff after each block is yarded up the slope. When a block is settled into position, Albert detaches the end of the winch cable and hooks it to the haulback line attached to the skiff. Logan reverses away from the shore, pulling the haulback line and the cable until the cable end returns to Billy at the Cat. Then they do it all over again. I keep out of the way and take pictures.

We're hootin' and hollerin' after all the blocks are in place. Two days to get the blocks, two days to move them up on the land. It's a great

Inlet Transporter fills our tank with propane every second month and moves large machinery, like Glen's backhoe, when needed.

feeling to have this massive undertaking over with, a giant step towards making our house dream a reality.

A couple of weeks later *Inlet Transporter*, a big propane fuel barge, picks up Glen's backhoe off his property next door and deposits it on ours. This prehistoric-looking machine carves big bites out of the slope to make room for the back of our house. Glen piles the scooped-out dirt to the right-hand side of the site. It's a mountain of dirt, ten feet high, thirty feet long and eight feet wide. I'm glad to be done with the roaring machines, but now I have a new task to add to the daily grind. Every day I barrow ten loads of soil down to the foreshore to level the area where the septic field will be. It's repetitive, tedious work, but while I shovel, barrow and dump I envision the garden that'll bloom by the sea some day.

It's February 20 when Albert muscles the first concrete foundation block into its hole. It's his birthday, and a big moment for the construction of this house. I fear it's going to take a long time. The bottom floor

of the house is now designed to be 44 feet wide and 30 feet deep. The second storey, with the kitchen, living room, bathroom and den will extend a further 14 feet back against the hillside. The bottom floor will be evenly divided into two spaces, a painting studio and a workshop, 22 x 30 feet. I've never had a painting space even remotely that large. The bedrooms for the Art Retreat I plan to develop and other guests will be a half-storey on the top back of the house. We're planning for enough space for everything we can imagine ever wanting to do.

Ted arrives from Lund in his speedboat, perfect weather all the way. He and Albert build forms for the concrete pads to support house posts where the granite slopes and blocks won't work. Next they set the cedar posts on top of the concrete blocks. There are twenty-five post holes, five posts each supporting five main beams. The 22-foot 2 x 12 slabs of hemlock are so heavy I nearly killed myself strip-piling them. Billy and I milled fifty of these monsters, because each beam is to be laminated to ten inches wide. We moved them from his mill onto the barge and from the barge onto our land. Just thinking about it causes me pain. Each piece of lumber had to be slid down the mill ramp, piled onto my skiff, or *John*, the prawn boat, or a barge, depending on the size of the load we were moving. We towed the load to our land, unloaded it piece by piece and strip-piled the lumber again near the house site. I feared my knees or shoulders would give out before it was done.

A careful worker, and thoughtful, Ted is not afraid to say when he isn't sure how to proceed. Every evening he and Al and I discuss the day's work, the next day's work and any problems. It's companionable; we're lucky to have him. Laminating the beams and setting them on the posts goes quickly, as does framing and sheathing the platform floor. Suddenly, three walls of my studio are up.

Ted arranges the 2 x 4 framing on the platform of the completed floor, nails it together and Logan and I hammer on 1 x 8 sheathing. I measure and cut the ends of each board to 45 degrees and he nails the planks diagonally across the framed wall. We leave spaces wherever there are doors and windows. When the framing and sheathing are complete, various neighbours come over to help raise the wall. We stand in a line along the length of it and when Ted gives the signal we all lift in unison, and up she goes. Ted takes charge of making sure the wall sits true and straight. With each new wall raised, the house becomes more visible, and I walk within rooms, furnishing them with imaginary items. Each wall we raise manifests my dream.

I run away for a couple of hours one sunny spring day, out to the Burdwood Group, my place of solace, endless stimulation, and solitude. Here I can ignore the call to hard labour. Not a breath of wind today. All is serene, warm and still. The tide silently claims its last few inches of ground without a ripple to mar its surface.

Afloat on the surface of the sea are small clumps of shell pieces, most less than a quarter of an inch across. They appear to ride on cushions; the water contours a subtle meniscus around them. Surface tension embraces these bits of beach; the tidewater slips under and lifts them as it rises. Three inches below, the shadows cast by the floating islands of shell dance on the bottom. Sunbeams refract through the meniscus and spread rainbow patterns, pink, violet, yellow and green, around the underwater shadows. One white bit after another drifts gently down, exhaling a minute stream of bubbles. It takes only the tiniest disruption of the water, the smallest ripple, to cause the surface tension to release its hold on the pieces.

One cupped pink wild rose petal floats nearby, an invisible force at work on it. It drifts one way, then the next, pirouettes, dips and turns, bumps against a fragile floating shell island, knocks a couple of pieces loose. I'd like to paint this, but I'm not confident I can. I haven't even been able to take a good picture of the numinous colour and light. Some things are just too ephemeral and I may have to be satisfied with observing this fleeting event.

The air is redolent with wild rose, columbine, paintbrush and monkey face flower in the wonderful "about to bloom" stage. Salt air enhances the moist green scent, cedar resin adds to it, and hot rocks and low tide kelp are the bass note in the perfect tidal perfume. Simply inhaling becomes an act of worship. A painting about fragrance appears in my mind's eye: the antique yellow cut glass perfume bottle Billy gave me lying in the sea grass.

Perched comfortably under the rose bushes, I quick-sketch wrens, golden-crowned kinglets and fox sparrows playing over the sun-warmed rocks and tide pools. Into this peaceful scene a hawk, with great swiftness, swoops out of the cedar tree behind and slams into one of the little birds directly in front of me. Instantly a scatter of birds. The one hit by the hawk plummets to the rock. The power and speed of the hawk's trajectory takes it halfway to the next island before it swings around. The little bird twitches, recovers and totters away under the bushes.

This scene, so fast, so brutal, takes my breath away. I'm awed, thrilled that the small bird escaped, regretful that the hawk expended so much energy for no immediate gain, and filled with gratitude to be in this moment: a lot of feelings to experience in the space of one breath.

Perched on warm rock, I write a bit, push the boat off the beach from time to time as the tide turns to ebb, contemplate the view from the close-up of the tidal edge, and across the rocks to the faraway islands, up Viner River estuary, and beyond to the slopes and peak of Mount Reid. As the light warms into an intense late-afternoon gold, I inhale again the island perfume. If I could only bottle it.

My thoughts turn towards the summer's fishing. Billy has sold *Twilight Rock* and bought a beautiful new boat named *Ocean Dawn*. He was worried I wouldn't like the head. I can't imagine why. Surely he must have been teasing me? The boat is spacious, with four bunks in the roomy bow. The head is forward by the keel and has a door that can be closed. On *Twilight Rock* the toilet was right beside the bunks. You could close the door to the wheelhouse when you were down forward in the bow, but if anyone was in the bunk, they had to get out if you wanted privacy. *Ocean Dawn's* wheelhouse is pretty much standard: stove, sink and counter to starboard where you enter; skipper's seat and starboard crew seat right in the front by the ladder down to the bunks; table and under-seat storage beside the port-side window.

The table and settee are too low so Billy is ripping them out and making a platform with storage drawers to rebuild the table and seats on. It'll be much nicer to sit level with the window, and there'll be an extra bit of storage. The fishing cockpit looks spacious, too, with a deep, rounded stern. *Ocean Dawn* is a wonderful boat, probably the nicest west coast troller you could hope for. I'm excited about fishing her this summer.

We've had a certain amount of stress in the last couple of months. I'm worried about both my children. Logan had to have his tonsils removed in Vancouver, and while we were there I met with the kids' father for a mediation session to discuss Logan's living situation. I also met twice with Theda's counsellor at her school in White Rock, the very caring Mr. Geary. She's been skipping school, my naughty child, and we discussed her post-secondary career options as well. Logan has been doing correspondence with assistance from the Echo Bay teacher. I help him as much as I can but the motivation must come from him. I'm a nag, but it's unavoidable. I believe strongly in the value of education and am committed to seeing he gets one. Logan helps a lot on the house construction, and I reassure myself that he is learning about construction and getting other intangible wilderness lessons. Survival skills I call them. Resourcefulness and independence.

But he's so sad, depressed and hurt, his state of mind concerns me deeply. I can't distinguish whether it's simply teenage angst or something more significant. There's only one kid near his age here. He has a few friends in Port McNeill, and we make sure he gets to spend time with them, but still, it must be lonely. I know he'll probably leave soon, and I dread it. Bad enough having Theda gone; having both of them gone is going to be hard.

This is one of the trade-offs you must make when choosing to live in a small remote community. What is best for your children? When Albert invited us to share his life here, we were overjoyed. It was obvious that living here was good for the kids in their younger years. Now, with Theda here only for short visits, I'm helpless to have an impact on her life in any useful way and I miss her dreadfully. Logan is deeply unhappy about being denied his desire to live in White Rock. They're both in high school, and the logistics of getting any kind of professional assistance are difficult. I work at trusting that all is well and my children will grow up to live happy, self-expressed lives. They're such different characters and strong individuals. Albert is absolutely reliable in his commitment to me

and my children. Thank goodness I have him to share my concerns.

Sun hangs low in the peaceful stillness of the Burdwood Group. I have what I came for, so it's time to go home and make some dinner for the hungry worker bees and prepare for my friend's arrival.

Deb makes her annual Echo Bay visit, climbing out of the float plane with a Japanese maple tree for my belated fortieth birthday gift. With Ted now in Theda's bunk, I am scrambling to make room for Deb.

"Logan, can you strip the sheets off your bed so Ted can sleep there, and we'll put Deb in Theda's bed?" I ask, sort of. "You can sleep on the couch, okay?" A long silence tells me this is not okay, and then he replies, "I want to sleep on the roof."

"Go see what Al says," I tell him, "but I think that could work."

"I really want to see some killer whales this trip," says Deb as she settles into bed after supper. Early the next day, I'm up with Albert, who is getting ready to go pull the prawn gear, and there, out across the pass, glowing in the morning sun, rise three plumes of mist.

"Deb, Deb, the whales are here," I say, shaking her gently.

"Why do they have to come now?" she moans, but drags her butt out of bed and gratefully accepts the cup of coffee Al puts in her hand. I start to write a note for Logan, but find one he's left on the table for me: "Gone fishing."

"Look at this." I show Albert. "Did he tell you he was going fishing?"

"Nope. Wonder where he went? Gotta go, call me if you need me." He swallows his coffee, kisses me and heads out the door. I fire up *Sea Rose* and Deb and I are off, puddling along with the orca family. It's a sweet morning, pearly like the inside of a shell. Morning works its magic on us as we idle down Cramer Pass, then around Islet Point towards Solitary Isle, where I shut the motor off. Six black fins rise and fall repeatedly beside the boat until they disappear after the last deep dive. Our stomachs growl, a reminder we could use a bit of breakfast.

"*Sea Rose, Sea Rose; Orca Air.*" I hear the tiny voice of Tom Langdon emitting from the VHF radio on the dashboard. I key the mike.

"*Orca Air, Sea Rose*. Wanna go zero six?" I reply, wondering, what the heck?

"Roger, zero six," Tom says. "Just want to let you know Logan made it here safe and sound."

"What? No, Logan's here, out fishing."

"No, he is right here," Tom says. "He just arrived in the skiff."

"That boy's got some explaining to do," I snarl to Deb. Apparently Logan had gotten up at 5:30 am with a plan: to run to Port McNeill by himself in the fourteen-foot aluminum skiff. And he did, through a fairly thick fog. A sixteen-year-old boy/man asserting his independence, I guess. He tells me later he could just barely see the sun through the fog and kept it in position over his left shoulder as he was crossing Queen Charlotte Strait. He knows I hear everything—almost!—even in my sleep, so he rowed away from the dock before starting the motor.

The weather comes up an afternoon westerly, making it too rough for Logan to run the boat back across the strait. Tom finds a seat for him on the afternoon "sched" flight, but we send him back with the plane to Port McNeill, to stay with the boat until he can bring it home. The following morning is clear and calm and Logan safely runs the skiff home, across Queen Charlotte Strait, something I'd never even *considered* doing in that little boat. Albert and I decide Logan needs a few more responsibilities around home, and maybe some greater freedoms. But we make him promise he will never not let us know his destination and ETA again. Resourcefulness and independence he has clearly demonstrated.

Billy says Logan can come with him on his next fishing trip, so he, too, will get to go to the Charlottes. They'll leave at the end of June. Logan's excited about this but I wonder how they'll do together. Hard to imagine my active, not fully coordinated son on a forty-four-foot vessel for a full month, even if there are shore parties.

Sockeye 93 Buys the Roof

BILLY AND LOGAN HAVE VERY DIFFERENT VIEWPOINTS about their July fishing trip to the Charlottes. They've had an interesting time together on the boat. Once while they were running the long days north to the Charlottes, Logan went out on the deck and after a while Billy went out to look for him. Logan was nowhere to be seen until Billy looked up over the wheelhouse and saw him about to try climbing the rigging. He needed something to do with himself and was sure he'd be perfectly safe. That hadn't gone over well with the skipper who'd envisioned telling me he'd lost my son. Then Logan got homesick after only a week's fishing off the west coast of Haida Gwai'i. He tried to talk Billy into taking him to land so he could come home. He had it all worked out: Billy could take him into Masset, a five-hour run, where Logan would call my brother, his Uncle Frank, who would fly him to Prince Rupert where he'd stay for a bit, then he'd take the ferry down to Port Hardy. Captain Billy put the kibosh on that idea, and said, "Nope. We are going to stay here and fish." Logan had a good time eventually, but I think Billy feared for my son's life again, when they eventually tied up at Masset and Logan went roaming. He found a Native boy to pal around with and didn't get back to the boat until 1:00 am in the morning.

On August 4 Theda and I run into Port McNeill, where I bus to Port Hardy to join Billy and Logan on *Ocean Dawn*. Theda runs my speed-boat home by herself, first time for her. Both my kids have now run a

Exploring in the little rowboat was a beautiful way to experience the dramatic shoreline.

boat across Queen Charlotte Strait, wending their way safely through the islands and up Cramer Pass to our homesite. It's an important accomplishment, and I'm proud of their competence, reliability and independence.

Logan meets me at the bus in Port Hardy, and at the Seafoods dock Billy is all grubbed up, iced up and ready to go. This fishing trip is for sockeye, and we leave immediately for Camano Bay. After travelling around the top end of Vancouver Island, we fish the west coast, Logan and I working in the cockpit and Billy steering. Periodically he comes out of the wheelhouse with pieces of chocolate bar, and Logan and I squawk like gulls, opening our mouths wide for the proffered treats. The wild west coast is hiding her wicked face. The weather and scenery are fabulous, and my fingers burn to paint, yet I must fish all day. Picture-taking is the best I can do, and I draw to store the memory of many dramatic images. One simmering hot day when we're anchored outside Sea Otter Cove we row to shore and explore into the long summer evening. Rowing back, I'm struck by the beauty of the boat's silhouette, black against

A Seafoods crewman unloading the iced salmon from the hold.

the gold sky, trolling poles spread wide like narrow wings. Spider-web rigging lines arc from the ends of the poles, lacing the boat together from stem to stern, mast to gunwales.

We tie off a mooring buoy inside Sea Otter Cove during two evenings of unsettled weather. I watch closely as Billy runs the boat up alongside the mooring buoy and Logan hooks onto it with the pike pole. The second evening we anchor there, Billy lets me take the wheel. Takes me two tries, but I get us hooked. At anchor, I'm glad for the solitude when the guys go off exploring, a couple of hours' relief from their boisterous way of relating, crude insults hurled across the deck and farting-inside-the-raingear contests. Alone on the bow I'm rewarded with close-up photos of sea otters, truly the most appealing creatures. Time too for a vigorous sketch of the surf beyond the entrance island.

We work our way east to end the ten-day trip and fish by Pine Island on a couple of wild and windy days that aren't good for much, so says the skipper. But I'm happy with my paycheque of slightly over two thousand dollars and ten more days of west-coast magic.

In Port Hardy at the Seafoods dock we deliver the sockeye. Handsome young men climb in and out of the hatch, bringing up the fish from the ice. They are sun-browned and muscular and work cheerfully with a lot of bantering, whistling and laughter: good material for genre paintings of fishing activities. Some day, inevitably, this way of life will end. This dock will be derelict and the bustling activity will be just a memory. Sad to think this way, but decreasing salmon stocks makes it a certainty. Habitat damage through logging, industrial effluent, dammed rivers, real estate development, overfishing of certain stocks, sea lice and disease from fish farms... the list is endless. All around the world, seafood species decline due to human activities, as human populations, fishing effort and technology increase.

Billy plans to go out for one more short trip, but Logan and I gather our gear and head for home. We make an excellent run from Port McNeill on a beautiful rolling sea, with a short stop to see Logan's friend Karen in Mitchell Bay. Good timing for this little jaunt, as it blows and rains hard the next couple of days. Logan is about to begin his grade eleven schoolwork and some grade twelve by correspondence. The books are here and soon, too, will be September.

Rafting the Wakeman

LATE SUMMER, IN THE GOLDEN DOG DAYS, the kids and I take a day out for an adventure. From time to time I chat with Steve Vesely, the watchman for the logging company Interfor at Wakeman Sound. Steve is a tall man, lanky with lean muscle close to the bone and clear dark eyes. He is past sixty now and has lived in Wakeman for years. He loves company and tells endless stories if he likes you, but he packs a shotgun and doesn't hesitate to raise it if he thinks you're getting too close to his crab gear in the sound. If you're in his good books, you'll be invited up to the house for a drink or driven a few miles up the road and dropped off to spend the day floating down the river in a rubber raft.

Steve's VHF call sign is *Gypsy Two*, and when he calls Billy on *Ocean Dawn* they switch over to channel 68 for what we call "the Steve Report." Steve is caring, almost paternal towards the chinook salmon that spawn in the Wakeman River, and he informs Billy about the state of the returning stocks, the geese, the wolves and the other beings living in the area. Some of his stories are hilarious. My favourite concerns an encounter with a grizzly bear as Steve walked one snowy winter day down the road to the dock. He told Billy, "A big old grizzly came bursting out of the bushes, didn't even have time to get my gun up. It just ran right over me, knocked me down on the road, stepped on my face, goddammit. I had to run and change my shorts!"

More than once Steve has invited us to come up and raft the Wakeman River, but there's always something going on that takes precedence. The Department of Fisheries closed the prawn fishing in Area 12 in July, so Albert and deckhand Theda pulled the gear out of the water. Albert trailered the boat from Port McNeill to Quatsino, and he is now fishing over there by himself. So Theda, Logan and I are home alone. The sun shines, the forecast is for light to variable westerly, no fog obscures visibility. We pack a picnic, fill the boat with life jackets, fishing rods, hats, shirts, camera and sunscreen, and are away by 7:00 am.

Steve Vesely, our guide and host for a day, sliding the raft in the Atway River.

It's a long run to Wakeman Sound: across to Penphrase Pass, around the corner and halfway up Kingcome, and then a left turn at Philadelphia Point. The land gets steeper and rises higher the farther up the inlet we go. It feels like a completely different country. A brisk little breeze flirts with the sea, strewing sun dollars all the way.

Steve is ready for us at the landing dock in his old pickup truck. We drive about eight miles along the Wakeman River and then alongside the Atway River. A couple of bears amble slowly off the road at our approach. Steve pulls into a shaded lay-by and parks. He and Logan slide the rubber raft off the truck bed and slip it into the river. We pile in with all our gear. The raft is half the size of *Sea Rose* and twice as full.

Adrift then—floating like a leaf down a lazy river—a rippling sun-spattered river surrounded by silent, dark conifers and the lighter variegated greens of shoreline shrubs and alders. Crimson leaves and vermilion huckleberries provide a colour surprise. Sun beats down golden-hazy

Logan on the stump in the Wakeman River holds the raft's bowline. If he'd let go Theda and I would've been swept on without him.

into the open space framed by the tall trees. Heat waves shimmer ahead and behind. Logan steers and I hang over the round side of the raft, mesmerized by the dappled patterns of refracted light on the pebbled river bottom. We let a sand bank snag us and put the fishing rods to work, casting inexpertly into deeper pools below the bank. The river stretches and coils in long sinuous curves. We pass underneath the great-timbered old logging bridge and turn another lazy corner, pull up to a bank strewn with lavender-violet flowers and eat our salmon sandwiches. Theda and I sunbathe while Logan wanders about stirring things up. Off again and around the next bend we come to the confluence of the Atway and the Wakeman rivers.

The delicious laziness and translucence of the Atway is overcome by the turbulence of the silty-brown Wakeman. This heightened energy is a lot more Logan's style. He tries several times to lasso us to one of the big stumps tumbled into the river by the burly winter floods. He is thrilled to make his sister shriek with every try. I can't help laughing, although I envision us dumped out of the raft and it bobbing down the river without us. On the fourth try he manages to attach us to a giant stump solidly lodged in the gravel, with roots pulsing sideways in the river flow. He climbs onto it while the raft pulls hard against the tie-up line, stands triumphantly atop and raises his arms in victory.

Big surprise around the next bend. There stands Steve, high on the bank, wearing only a small Speedo-style bathing suit. Looking pretty good, I might add, nut brown and sinewy.

"Just checking to make sure you're okay," he shouts against the river's noisy conversation with its banks. "It's a little farther along where she swings wide to the left. You gotta come in there, or else you'll be swept down to the estuary and it's a mess, full of big old roots, and I can't get you out of there." I'd been wondering where we were supposed to get off the river. Shortly we glide into the slow current near the bank, and there is Steve to help us out. He lets Theda, then Logan, drive his old truck up and down the road while we visit at his house.

The afternoon is melting into liquid blue and gold as we head down the inlet. An ebullient chop kicks up, but I'm not worried. I know my boat now, and she is seaworthy. *Sea Rose* bangs determinedly down Wakeman Sound, picks up a little speed in Kingcome, then goes slower the rest of the way, across the mouth of Fife Sound and finally safe home as the sun hovers over Baker Island. Theda and Logan are mostly silent, not much noise and activity now. We are all full to the brim with river joy, dizzied by the beauty of the day. I can only hope it will be as memorable for my children as it was for me. I hope they store some of the good stuff, like today, along with the parental horrors.

Dring, dring, dring.

"Yes, hello? Can you deliver twenty thousand board feet of lumber to our home on Gilford Island? Tomorrow? Lovely! Thank you very much." I wake up from this beautiful dream remembering I'm going to Billy's again to mill sheathing and siding and panelling, thousands and thousands of board feet of hemlock, yellow cedar, red cedar, spruce, fir and pine. Billy mills our lumber for three hours almost every good weather day. I pull the lumber off and strip-pile it on the mill deck. The miraculous lunch call from Yvonne signals quitting time.

"Well, look who shows up when you haven't got a gun," says Yvonne as I walk in the door pulling my work gloves off. I pile her good canned

sockeye on homemade white bread and slather it with mayo. We sling verbal abuse at each other as we eat and laugh until we choke.

Glen Neidrauer's clumsy old punt works well for transporting lumber the short distance to our foreshore. I can feel the pain and weakness in my right shoulder and arm after a day of dragging those friggin' hemlock beams off the punt onto the land. Yvonne P. keeps telling me, "Let the men do it," and I'm thinking she's right. They do have superior upper body strength, after all. Most of the big beams are done now, thank goodness. We're currently milling flawless yellow cedar panelling. It's great until the wind blows southeast and we're eating sawdust.

Al is home from Quatsino. Fishing was poor and he got tired of fighting off the hagfish. These are horrendous long, pink, slug-like creatures that exude mucous from pores along the sides of their bodies when disturbed. Al has devised a technique of gingerly loosening the trap opening and then stealthily slipping his gloved hand under the creatures and abruptly flipping them out the opening. If he doesn't do this, the mesh trap is covered in mucous in about fifteen seconds, and it's a terrible job to get it off. It only takes a teaspoon of water to turn hagfish mucous into vast masses of snot-like slime. He's happy to be working on the house again.

Ted, Logan and I install 2 x 10 floor joists, then Ted and I nail up the rafters for the front section of the studio. Albert and Ted set up a main beam on the posts to support the second floor. The house rises slowly, but it rises. I love walking around the studio space, peeking out the open window spaces.

In October we take Al's prawn-fishing money and my sockeye dollars, rent a truck and make a buying trip to Courtenay. We find four beautiful doors at Wacky Willy's on the old highway just south of Campbell River. We'll use these for the upstairs guest bedrooms and the bathrooms. A big stack of nine-foot-high arched windows leans up against the wall but one in mid-pile looks to be a couple of feet shorter.

Al and the salesman and I wrestle four of the nine-footers out before they find the seven-foot one. It will be perfect for the window beside the bathtub. Elegant and graceful, it will flood the room with light. Already I can imagine the bliss of lying in my tub with a book and a glass of wine, raising my eyes to the trees on the hillside and the blue sky beyond. Night time, I'll see the moon rise beyond the tips of those trees.

We also find a pile of old brass-paned window units. One with an arched top will be for the bedroom, to frame the moon as it sets over Baker Island. Albert thinks they can be sandwiched between two pieces of glass and will work for all the windows across the front of the main floor: living room, bedroom and study/den.

Our last stop is at Tracy Clair's Comox Valley Wholesale on Back Road to see what styles and colours of tin roofing he has. We like the turquoise roof and buy that along with all the flashing and hardware. I saw Monet's pink stucco, green-trimmed house in Giverny, France, in 1985 and loved it. Our west-coast interpretation will feature red cedar siding and a turquoise roof, downspouts and gutters. The roofing panels will come up by Overland Freight to Port McNeill. Glen offered his barge, again, for us to load them on to bring them home.

At One (?) with the Universe

ALBERT AND I CELEBRATE THE FIRST YEAR of our marriage on September 19. Celebrate our house-building efforts too. Apparently we're not the only couple whose commitment has been challenged by house construction. A visitor to see my paintings inquires, "Are you still married?" when I tell her about the argument we had over non-existent windows and other problems we've encountered trying to shape house idea into house reality.

In October I attend Theda's grade twelve graduation ceremonies—barely. Wednesday I purchase a Pacific Coastal ticket for the early-bird flight to Vancouver on Friday morning and spend the night with a friend in Port Hardy. The day before my flight I sell a painting and pick up a cheque for another painting sale from Graphics West. Feeling at one with the universe, I be-bop cheerfully around town taking care of business. In the middle of the night, I awake with the memory of my ticket purchase running through my dream. I see myself clearly, saying "tomorrow" instead of "Friday" as I bought it. So I've missed the flight I booked and have no ticket for the right day. I wait in the airport from 7:00 am Friday and finally get a seat on the 3:00 pm flight to Vancouver. Deb picks me up. We speed to the hall where Theda's grad ceremony is about to take place and slip in just before the doors close.

My garden, another manifestation of oneness with the universe, is evolving. In September I planted rose bushes selected for fragrance and rain resistance. Most needed to be transplanted to a permanent site from their original "temporary" spot. I had no idea what the word "rambler" meant as a rose descriptor, and the Albertine has stunned me with the enthusiasm of its rampant growth. The four-foot-high trellis I built to support it is sadly inadequate. I hope red and white striped *Rosa mundi*, an ancient rose from the far east, and modern hybrid 'Sharifa Asma', with its pearly pink petals and warm heart, thrive in their new positions. A rose-pink rhododendron, *Roseum elegans*, that Logan brought home for Mother's Day years ago flourishes in front of the house. And the very first rhodo, 'Nova Zembla', uprooted from its planter on the float, has taken hold vigorously. Logan and I came out one dewy morning to find a sleeping bee in almost every blossom and we renamed it Nova Zembla Bee Hotel. The sugar maples Irene and Dave Myers gave me from their trip to Quebec have settled in and stretched. Their leaves in fall glow a brilliant orange-gold and provide mulch as the tree gets larger. Billy gave us a red osier dogwood, which in two years has grown so much it has needed to be moved twice.

Billy takes neighbour Pat Steernburg and me into Twin Lagoon in his speedboat one day. The lagoon has a narrow entrance off Fife Sound with a steep outflow when the tide is falling. Access to the lagoon is through a narrow channel bounded by a steep shore on the right and treacherous rocks just under the water's surface to the left. Billy pushes the throttle forward, and the boat leaps like a live creature. Sixty horses race barely an arm's length from the granite wall, up the glossy rushing slope of the outflowing tide. Over-arching trees slap at us as we duck and squeal. The louder the passengers shriek, the more Billy grins. The thrill lasts barely thirty seconds, but it's enough to get us high. Inside the lagoon all is still and mysterious. Thousands of moon jellyfish pulsate in the shallow waters. Billy beaches the speedboat and leads us on a narrow forest trail to a hidden beaver pond. Dragonflies linger; a kingfisher plunges and rises with a small silver fish. Around the edges of the swampy area grow sundews, a carnivorous plant. The pond supports cattails, yellow water lilies, sedges and grasses; it feels primordial, unsullied, as if a dinosaur will roar out of the forest any minute.

Pat comes with me later in the week on a painting trip to another

lagoon, Booker, near the entrance to Fife Sound off Queen Charlotte Strait. At the long rock entrance a stone man stands, like an Inuit in-ukshuk. It has stood there as long as I've been here, and nobody knows really who built it. We humans like that kind of thing, a distinctive marker on the landscape, mysterious and intriguing. I tie the boat to bull kelp, and we sketch the stone man. I like running my own boat around, reading the charts to make my own decisions about what to avoid and where to go forward. A powerful tidal flow fills this lagoon as well, so I boot it through the entrance channel. A second narrow channel provides entry to Booker. Here steep walls are washed by oxygen-rich tidal currents twice a day. They're quilted with an incredible patchwork array of multi-coloured sea life hanging off the vertical wall. Low tide reveals this amazing glory of life. Not a square inch of rock is without coverage by some kind of animal, plant or synthesis of both.

"Can you do me a painting with a central panel of a wild rose surrounded by a border of smaller paintings of other wild flowers?" Bill asks, one day. I love his idea! I get right to work on it and do a painting for him of the wild rose surrounded by monkey face flower, columbine, calypso orchid, pink fawn lily, blue-eyed Mary and other wild flowers that bloom on the windblown rocks, a wonderful way to get to know more of them. I love the wild garden as much as I do my domesticated one.

All through December I've been able to indulge in an activity close to my heart: directing the schoolchildren in songs and a play that they present to wild applause at the Christmas concert and potluck dinner. Underneath the basketball hoop at one end of the hall stands a brightly decorated Christmas tree. Under the hoop at the other end sits the stage. The doting audience loves the kids' robust version of "We Three Kings" and Billy's favourite carol, "Silent Night." Two parents leap up to help open and close the curtain when it catches on the cable strung across the room. Ten children attend school here, five from Echo Bay and five who come down Cramer Pass from Gilford Village (Gwayasdums). Echo Bay Hall is packed full, warm from the wood heater, the heat of so many bodies and our shared pride in all these children's accomplishments. I can never watch them without tears stinging my eyes.

The last evening of 1993, all is quiet inside and out, except for one lonesome owl hooting in the bush. Logan is down with stomach flu and fever and in bed. Theda's reading and Albert snoozes. I'm lying in the bath with a glass of wine thinking about the last couple of months. We've accomplished so much on the house. It has consumed all our energies and resources. Ted has gone to join his family for Christmas but before he left we raised the final two walls on the top floor, then milled, moved and installed seven 24-foot long 3 x 10 rafters over the living room. My children are clearly glad we reunited. Both of them have had a good year. Fishing with Al was good for Theda; she learned to exercise patience and took on new responsibilities. Fishing with Billy was good for Logan, too; it got him out of here and into new experiences. This last year has felt more like running with, rather than bucking, the tide.

Another hour and it will be 1994. I hope by this time next year we've moved into our house. I have big plans for art retreat guests and big paintings in the big studio… get a grip, I tell myself. All in good time.

Gaining the Summit

WE'VE MADE IT TO THE TOP OF THE HOUSE! On January 21, the last of the rafters are set in place by the taciturn team, Ted and Al. Like twin brothers, side by each, they muscle the beams into place. Billy and I pound down the last piece of fir sheathing on the upper eastern corner of the third half-floor.

Completing the last of the rafters and strapping is a significant milestone. The turquoise tin roofing sits inside the house waiting until we're ready to put it on. Construction slows down for a bit when our neighbour's boat, *New Fraser*, sinks at the dock in Echo Bay. Luckily Pat and Fraser, and their kids, Robalin and Eric, were out to town on their tug and not sleeping in the bunks when the bilge pump quit. We've all been over helping raise the vessel and drag it to the park beach. Billy punches a hole in the hull with his Cat at low tide in order to extract the motor. Fraser hopes to rebuild it. It's sobering how quickly disaster can strike. There are so many sunken boats around here. Although you cannot see them all, it is a graveyard of ships here in the Broughton Archipelago and the cause is rarely due to wild winds.

March 12 is a big day, too.

Billy comes over with a big smile, waving a piece of paper. "They finally approved the subdivision." It's official now; we are recognized landowners in the eyes of the state and the world at large. Albert and I hang over his shoulder reading out loud. It took the personal interest of Gordon Wilson, currently the elected representative for our provincial riding, to bring the Deputy Minister of Highways out here, at Wilson's own expense, to show him that putting a road in as a requirement of this subdivision (standard operating procedure) is plain craziness. Rules should be for a functional purpose, and in this case the bureaucrats cannot comprehend that "water access only" is a statement of practical fact. One bureaucrat in the ministry told me earlier that we would need a road for our children to walk to school on, in case it blew too hard for us to go by boat. It was gratifying to be able to show the deputy minister exactly where a child would have to walk, amongst whipping branches or falling trees, if it was blowing too hard to boat to the school.

"The day after school let out for Easter break in 1989, it blew so hard a tree fell and crushed the swing set on the school playground," I tell him. "Picture a kid walking to school in that."

I've felt uncomfortable taking our house so far into the construction

Our float house in the foreground. On land the new house slowly rises from its foundations. The generator shed is on the right.

Theda checking out the crushed swing set in the schoolyard.

process without the official sanction of subdivision approval. I'm not much of a maverick in these areas, but both Al and Bill were confident it would happen eventually, and if not, we'd at least have a house. If it doesn't kill me first, I guess we will. In amongst the murderous labour there are kernels of fun.

As the month of May flowers, I'm gone to sea and far from home again. This time Billy and I are ling cod fishing in the mystical Scott Islands. I'm loving the daily pleasure of new vistas to explore, new treasures to find, new things to learn. Billy is a walking encyclopedia of nature lore. He knows so much about the weather, the birds, the flowers, the sea and the creatures therein. I love being the deckhand. I never want the responsibility of being the skipper, although it's fun to pretend I am on a long journey, when Billy leaves me to run the ship alone and goes down to the bunk for a snooze. I'm the Queen of the Sea as we run, riding the gunwale of the cockpit, rising up and sinking, sliding down the long slope. In the valley of the swell the glossy mound of sea rises up, way up behind us, much higher than the boat. A powerful surge lifts the boat to the crest. We hang at the top of the arc for a long breathless moment, see sea for miles and then, d-o-w-w-n we go again, into the valley of the swell.

Ling cod fishing is different from salmon fishing. Billy put a watertight bulkhead in the hold of *Ocean Dawn* to create a live well, or tank. When we catch the ling cod, we don't have to kill them; we slip them into the "swimming pool" where they are supplied with a constant stream of pumped-in oxygenated sea water.

We use pink and blue hoochies as lures; sometimes an orange one works, or a cuttlefish, which is larger than a hoochie. We also use a home-made wooden lure, painted orange with yellow spots. It's in two sections, each with a hook and a small tail at the end of it. The most effective lure is the "drag" Billy makes. He cuts pieces of halibut skin into a fringed shape to resemble little squid and attaches them to the hooks. The drag has eight hooks on it, spaced six feet apart, and it is snapped onto the cable with a three-way swivel six feet above the cannonball. I lower the drag carefully over the side, then flip the brass lever to lower the cannonball and the drag into the blue deep until I can feel through the cable that the cannonball is bumping along the seabed.

"When you feel it bumping on the bottom, you raise it just a bit," explains Billy. "Keep checking for the bottom and bringing it up a bit."

With my fingers curled gently around the gurdy wire, my consciousness plunges down the wire to the seabed below. Every nudge, tremor and bump transmits meaning. The cannonball hits bottom with a distinctive thud; I wind it up a little. A big bump, bumpety bump means the terrain is rising quickly; I wind it up a lot. A gentle vibration of the gurdy wire means the cannonball is slipping along right where it should be, just above the bottom, leading the drag, luring the cod. Energetic side-to-side jerking motions signal a ling cod is on the hook. Flip the lever into gear, and up comes the whole works. Surprise! Often there are four, five, even six ling cod with their spiny-toothed mouths stretched wide. "Bucket heads," Billy calls them, due to the huge wide-lipped mouths and bulging eyes of the females. Their skin is beautiful with an amazing array of

147

colours: spotted, speckled golden, greenish, amber. Some are a bright turquoise. Theoretically this is because of what they eat, although I'm not sure that is the case. Some large females can be up to five feet long and average eighteen to twenty-five pounds. The male of the species is noticeably smaller.

Billy and I are competitive, but in the friendliest manner. I love to out-fish him, knowing full well it has nothing to do with skill. I note in the log for May 5 that "Billy got the biggest, Yvonne got the most."

We roll along with a stiff southwest breeze and all the gear in the water, the rigging singing a wind song, everything happy, and then, bam! The boat gives a hard jerk, all the gear snags and the boat almost stalls. Panic ensues. Billy throws the motor out of gear and we both engage the gurdies to bring up the drags.

"I've got one on," I tell him, peering over the side. "It's a big one! There's another one behind it, and another one."

"Me too," says Billy, heaving in a big ling cod. Billy's side has a fish on every hook. Mine is short one, for fifteen cod in one drag. We must've run right into a big bunch of them feeding, for their combined weights and the suddenness of the bite to outright stall our forward motion.

"Wait 'til the boys back at the club hear about this!" says Billy, the hilarious expression he uses whenever one of us does something re-markable, funny, heroic or just plain silly. "Pretty good for Friday the thirteenth."

We must have used up all our bad luck yesterday, by fishing the ebb tide instead of the flood tide. The ebb is stronger; and the fish lie quiet in the shadow of the seamount. They feed when the tide turns to flood. Billy beat himself up about that for a while but the weather turned snotty anyway, a lot less than pleasant with greasy big swells and a gloomy fore-boding sky. We anchored by Lanz Island, and although I'd rather have had a snooze, we rowed in a snarly swell to the beach. Billy noticed I was looking a bit grim clinging to the sides of the rowboat.

"Smile," he said.

"I'm here, aren't I?" said I. "Do I have to smile too?"

At 3:00 am, when the wind changed from southeast to southwest, we pulled the anchor and reset ourselves where the unceasing lump was less offensive. So Friday the thirteenth turns out to be bonus. Our day's catch of sixty-three ling cod bumps up our total to one hundred and sixty-seven and this is our biggest day's catch for this trip.

Fishing only the flood tide leaves plenty of time for exploring which-ever interesting bit of land is nearby. This is the great thing about fishing with Billy. One day we land at Barge Bay on Cox Island, so named due to the rusted hulk of the *Rivtow Norseman*, her cargo of logs lost off Cape Scott when the towline broke in an October storm in 1971. The barge washed up on the beach here and her bent and twisted metal plates graphically show the elemental power of the sea. In ironic contrast a large Japanese glass float, a real beauty with dimples on both sides, lies serenely in a tide pool. Here the Queen of the Sea takes a rest and the artist spends three lovely hours in the heart of a wild creekside garden.

Halfway through the trip, we deliver half the load (127 fish, about 1,540 pounds at $1.50 per pound) to Coal Harbour, where the buyer meets us at the top of the dock with his water-filled truck. Billy nets the cod out of the live hold and dumps them head first into large green garbage buckets. Some of them are so big their tails stick out the top and they twist and wriggle in a writhing mass. Dead low tide steepens the ramp to an excessive angle and it takes both of us, me dragging from the top and Billy pushing from below, to get the heavy bucketsful to the top of the ramp. Billy presses his shoulder against the bucket to push. A twisting ling cod tail whaps him upside the head.

"Jesus Christ!" he curses as his glasses go flying off his nose and over the side. After we get the cod unloaded he tracks down a local diver who shows up a couple of hours later.

"A hundred twenty-five bucks, no guarantees," says the diver. Billy pulls out his sunglasses and wears them the rest of the trip. My glasses almost join Billy's when a muscular tail delivers a stinging slap to my face. Ouch!

Coal Harbour, an old whaling town, isn't exactly a wilderness shore party, but I stroll around, admire the giant whale jawbones and billows

of wild bleeding hearts. We set the hook in Hansen Lagoon too late to fish, so a shore party is the only option. We prowl around looking for "new to us" wild flowers and find one: the rosy twisted stalk, a delicate arching branch hung with the palest pink bell-shaped flowers, each attached by a green filament with one angled twist.

One lovely day we anchor at Guise Bay for the ebb tide. This bay closely resembles a tropical lagoon, the water so turquoise, cobalt, cerulean blue, and the sand so fine. Over the side goes the dinghy; it's a short row to the welcoming shore. Out of the bay southwestward, lacy white surf edges each swath of azure sea. After a short walk on the golden sand dunes across Sand Neck to Experiment Bight, we gaze northward across the Pacific into blue-grey infinity.

The beach at Guise Bay with its blue and gold tropical good looks is fiercely inhospitable in winter. No wonder the Cape Scott settlers finally left—with, I imagine, the greatest regret—when all hope of survival here was lost. Even the Native villages had been deserted over a hundred and fifty years before, long in advance of the European settlers' arrival.

These unhurried meanderings on distant shores will stay with me always. And after the return to the nest, the boat which we cannot do without, up comes the anchor and we're off to sea again. The joy of that rushes through my veins.

In the cockpit fishing one late afternoon flood tide, I sweep my gaze back and forth across the expanse of glittering sea, searching for anything of interest. Sailing out of a wash of sunlight are numerous glistening small sea creatures that look like little model sailboats.

"Billy!" I shout. "There's hundreds of tiny little boats out here."

"Velellas," says Bill, peering out the wheelhouse door. "I'll get the book."

They're like little blue rafts, only a couple of inches long, made of a semi-firm, jelly-like substance on which sits a bit of jelly-like "sail." The sail is less blue, glossy, more transparent, a semi-circle with the long edge perpendicular to the floating oval raft part and attached with a slight "s" curve. Their common name is "by the wind sailor," or sail jellyfish, although they are not technically jellyfish. The Latin name is musical: *Velella velella*. They sail across the glossy swells towards us, hundreds of them... a miniature flotilla.

Beneath the surface, the pictures form a different way. What once was uncharted and unknown territory, for me, becomes familiar after a week. Uncountable complex bits of information piece themselves together to form a three-dimensional puzzle. When we arrive on the fishing grounds, at first we see only a vast expanse of heaving, pewter ocean. It's like the cover of an unopened book. We check the charts, locate some humps and bumps in the way down deep, shallow plateaus that are surrounded by great depths. We fish on the flooding tide by approaching a hump slowly with all our gear let down. Sound the bottom electronically, sense the bottom through cannonball messages flowing up the gurdy wire. Ah ha, some action. Must be a cod. Flip the gurdy lever and up it comes.

After a pass or two, we line up visual range marks, looking for the way a certain bump on the horizon lines up against Lanz or Beresford Island. Find a landmark behind Cape Scott to line up with the lighthouse. Billy prefers to have at least two visual range marks. Three is even better, so he can make pass after pass over the same spot. We're onto something good when we consistently pull up three or four cod with each pass. Enter the range marks in the GPS, which permanently marks the spot to return to. Do this in several spots over a couple of days and a memory map is created. Modern-day electronics may offer certainty, but a fisherman who has spent many years working the same territory will never forget the visual line-ups for a productive set or drag. And the plotter may just quit on you.

I now have an intimate three-dimensional knowledge of the configuration, population and vegetation of this area of seabed and the waters between there and the surface. My relationship with this small spot of water-covered land has completely taken over my thinking. When I lie in my bunk at night, before I fall into sleep, the pictures in my mind are of the deep sea, the bottom, the dark, the fish that swim down there, eat and live, the fish we lure to our gear with false promises. It's a complicated feeling, and not without guilt.

A Grateful Elation

And the sea also glowed from below.

—Pierre Loti

HOME A MONTH NOW FROM LING COD FISHING. Midnight has come and gone. Albert is away fishing prawns, and I'm sleepy, but my thoughts tumble around like clothes in a dryer. A golden crescent moon hangs above the gap on Baker Island. Gauzy strips of cloud like illuminated ribbons drift above and below the moon; a wash of pale light stains the sky beyond Mount Stevens, and big, bright stars shine. Their reflections dance in the slight swell, and soft plunking noises mark the nocturnal movement of baby salmon. A nightbird calls quietly, a sweet mewing peep, probably a little murrelet; another answers. My spirit is soothed by the serenity of this June moonfall.

I've been working with some of the drawings and photographs I collected on the ling cod trip. My favourite is of the little creek in Barge Bay on Cox Island. Painting and drawing are methods of "time travelling," beautiful ways to return to meaningful places. Lying awake, I travel to Barge Bay, and I revisit the gaily chattering creek set back from the open shore. It is screened from the casual gaze by a row of twisted, stunted spruce trees. In front of them, ranks of drift logs are rolled up and stacked in tiers, from the lowest high tide to the highest wind-driven levels. It's tricky scrambling over these delicately poised logs in my gumboots, packing my painting gear. The logs form a barrier that protects the multitude of wild flowers and mosses cloaking the rocks around the

Inside the forest canopy by Cox Island stream.

edges of the little stream. Behind the outer logs I find one hardy, elegant yellow iris plant (*Iris pseudocorus*), which probably arrived here via the settlers at Cape Scott. Strange to see it in this wild setting, yet it looks completely at home.

Sound changes as I duck under the spruce branches to gain the bank of the creek. Outside the spruce barrier, the surge and retreating suck of surf on rock, kelp and gravelly shore rumbles unabated. A perpetual wind thunders through the trees on the high ridge above, drumming through my body. The spruce barrier muffles those sounds; the stream murmurs a sweep of stringed instruments. Small rustling noises in the bush, flute or piccolo, add another layer to the creekside melody. I sit for a long while, listening to the woodland orchestra, breathing the fragrant greenness of the air, noting the variety of verdant leaves and innumerable tiny flowers. Small birds, encouraged by my stillness, creep and flutter out from the underbrush to busily resume feeding. I'm loathe to move, to destroy their perfect confidence with my intrusive presence.

Finally, out comes the camera to gather the visual information. Next, I perch on a dry rock about fifteen feet up the stream to draw the creek. Uncounted minutes, hours, pass. I know it's time to quit when my bottom goes numb.

How blessed I am to have these opportunities to be in wild secret places. *This* is where I hear God, or whatever you name the great creative energy, most clearly. This ravishing world is the gift to us, not an imaginary heaven that awaits us after death.

I feel such pain in my heart when I'm made aware, so frequently, of how we humans are unable to cherish what we have, but only ravage, abuse and destroy. The paradox of our being is that we can't exist on this earth without leaving a footprint with some degree of impact. The great irony is that even when we do manage to preserve some unique place, people want to see the natural treasure and that creates damage. The Lascaux caves with their rock paintings, for example, damaged by the exhaled breath from thousands of visitors. Or BC's Carmanah, valley of the giant trees: too many visitors to the valley has become a hazard in itself.

So good to rant to the moon; it won't rebut my opinions, nor will it argue.

I'll do the Barge Bay drawing on the watercolour paper tomorrow and begin. I'm in bliss when I have a strong feeling about a painting, an idea that's been growing. Preparations complete, I'm ready now to give birth to the image, set it down on the paper. Billy wants another painting in the style he envisioned, a central scene surrounded by different wildflowers. The little creek on Cox Island will be the centre for this one and around it I'll paint the flowers we found on our ling cod trip, in particular the pink-belled twisted stalk in Hansen Lagoon, skunk cabbage and yellow iris too.

These days the teacher in me gets to show up. A well-attended watercolour workshop in Sointula gives me a break from grunt work for a few days, and on the fourth of June my first-ever art retreat guests arrive. The house is still under construction, although we eat a picnic dinner within the walls one evening. My art retreat guests, Suzy and Linda, stay with Chris Bennett at his fishing lodge half a mile down Cramer Pass. He feeds and houses them, and I teach each day. Billy takes us to Bond Sound on *Ocean Dawn* for a combination scenic tour/plein air painting session.

During the week I spend some evenings with my guests at Chris's lodge. One night I linger long after dark, not realizing how much the wind has risen. The moonless night is as black as the inside of an ink bottle; a southeast wind blows down Cramer Pass against a rising tide. I motor slowly, but spray flies against the windshield, and my heart rate kicks up a notch. After my pupils dilate, I see there is some light. Sparkly white spume blows off the tops of breaking waves. *Sea Rose* rises to each wave, moving slowly into the rough slop breaking against the bow and along the sides of the boat. Everywhere the water flares with glitter. A bright gleam in the depths of the black ocean catches my eye; it's swelling, rising towards me. It expands into a billowing glow, a slow motion volcano, galaxies of stars compressed into an expanding cloud. It hits the

surface with a tremendous flowerburst of light. Shivers run up my spine, and the hair on the back of my neck is stiffly erect. I pull back the throttle to dead slow. Crazy ideas flash through my mind. Is it a whale surfacing in a phosphorescent glow? Can't be: there's no defined shape, no "suit of lights" such as when we see dolphins in phosphorescence running by the boat. I motor on with my heart racing triple time, hardly able to believe what I've seen. When I finally pull up to the dock, Albert is there with a flashlight to meet me.

"Get in the boat, get in!" I stutter. "There's something out there you've gotta see." I try to tell him about the cloud of light in the water.

"No, no," he says, hugging me. "Just come inside, you're home safe. We're not going back out there now." He is the voice of reason, but I am caught in the otherworld of mysterious lights, wondering if my own mind manufactured the event.

Cramer Pass widens out just before the lights of my house become visible. The terrain below the surface there drops off from shallow to much deeper. The theory we come up with is that a mass of bioluminescent plankton was propelled upwards by the flooding tide at the undersea wall just as I passed over. The brilliance was due to the extreme agitation of the wind/wave conditions at that moment. Likely I'll never see another cloud of luminosity like that. In Lyall Watson's book, *Gifts of Unknown Things*, he writes about a sea journey by night during which he and other people see mysterious underwater lights. His experience of, not fear but a "synthesis of honor and awe," perfectly describes my own feeling: a "grateful elation that is very close to worship."

Miraculous Wonderful Sockeye

*There was a time when fisheries managers thought a
sockeye was a sockeye; that a salmon from one river
was not different from a salmon from another.*

—Mark Hume *The Run of the River*

MIDSUMMER, LOGAN GOES TO WHITE ROCK to see his dad. Albert fishes
prawns with Ted as deckhand, and I'm off to Port Hardy August 2 to
crew the next trip with Billy. This is a sockeye opening, and we prepare
by tying many leaders. We head for San Josef Bay on the west coast of
Vancouver Island the first day and fish from Topknot to Kains Island.

Sockeye fishing according to Billy:

- The ideal temperature for sockeye is 50 to 54 degrees: any
  hotter and the fish go deep.
- The clearer the water the better for sockeye and pink. Coho
  and spring like dirty water.
- Sockeye bite better when the water's surface is rippled with
  a wind.
- Watch for upwellings. Good spots are tide rips at the change
  when the water is in pyramid peaks.
- The best bite is going west.
- Sockeye come in two days before the full moon and peak the
  second and third days after.

Sockeye fishing is characterized by having many hooks with flashers and lures on them in the water. The fisherman hopes the sockeye will believe these are a school of small fish. Ideally, experience guides you to the right place at the right time, the boat's electrical charge attracts rather than repels the fish, and they are in the mood to bite. Sixteen leader lines to a gurdy line, three gurdy lines to a side: that's a lot of fancy flashing. One of Billy's rules for being a highliner is to be first on the fishing grounds; another is to be on the fishing grounds at first light.

Three o'clock is a beautiful time of day for the morning person. I'm sipping hot sugared tea and pulling on my Helly Hansen rain gear. We're in the cockpit as dawn's grey blushes to a pale creamy rose. The sea quivers like pink mercury. A faint rosy-hued aura shimmers around the edges of the forest greens. My body may be fishing, but my mind is painting.

When we drag all that flashing fishing gear through the water it has to be at the right depth.

"What is right?" I ask.

"Where the fish are," Billy answers. We check the sounder screen for the distinctive blue streaks that signal sockeye; check the water temperature; ponder over the colour of the water (too clear and the fish are spooked, too cloudy and they can't see the flashers) and whether there is enough surface ruffle. If it's too calm the fish will see defined shapes rather than the distorted image puzzle created by a choppy sea surface. When the trolling poles start to bump and twitch, the salmon are hitting the gear. We bring those lines in, nice and quick and steady. Up comes a sockeye, swimming, looking just like a mini-submarine, built for speed, determined and focussed, but he's hooked. I lean over the side of the boat, stretch out my arm, grab the line, make a quick twist and fling the fish onto the deck in a spraying silver arc. Bonk it dead, remove the hook, unsnap the leader from the gurdy line, snap it into the bucket. Flip the brass lever that runs the hydraulics and bring the line up two fathoms (twelve feet), reach over, fling another in. If the fishing is hot, there'll be a dozen sockeye or more on every line, and it takes a couple hours to get them all in the boat. It's not long before the deck is covered with slithery, shiny sockeye.

After the entire line is in and cleared of salmon, we reset the line, and get the gear back in the water quicker than quick. Bring in the mainline first, unload, put it back down. Next is the shear pig line that floats the gear out to the side and back, held in place by the rectangular Styrofoam pig. The third line, the back pig, floats a longer distance astern, also kept in place by the pig. We fish all six lines, gear in, get the fish in the boat, gear out, no time to even pee, no stopping for anything, we're in the money now.

With special purposed boards slotted into place on the deck, we create small square pens, called checkers, to contain the fish. A mountain of sockeye slithering around as the boat rolls is dangerous. The checkers help us manage the catch in the first busy hours. Another important item is the ice blankets. We don't want to leave all those fish exposed to sun as the day heats up, so the deckhand (me!) makes sure the salmon are covered until we have time to clean them. If the fishing is spectacular, once we have worked all six lines, we pull them all again. In most cases though, after the morning bite, fishing slows down and I prepare toast for a quick breakfast.

A *really* quick breakfast, because it's important to clean the fish and dress them, an odd phrase meaning to cut open the belly and remove the innards. I visualize designer outfits for the sockeye, fishnet stockings, ruffled skirts, ascots and natty, nautical hats as I hose them down and scrub clean the insides of the fish Billy guts. In front of the cockpit is a wooden trough and it's easy to hold the fish in the trough to clean (dress) them. I aim the saltwater hose inside and out to get rid of the blood and guts. The water drains directly from the trough into the sea. We slide each dressed sockeye forward into one of the checker pens. The salmon get a second hosing down, just to be certain no clots of congealed blood or bits of innards are left behind.

When all the sockeye are shining clean, no bloody bits trailing around, Billy dons thick orange freezer gloves and woollen toque and climbs down into the ice-filled hold. I slide the salmon down the hatch one by one, counting as I drop them. Billy is down there for an hour, carefully laying the salmon on their backs on the ice and filling the spread bellies

with ice. The care he takes now will make a big difference when the buyer, Seafoods, is doling out the bonus for quality fish. I hose down the deck, write the total catch in the log and prepare our next meal.

The fishing is pretty so-so to start; we bring in eighty-nine sockeye the first day. With fifty or sixty salmon on deck, it is easy to see distinct colour variations in the fish. I arrange them in the checker pens so I can see the differences en masse. Most notable are the biggest sockeye, which shine an iridescent green from the centre-line of their sides up and over their dark backs. Greenheads, Billy calls them.

"Those are the Adams River run, and the large dark blue ones are from the Chilko River." Billy also points out the slightly brighter blue, longer-nosed Stewart River sockeye. Even within the larger groups there are subtle variations and I sort these, too. He says they are probably all

Billy and me bringing in the sockeye. Photo Theda Miller.

returning to the Fraser River, to one or another of the twenty-four natal streams. I'm in the cockpit a long time sorting and studying the sockeye. I could never have perceived these variations by catching one or two. My awed respect for the "salmon designer" goes up another notch as I comprehend the variety, subtlety and precise adaptations of what we loosely call "salmon." Environmental factors such as depth, colour and pH (alkalinity or acidity) of water, composition of the bedrock, turbidity, speed and glaciation of natal stream, and in particular, what they eat, all go into shaping the size and colour of the sockeye (and other species).

I've gotten better at distinguishing which species of salmon is on the gear when they are still deep out of sight. If a big spring has hooked on, there's a lot of drag; the line is pulled back taut, and when I bring up the fish, it fights with powerful, pulsating resistance. The smallest, the pink salmon, fight energetically on the line and flip all over the place, which

This one was a real beauty. Photo Theda Miller.

translates into a jiggling movement on the gurdy wire. Coho and chum are difficult to distinguish although once they are close up to the boat the silvery coho fight much harder; the chum lie there like a slab of meat. The sockeye move just like a torpedo, sleek, straight and undeterred in their forward motion. I'm touched by what seems a sort of stoic commitment emanating from them. I cheer when one gets off the hook as I'm bringing it in and slips away into the blue-green deep. Once in a while we get an odd-looking fish that Billy calls a "chumpie": a cross between a pink salmon (otherwise known as a humpie) and a chum. Evidently there's some hybridizing success when sperm and egg get mixed up in a heavily trafficked spawning stream.

The second day we run all over the place, end up at Cape Cook for seven sockeye. We never lay eyes on another fish boat the whole day. The weather is awful, southeast wind and rain. No fish either. But we do see a couple of huge, white-faced, dusky birds Billy says are albatross, the ocean's nomads.

These are black-footed albatross, the only species of thirteen worldwide that frequents the North Pacific. I'm enthralled, watching them soaring, gliding, sliding along an invisible cushion that shifts with the changing shape and angle of the sea surface. The poetic flight of the albatross appears effortless. Their long narrow wings span seven feet yet neither wingtips nor feet ever touch the water. Their attunement to wind and wave has been named "dynamic soaring." The albatross's flight is so perfectly aligned to the sea's movement it can soar this way over thousands of miles without ever flapping its wings or needing land on which to rest. Today, the albatross follows the boat for hours, hoping, I guess for some goodies, though we have nothing to offer. Their main food is caught at night, when squid, fishes, cuttlefish and other sea creatures rise to the surface. Another miracle of the albatross is that they drink salt water. They're fascinating, wonderful, and I want somehow to celebrate their presence near us on these restless seas. I raise my arms to the sky.

"Albatross! Albatross! O mighty winged one!"

Billy rolls his eyes, but I know he feels the same.

By late afternoon we're so close to the fabled weather evil of Solander

Island that we take a little cruise to get up close and personal. The island is a formidable piece of crumbling rock jutting up from the deep, black and invincible, supporting a varied array of wildlife. A large group of sea lions loll about high on the rock (how *do* they get up there?), and half a dozen sea otters resting comfortably on the big swells regard us, unperturbed. Billy decides the sea is calm enough to spend the night anchored by tiny Hackett Island, but in the early hours past midnight the wind shifts from a gentle offshore breeze to a snotty southeast. Rain pours down hard as the wind swings around, and the anchor drags. The skipper and I are out of the bunks and up into the wheelhouse in a flash. Billy pulls on his rain gear and goes out into the slashing rain to raise the anchor while I steer into the swell. We jog into the slop until dawn and during that dark time Billy gets a great idea. We'll go to the Charlottes again.

On the way in to Winter Harbour to stock up on grub and fuel, we anchor for lunch at a golden stretch of sand, Grant Bay. Billy scoots the bow of the rowboat up to the black rocks and has me leap out on the rise of the swell; got to be quick! My camera, slung around my neck, bangs hard against the rock as I jump. He backs away on the receding swell and rows the boat in to the beach. He tries to time his landing, but a big roller catches him, and over he goes, scrambling out in a wet flurry. He dries out quickly in the hot sun. The edge of the telephoto lens is dented, but at least I won't have to replace the body, again. Salt water isn't good for cameras.

Who doesn't love a picnic on a sunny sandy beach? Rolling surf plays bass under the scree of gulls, wind sighs through cedar trees, hot sand warms my toes. After lunch I roam about collecting beautiful things: shells, feathers, sea glass, twisted bits of sea-polished driftwood, kelp and stones. Kneeling in the sand, I place these items just so, governed by an ephemeral inner command.

"What are you making?" Bill asks from under the shade of his cap.

"Art," I say. "This is art from found objects. It's like beachcombing, only smaller." This is the most fun of all-art making, its only purpose the joy of creating. Wind and tide will scatter these pieces and leave no trace.

I'll never have to make a frame, hang it in a gallery or find a buyer for it. After a while Billy is making art in the sand, too, finding small bits and pieces, and arranging them just so.

On this sunshine shore we feel like the only ones for a million miles around, until a couple of fellows burst out of the bushes and walk across the top of the beach. Shortly thereafter, a helicopter lands and disgorges half a dozen people. I imagine they all have the same feeling we do; their expectations of a deserted west coast beach are dashed. They probably paid a lot of money to arrive here and find us.

The invasion of the helicopter tourists spurs our reluctant departure. Off we go, by Kains Island Light and into Winter Harbour, the sweetest little village spread along the waterfront of Forward Inlet. Billy takes off up the dock to find a buyer and is gone long enough for me to explore the harbour waterfront. Finally he jumps aboard and fires up the motor.

A Long Hard Voyage

No one has ever described the place where I have just arrived.

—Paul Theroux, *The Pillars of Hercules*

WINTER HARBOUR DISAPPEARS ASTERN, as we begin the long journey to the mystic isles. Kains Island Light slips by again and then the outer coast of Vancouver Island. Seeing Cape Scott Lighthouse recede gives me a pang. There are still islands ahead, to be sure, emerald jewels set along a glittering band of western light: Beresford Island, Lanz and Cox, and beyond those, terrible Triangle Island, island of hurricane-force winds, destroyer of railroad tracks, lighthouses and cows. Triangle Island, aptly named, surges straight up, its powerful diagonals piercing the skin of the sea. It's as if colossal waves had solidified and been sharpened to a fine point by the unceasing rasp of wind and water. In the late afternoon haze, Triangle Island looms formidable and adamant. This is the top of a mountain, ascending from the deepest sea. Billy brings the boat close in so we can see through the great stone arch. Dark falls with sudden tropical violence after we swing round the island and set our course for Cape St. James.

We're in for a long, arduous night. The farther north we travel, the rougher the seas roll, slopping and slapping us around. We take two-hour turns at the wheel. Billy goes down to the bunk to snooze. Soon I hear cursing from below, see his face peering up the ladder.

"Damn sea nearly threw me out of the bunk," he glowers. "Can't

get any sleep like that." He pushes a mattress up onto the wheelhouse floor and settles down on it. I sit in the faint glow of the electronics in the darkened wheelhouse, watching the compass through the midnight hours. I plug Emmy Lou Harris into the tape deck, or Bonny Raitt, while *Ocean Dawn* slams up, crashes down, pitches to port, yaws to starboard, in no predictable order. On Billy's watch, I snug into the sleeping bag on the floor, roll the short distance back and forth between the base of the stove and the drawers under the table, breathe the sour smell of diesel, doze (sleep is not possible) to Billy's choice of tunes: Boxcar Willie, Hank Williams, Johnny Cash. These are familiar voices from my childhood. I can hear my father and Uncle Jimmy singing cowboy songs, their voices offering comfort through this interminable, uncomfortable night.

"It'll get better when it's morning," Billy assures me. Leaden daylight dawns, and I wish for darkness again. The seas that felt huge now appear gargantuan. Monstrous green surges break over the wheelhouse roof and pour down the windows.

He tries again. "It'll get better when we get closer to Cape St. James." While Billy is never wrong, in this instance, he's not correct. The closer we get to Cape St. James, the steeper the mountains of water. Great relief envelopes us when we finally anchor in Luxana Bay. We crash as if bludgeoned into the bunks. After a three-hour nap, still feeling like we've been beaten up, we pull the anchor and set off again.

It's still blowing over forty knots when we depart Luxana Bay to work our way up to Houston Stewart Channel. To reduce the side-to-side roll of the boat, Billy puts the heavy triangular stabilizers in the water. There's a tangle in the starboard lines where the stabilizer hangs from the outspread trolling poles. The heavy piece of plywood, weighted with an attached half-cannonball, is supposed to sit just under the surface as we run, but it won't settle properly. Billy stops a couple times in the confused jumble of cross swells to try, without success, to adjust its position, but the erratic motion makes for unsafe footing on the wet deck.

"I'll deal with it when we anchor tonight," he grumbles.

We continue on our slow way until an exceptionally turbulent swell flings us over in a deep roll to port. The heavy stabilizer rips out of the water and is propelled like a missile across the deck to crash against the gunwale. Now Billy does have to mess around with the stabilizer. I steer the boat through the breaking seas while he wrestles it into reluctant submission.

Cooking in such sloppy seas is a challenge too. I'm having trouble preparing our bacon and eggs, getting thrown around as I stand at the stove. If I brace myself against the back of the captain's bench, I have to reach out just a bit too far to easily turn the bacon. Billy roots around in the box drawer under the settee and comes up with a roll of gagnon, the all-purpose sailor's twine. He fashions a strap like a bus strap, fancy-knotting a piece of gagnon that he then attaches to the ceiling beam. It hangs down above the oil stove and I hang on to it as the boat rocks and handle the pots, pans and tools with my right hand. It's a small fix that makes a big difference.

We still have a few days before fishing opens for the whole coast on August 11, so Billy takes us up the ironbound shore to explore the lagoons and protected coves that break into the rancorous, sharp-toothed western face of the Charlottes. From the southern tip of Graham Island up to Tasu Sound there are several small inlets within about fifteen nautical miles that are characterized by apparent inaccessibility. We don't have enough time to explore all of them, but Pocket Inlet and Puffin Cove are on our must-see list and we're lucky with the weather. We anchor in a small rockbound cove, climb into the dinghy and row through a high-sided, narrow channel, surfing the waves until the little dinghy is thrust out of the narrows onto a shallow unwrinkled lagoon. Spread before eyes fatigued from squinting against a shimmering, vibrating skin of ocean is a stretch of perfect golden sand lapped by water the bluest of tropical blues. This is Puffin Cove, a safe, secluded small harbour with a driftwood house built by Neil and Betty Carey, well known to any reader of coastal literature. It does not disappoint.

Billy and I eat lunch here. After we go our separate ways on the beach, I explore and investigate, photograph and sketch for a happy three hours while Billy has a short siesta in the noonday sun. All too soon we must leave. How many others have had the same feeling of gratitude to the

Careys for the spirit and fortitude it took to build a house in this inhospitable landscape, a house that they leave open for passers-by, a surprising number of them. I write our names and *Ocean Dawn* and the date in the logbook lying open on the table and read the record of passage of other visitors through the years.

Running south from Puffin Cove I watch for puffins, finally seeing a small colony on a cliff. Sun blazes down hard. It's *hot*. Billy wants to show me Pocket Inlet. He came here when he and Logan fished the Charlottes.

"Yvonne," he says seriously, "this is the most beautiful place I have ever seen in all my life, I swear." High praise from a man I know to have a great appreciation for the beauty in all things, from a little clingfish to a blazing red and gold sunset. We enter a channel just wide enough for the fishing boat. Inside the opening, Pocket Inlet swells into a short, wide… pocket. Set the hook, let down the dinghy from the roof of the cabin, gather up camera, hat and sunglasses, over the side and into the dinghy and row to the shore.

With a short climb, we crest a hill strewn with wind-stunted pines. A scene of epic grandeur lies before me. Everywhere is wonderful to gaze upon. The silver-foil sea stretches to the delicately arced horizon; frothing surf swirls below to a row of sharp-toothed rocks in the distant sun haze. The rounded horizon proves the earth *is* a big blue ball. The short pines frame several ponds, each draining into the next. Red and green dragonflies and electric blue damselflies hover everywhere. Growing out of cracks between lichen-covered rocks are cobalt blue harebells, two nodding flowers to each six-inch stalk. Dwarfed and twisted spruce trees soften the stony profile without obscuring the view. Mysterious six-foot towers of hard-packed soil rise here and there. We wonder what they are. Billy leans up against one to watch the surf boil below as I amble about, feasting my eyes. A sudden shout alarms me, but Billy is laughing as he curses, brushing wildly at his clothing with his cap.

"Ants," he shouts. "These are ant hills, dammit. They're all over me."

How lucky I am to be here, so far from anywhere. I'll think about Pocket Inlet many years from now and know that there'll be few who

While we are waiting for the season to open Billy and I explore some of the small inlets on the western shore of Moresby Island. Pocket Inlet (above) and Puffin Cove are on our must-see list.

tread this windswept, moss- and lichen-encrusted rock face on the western coast of Haida Gwai'i. Pocket Inlet now has the same status in my book as in Billy's.

He and I sit in replete quiet, fulfilled by beauty, as we motor south towards Anvil Cove. We listen to the fishing update. One more day to explore before the work begins. It's so hot we can hardly bear to have the stove on. I prepare dinners for the next three days and put them down the hatch in the ice: baking powder biscuits stuffed with salmon, cheese and onions; bacon and egg quiche; two pans of chocolate chip cookies: food we can eat cold, with a salad.

Opening day; fog so thick you can't see the nose on your face. After our dreamy holiday poking around inlets and coves we are all business.

It's time to make some money, bring in some fish. We put the gear in the water near McLean Fraser Point, one of the most hellish-looking places I've ever seen. We only get a brief glimpse of the wicked rock fangs, but we know they are there, lurking. The blazing sun has had its power sapped by the muffling cotton of the coastal fog, and Billy is in and out of the wheelhouse like a jackrabbit, watching the radar and the depth sounder.

We're tooling along southwards, working the gear, both of us glancing up frequently to watch for boats coming towards us. There are many here hoping for good fishing, all congregated in the same spot. A ghost ship looms out of the fog dead ahead, another fishing boat, massive in the enveloping greyness. Billy sees it the same moment I scream. He wheels the boat hard to starboard, and luckily the skipper of the *BC Sun* does the same. Barely a kiss of the tip of the spread trolling poles, and we swing apart and pass. Billy and I are left weak in the knees and shaky but no harm done. Some other boats aren't so lucky and clash their poles together.

Later in the day, in the thinning fog, I see a mirage-like being. A leviathan volcanoes up like a new landmass from the water, curves over and dives. Lifting its colossal tail high in the air, it sinks in slow motion. I run in and draw a quick sketch of the tail.

"Sperm whale," says Bill.

"Wow! I can't get over how huge it is. It's giant, it's gargantuan. Wow!"

"Waoow," says Bill, mocking me.

"No more chocolate chip cookies for you," I threaten.

"Whales," he says. "They go up. They go down."

Hundreds of Pacific white-sided dolphins and a juvenile humpback whale hang about for a while. Lots of puffins and other seabirds, too, but not many sockeye. We got 269 on our first day fishing, and Billy is happy with that, but the tally peters off quickly, and by the evening of the second day there are few boats left at McLean Fraser Point. With 576 sockeye iced down in the hatch and most of the other boats gone, Billy decides we should make a run for it to Pine Island via the Goose Bank.

I'm not too excited about this plan, with the memory of our last brutal all-night run freshly stored in the cells of my body. However, by the time we motor our way to the eastern side of the islands and begin the endless crossing of Hecate Strait, the evening light is almost mystical, the sea miraculously calm. Sky colour slides from lavender to rose, peach blooms into palest green, teal to blue-black. Stars twink on their small glitter. First a few, then more, then great smudges of uncountable millions spangle the immense bowl of velvet black with their faraway light. Sea melts into sky as the earth turns. Again we take two-hour shifts running the boat and snoozing on the wheelhouse floor, but this night run is magic.

Pine Island at last, in the wee small hours of August 14, and we throw the gear in the water. We've made the right decision, hooking onto almost two hundred big beautiful sockeye on the first pull. To make the cake sweeter, rumour has it the price is rising, possibly as high as $4.10 a pound. We'll see. We make a quick run into Port Hardy to deliver our catch, and pick up another deckhand: my daughter Theda.

Fishing season 1994 at Pine Island is an unforgettable experience. All three types of salmon fishing are in use simultaneously. Trollers like us traverse pretty much a straight line. We turn around and work back, turn back again, as we follow the blue streaks on the sounder and the flow of the tide, ever watchful of oncoming traffic. The big seiners roll out their nets in giant circles, so we must all go around them. That creates a big jog in the traffic flow. The gillnetters, which traditionally set at night, have daytime openings as well here, and they set the drum rolling and head right across the path of the trollers as they let out their nets. Picking up our gear as fast as we can while making a hard turn or going into reverse to avoid running over a gillnet keeps stress levels at the top of the scale. Tempers flare. Plenty of blue-streak cursing from the skipper, so Theda and I try some creative cursing of our own to make him laugh. "Bastard, pig-f*#&!ing jackass, pr*#k!"

He does laugh but he is not so amused when the owner of the gillnet we overrun, due to the gillnetter setting right in front of us, stands on his bow and curses us as we work to untangle our gear from his net.

"Jesus, the bastard could help," Billy mutters, as we frantically tease hooks and flashers from net webbing.

At night we anchor by Vansitart Island, and the mast, running and cabin lights from hundreds of boats anchored in Shadwell Pass look like a small city, an uncommon and lovely sight. Rarely are all gear types fishing the same area and the same opening. The lights of the boats and their reflections form a human version of the starry sky.

Since our shore day on the fifteenth when I received my paycheque of almost three thousand dollars, we've caught only six, thirty-eight, five and four sockeye, respectively. Not good. In those four days, the water temperature has risen from 49 to 55 degrees, which Billy says is a bad sign. The skipper is bummed, and so is the crew. We head south towards the backside of Malcolm Island and do a little better fishing the rip at Egeria Shoal. Billy tells me how well people used to do, fishing "the Bank" at Blackney Pass as the tide turned to flood down Johnstone Strait. Nobody fishes there anymore but since we still are not doing well, we make up our minds to slip away from the other boats in the fog and try it.

"The big problem," warns Billy, "is you've got to make sure the gear doesn't get tangled. It'll be a helluva dog's breakfast if that happens." The tide here creates a boiling cauldron when millions of gallons of water suddenly pour from Blackfish Sound through the narrow neck of Blackney Pass into Johnstone Strait. The swirling rips create havoc with the gear, sixteen leaders with flashers and hoochies, and hooks, hanging off four or six deep lines.

Billy checks the tide book and we get ready to move when the flood begins. Only the main line and the shear pig lines go out and we shorten them up to permit the tight turn Billy makes. It's thrillingly successful. Over a hundred sockeye climb on the hooks. Our second pass results in a fuck-up of major proportions, and we spend the next two hours untangling a mess of balled-up lines, flashers, hooks, hoochies and lures. While we're untangling, I take a break to make us some tea and notice a huge blip on the sounder less than a quarter mile away. My body jerks when a foghorn boom erupts.

"Holy shit, Billy!" I run out of the cabin. "We're going to get run down by a cruise ship!" Billy has already changed course but there's not enough room to feel we are well out of the cruise ship's path. I never have seen *anything* look so deadly as the ghostly hull of that vessel looming like a moving cliff out of the fog. A few greyed figures stand by the rails looking down at us, their shock and surprise obvious in the open-mouthed "Oh!" in the lower half of their faces. A wall of windows stretches high above, and the behemoth takes forever to pass by. As abruptly as the vessel appears, it is swallowed by the fog. A slight ripple and the acrid breath of its exhaust are all that mark its passing.

Billy is so frustrated by the fact that nothing works—watching the blue streaks on the sounder, plotting with all his years of experience, being creative and innovative, and still coming up with a poor showing— he decides that's it for now and we run home to Echo Bay for a break from the dismal crush of the week's fishing.

I'm glad to be home to reap the rewards of the summer, to can fish and peaches and make pickles while Logan crews the next trip with Billy. But it's a short reprieve. Billy phones through the Coast Guard radio telephone a few days later to ask if I'll do one more trip. The radio transmission is poor, but I get that there's a two-day opening at the mouth of the Fraser River and Billy wants to make the run down there. I say yes and when and where. He and Logan are already halfway down Johnstone Strait so he'll pick me up in Campbell River the next day.

I've a bit of organizing to do to pull this off. I'm home alone since Albert is fishing in Quatsino and Theda's left for White Rock. An hour after Billy phones, our hatchery manager, Clint Montgomery, comes by to borrow some canning lids. I seize the moment to ask him if he can stay at our place for five or six days. I need someone to feed Buddy the dog, can the peaches and do the pickles for me. A tall order, I think.

"No problem," says Clint.

I book a seat on the afternoon sched flight to Port McNeill and throw my gumboots, rain gear, licence and freshly laundered fishing clothes in the kitbag. I meet Billy and Logan at Redden Net in Campbell River, a bit breathless from the sudden rush of preparation and travel. The long

hours motoring for the mouth of the Fraser River will calm me down.

In the late afternoon sun Logan asks Billy to stop long enough for him to dive off the boat and have a swim.

"What the hell do you want to do that for?" Billy cries. He doesn't swim, never runs his speedboat far from the beach unless he has to. He cannot imagine why Logan wants to dive off the boat into water unimaginably deep. He obliges, though, and puts the boat out of gear. For me it's a beautiful moment, watching my young son dive in the late afternoon light off the side of *Ocean Dawn* into the spangled indigo sea. Like a seal he shakes golden drops off his hair as he surfaces, climbs up the side of the boat and dives in again. Perhaps, like me, he remembers diving off Albert's boat years ago in Nepah Lagoon.

The light fades to rosy dusk, then deep violet twilight and night brings a sudden squall overloaded with summer rain. Billy watches the chart, the depth sounder, the radar but can see nothing through the water-swept window. We are somewhere near Tribune Bay, Hornby Island, but how close? I go out the door and peer ahead to where the spotlight's erratic beam lights up rain-pocked seas, and barely visible, sea-washed flat rocks.

"Rocks, rocks to starboard!" I yell. Billy wheels hard to port. This close call rattles us so much we decide to anchor for a couple hours and carry on in the dawn light.

It doesn't take long to arrive at the south arm of the Fraser River in the morning. We come upon a scene of apparent mayhem, boats running everywhere and American Coast Guard vessels out in force, armed with loud speakers and guns.

We are scrupulous as we fish, 100 per cent certain to never get too close to the boundary line. The big American vessels mean business, and we hear on the radio that a couple of vessels have been boarded and detained. Good catch the first day: I enter 167 in the fishing log. The second day is a bust and we three vote to get the hell out of there. We head north to finish off the trip in our home waters.

I reflect on the territory I've covered this summer, the scenery I beheld as I journeyed from Echo Bay to Cape Cook on Vancouver Island's west coast, Winter Harbour to Triangle Island to Cape St. James, from the western sea of the Queen Charlotte Islands south again to Pine Island, and on to the southern arm of the Fraser River until the final voyage home. Johnny Cash's song "I've Been Everywhere Man" loops through my head. I'm bursting to paint some of what I've seen and felt. Clint did all the peaches and pickles while I was gone, and they sit glowing on the shelf. Thank you, Clint.

Stand-Off on the Boomstick

I'VE WORKED HARD ON THE HOUSE SINCE EARLY THIS MORNING, when Albert, Logan and Ted left for town with Billy. Insulation is the work of the week, a nasty, nasty job. Every day since my return from fishing we've laboured to make the structure habitable. We place the long pink batts of fibreglass between every 2 x 4 in the walls, carefully cutting around electrical boxes and plug-ins. The entire bottom floor, the inside walls and the ceiling must be done. Underneath the house is the worst. I've dragged a tarp under there and crawl onto it after I shove the fibreglass bundle in. Lying on my back, I press each pink batt up in between the floor joists. Once I get a section of batts in, I push or pull the long roll of house wrap under there and—still lying on my back—unroll it in short sections, then staple it up onto the floor joists. Wearing eye protection and a mask makes the work even more difficult. I can't get as much breath as I need for the amount of work I'm doing; sweat burns my eyes, and my stomach muscles and back are crying for relief.

The gabbling chatter of Barrow's goldeneyes along the foreshore carries clearly under the house. Time to take a break from the bloody pink batts, I think, just a couple of minutes. My jeans and long-sleeved work shirt, tucked into gloves at the wrist, are covered with stones, twigs, soil and insulation wisps. Too much trouble to change, so I remove the Liberty silk scarf from my nose and mouth, walk to the creek for a drink of water, walk back and plop down on a stump on the shore above the busy birds. No rain yet, although it's coming. The sky is a wet warm grey, and Mount Stevens looms indigo blue.

Thick masses of shiny little black mussels grow all over the boomsticks that hold the float off the land. Due to the falling tide the sticks sit at a steep angle. Five or six crows are perched on the top side, pecking away at the mussels, and half a dozen black and white male goldeneyes do the same from the water. Looks to me like there's plenty to go around, but the crows don't agree. They jab their beaks repeatedly at the goldeneyes to make them back off. One old crow and a big goldeneye are having an intense confrontation. Whenever the goldeneye advances purposefully to the mussels and grabs a quick bite, the crow jabs his beak at him. Finally the goldeneye has had enough. He swims under the boomstick, surfaces behind the crow and pulls its tail! I laugh hard, retie my scarf over my nose and go back to insulating, re-invigorated, thinking about volition, revenge and deliberate action in bird brains, clearly an undeserved insult.

Later I get halibut marinating in ginger, garlic and soy sauce, enjoying a short quiet time before the guys get home from town. Yesterday a neighbour asked me why I deckhand for Billy and but not my prawn-fishing husband. I love to go on excursions with Albert, but experience has shown me deckhanding for him is just trouble; it's our working styles, I think. We get into too much conflict because we do things and think so differently. It's better if we divide up the work according to our preferences and abilities. As well, now that we are planted here, Albert fishes near home; I dearly love to voyage to new places and Billy is the only one going anywhere. I can be married to Albert or deckhand for him but not both. This gives my kids a chance at the prawn deckhand job anyway.

I've come to realize that many human interactions are simply a question of habit compatibility. We've been framing the house with Ted's help, and Billy's been helping me nail on siding. All four of us work on the roof on the big push to lay the turquoise sheets of metal roofing. Billy and I work side by side nailing down fir sheathing on the rafters. We're working like a well-oiled machine, talking, swearing and chuckling, sometimes laughing so hard we have to stop for breath, but steadily banging in the nails. I look over towards Al and Ted, who resemble twin

Billy brings in the ramp we built to go from land to the float.

brothers, side-by-each with their reddish hair and mustaches. They are completely silent except for the odd grunt. They're working like a well-oiled machine without saying one word, completely happy setting the last few rafters in place over the main floor. This is working compatibility, each to his or her own style.

Billy makes a ramp for us just before our move into the house. He sets the two fifty-five-foot fir logs he beachcombed on the cradle of the boat ways and Albert and I nail down decking across them. On a good high tide Billy lowers the cradle, floats the ramp off and tows it to our place with his speedboat. Standing on the floating ramp, he pushes with a pike pole to manoeuvre it into position. He and Albert use the come-along to pull the high end up onto the shore and the low end up onto the logs of the float. They attach boom chains from the float to a U-bolt on the shore, on one side, and to a stump on the other. Logan and I run up and down the dock twenty times, jumping up and down crazily. What a difference it makes having easy access to the land! When I think of how long we've been "dinghying" over to the shore, having disasters with the dropping or rising tides, I think we were nuts not to do this years ago. We've hauled enormous boatloads of lumber over here, and packed it up the bank, piece by piece. All that work would have been a thousand times easier with a ramp. However, we have one now and the future can only be better for it. Just hope my knees hold out.

Billy and I completed the cedar siding for the first floor and we're well

Ted and Al working on the roof beams, like twin brothers, side-by-each.

on our way up the second floor. We're adding to the scaffold as needed, spiraling our way around the house. Albert is working, in marathon shifts as is his style, from 4:00 pm to 4:00 am installing wiring right now. He's amazing the way he sits down night after night to read and plan and then, bam! wires a house right to code. Billy has named him my "Hercules," appropriately so, after the patron god of human toil. Another nighttime activity that's been fun is arranging small-scale furniture cutouts on the floor plan I drew of the bottom level. Albert and I move the cutouts around trying to work out the most functional arrangement. Everything fits compactly… on paper. Hope it works for real.

Albert salvages miles of discarded school carpeting from the dump/recycling depot north of Port McNeill. We have not done the insulating above the first floor yet, so his plan is to roll out the carpet on the second

Billy and me working on the roof.

story floor, to keep the heat in. He and Billy load up *Ocean Dawn* with thirty or forty rolls of it. When we tow Glen's little barge over to Billy's boat to bring the carpet home, I see that the deck of the *Ocean Dawn* is *completely* covered with rolls of the heavy, dense brown carpet. We pile every piece onto the barge. Billy opens up the hatch cover, and oh my god, it's full, too. I can't help it: I burst into tears.

"It's impossible, there's too much, we'll never get it all over there," I sob.

I'm wrong. Thank goodness for strong young sons and good neighbours. Al spends the next several days stapling down roofing paper on the floor above the studio and rolling out carpet to fit.

Christmas Eve is an unusual day to move house but I had set the end of 1994 as our target date and we do it. To make furniture removal easy,

Moving day, Christmas Eve. Bill and Albert pack the hot water tank out the hole Albert bucked in the wall.

Albert bucks out a big hole in the back wall of the trailer we called home for five years. I'm the energizer bunny, up and down the fabulous ramp without stopping, shifting all our belongings into the new home. The floor plan is tacked to the wall to guide the movers and everything goes into place like a hand into a glove. Within six hours Billy, Clint, Albert, Theda, Logan and I have our entire household neatly packed into one room of the new house, my studio-to-be.

The kids' beds lie head to head at right angles in the southwest corner of the studio. Our bed is against the other wall. If one of us wants to change clothing, we call out "privacy moment" and the others turn their backs. The kitchen fits perfectly along the lower section with the table overlooking the wreckage of the trailer on the float and beyond to Mount Stevens. Buddy takes up a position right outside the door, lying in a kingly fashion with his paws crossed. He's happy over here with room

Albert and Billy use a come-along and leverage to get the ramp log ends settled up onto the float.

to roam. I can't stop crying tears of joy, relief and exhaustion. Part of me had begun to think I'd never actually live in this house but would only be working on it into eternity.

A small Christmas tree glows on a sheet spread on my camphorwood trunk. The kids and I decorate it and string the lights and Albert fires up the generator when darkness falls. I go outside briefly to see the tree lights through the window from the darkness. Around midnight, tired out but warm and safe under our new roof, we slip under the covers and call out "Good night, Merry Christmas."

The Ling Cod Trip from Hell

JANUARY 1995 BEGINS WITH AN EVENT with high entertainment value: the moving of a house. This can be either from land to a float or float to land. In this case, it's the moving of the Neidrauers' house from its float to a position on land.

The tide is high, the float sits near shore in the best position to slide easily and a complex array of blocks and cables is organized to multiply the pulling power of the winch. You never know when a cable is going to snap or just how much stress the floor joists or window can take. It's a pleasure to watch a move that's well-orchestrated like Glen and Marg's. Everything goes smoothly with lots of expertise from Billy and able assistance from neighbours. I lurk, taking pictures, and I'm pleased with one of Pat, Fraser and Billy yarding on a cable. Pat is not a big woman, but she has a lot of oomph, and she's putting her heart into the job. Glen and Marg's little grey house was dragged from its position in the centre of its float to perch on a low rise up from the shore on the site he had cleared. Their house used to be one of the Echo Bay forestry station houses. It had been yarded off the land onto a float years ago. Houses out here don't get demolished; they simply get new underpinnings, whether on land or logs. When they're abandoned, they become the coastal "Home Depot"—we scavenge for windows, toilets, hardware fittings, hot water tanks, even old chairs and dishes.

Our own new home, of course, is the focus of most of our attention and effort. Every erg of work shows in one way or another. Days without rain, I set lengths of golden-brown cedar siding on sawhorses and brush a mixture of diesel and transmission fluid on both sides. The idea is that this will preserve the wood as well as the rosy colour and discourage bugs from dining on it. The oils quickly evaporate, then the siding is ready to nail up. We're finishing the second floor now. Billy comes over after his lunch, and we saw and nail for a couple hours. All the 2 x 4 trim around the doors and windows has a decorative 45-degree angle cut on each side of the horizontal top piece, so the corresponding pieces of siding must be cut to match. We're up about twelve feet on the scaffolding in some places, but I'm used to it and have no trouble as we work higher. Billy's taught me how to handle a handsaw, and I can rip a nice straight cut and saw complex angles. Albert is the quality control man. I tackled the first outside window trim without consulting him and proudly showed him my handiwork. He was quiet for a minute, looked at me, obviously dreading my wrath, said, "It's not square."

Glen and Marg Neidrauer's house all set to be yarded up the rollers.

"Oh, that's okay," I blithely replied. Albert hesitated, looked doubtful but said nothing more. Even though I knew he was right, I was pissed off. I rode my anger to wrench the trim off the walls and squared it up before I cooled down.

For all of short February, we work like demons. My days are all about siding and staining, staining and siding. One day the generator refuses to generate electricity. Billy has some carbon brushes that Al cuts down to size to fit our generator so all is well. The steering cable on my speedboat breaks, and Billy just happens to have one that will work until I get a new one. There's one mini-disaster after another. I am agitated but after listening to the news on the radio I remind myself I live in a heaven where we have a neighbour who has one of everything we'll ever need.

I'm frequently out rooting about in the muck, creating soil, nooks and depressions to fill with plants. The rocks on our property are in-finite, every size and shape. Large ones emerge out of the steep slope and will be wonderful for retaining walls. The garden ascends the hill in

I stained every piece of cedar siding with a mixture of diesel and transmission fluid, to protect the wood from weathering and bugs.

terraced, horizontal beds. Albert and I have sore backs from filling and hauling buckets of rocks from the creekbed to fill the drainage trenches for the septic field. Three fifty-foot trenches are required, and we have just enough room on the lower garden level to fit that in. Clint Montgomery gives us a hand with various grunt jobs, including picking rocks but in the end, I pay a dollar a bucket to Logan and any young fellow in the neighbourhood willing to help.

March is a blur of hard work, yet I've plenty of time for painting, and visiting too. Mid-month, Billy and I run up to Wakeman Sound to see what we can see of the herring spawning. Billy scoots around the edges of the wide sound, looking for the clouds of pale opaque green that signify herring milt. We locate several billows of the distinctive colour, but not nearly as many as Billy hoped. A nasty wind picks up while we're poking about. It's a silent ride home as we hunker down in the speedboat, trying to keep ourselves from banging around as the hull slams against the chop.

In April, Billy and I set off to the western sea to fish for the wily ling cod. We head for Cape Scott but get only as far as Shushartie Bay. I've got a bad feeling about the throbbing pain in my tooth and tell him I need to find a dentist in Port Hardy and get drugs. Going to sea with an incipient tooth infection is just plain dumb. Billy hates to go back once he starts forward but he turns the bow towards Hardy in good humour, and after phoning around I find a dentist who'll fit me in. I'm relieved the tooth began to hurt badly close to Hardy, and not way out by Triangle Island. I get the antibiotic prescription filled. Billy picks up some more chocolate bars and we're away again. Take two on our departure is uneventful; we make good time and anchor in Hansen Lagoon. What an exquisite stretch of real estate on a sunny day. No wonder those intrepid pioneers believed they could make a success of homesteading here.

Billy is eager to fish, so we don't take much shore time this trip. We spend one night at Barge Bay on Cox Island, where I find the little yellow iris sadly exposed on its small sand dune. Last winter's high tides rolled away the protective wall of drift logs, washed out the sand and exposed the roots. I carefully unearth the bedraggled little plant and carry it to the moist shelter of the creek, where I divide the corms, and plant them along the stream's bank. I'm careful, but one small stalk breaks off from the main root, so I slip it into my paint-bag and take it back to the boat with me. There I place it in a ginger ale can half full of water and set it behind the retaining line on the window sill in the cabin. If I'm lucky it will flourish in my own garden some day.

The pain in my head slowly recedes, but despite good fishing and one lovely day after another, things don't go that well. Billy is having dizzy spells, and I'm a little short of breath. I worry a lot for the next two days while we get our load of cod, anxious about what I'll do if Billy loses his balance and falls over the side. Breathing gets harder, and my chest feels tight. Billy decides to deliver to Port Hardy instead of Coal Harbour so I can see a doctor. Not much conversation in the wheelhouse as we make the run across the bar, and tie up at the Seagate Wharf at 10:00 pm. Billy doesn't want to leave the boat, but I need him to come with me. I'm having so much trouble pulling in a good breath of air I'm afraid I won't make it to the hospital without him. It's pouring rain. We wait an hour and a half for a taxi, after the dispatcher tells us ten minutes, hanging about in front of the Seagate Hotel soaking wet and miserable, me short of breath and Billy irritable and dizzy. What a crew.

Finally, I'm lying under crisp clean sheets in the comforting white cave of curtains in Port Hardy Hospital emergency ward while a doctor examines Billy in the next bed. As in a dream I hear the low murmur of masculine voices drifting from behind the curtain. After a long hazy time the doctor comes in to me, puts a little gizmo up to my face and tells me to blow. And again.

"Well, this isn't good," he says. "You've got a viral lung infection and are using only 40 per cent of your lung power. There's not much I can do for you except give you some lung-expanding puffers for asthma."

"How is my skipper?" I ask.

"Oh, he has a viral ear infection," the doctor replies. My last query, "Would it be alright to go back out fishing?" is met with a pause and a look that says, "Are you nuts?" Aloud he mildly replies that while I'll have to make my own decision, the best thing for me would be to go home and stay in bed for two weeks. And that is what we do, though

Billy is not too happy about it. It's a good thing the doctor says two weeks, because if he'd said only one, I might've treated it like a cold and tried to tough it out. I know Billy wanted to. But I've been exceedingly ill, almost delirious for more than a week. One afternoon I wake from a snooze to see Logan standing by the bed.

"Billy's really sick," he says.

Theda chimes in, "He's in bed and he can't even walk."

"Thank goodness!" I exclaim.

They're a little taken aback and think the drugs have got to me. Maybe they have. But, what I mean is, thank goodness it's not only my health but Billy's as well that made us abort the fishing trip. I'd hate to be the only one responsible. It's much better that *he* should be so ill that he would think "Good thing we came home."

In the space of a week, I've been to Port Hardy twice and Cape Scott

Logan bringing in a big female "bucket head" ling cod.

188

and home again. I'm tucked cozily into my bed slurping cherry jello, my family around me carrying on with their lives and business. I've been lucky with this virus. Joanie is working as the medic at Scott Cove, and she medivacked a fellow who had a viral heart infection. Maybe the same virus got us all but in differing weak spots.

"Now that it looks like you're going to live," says Al, coming into bed, "Theda and I can leave for Nepah Lagoon tomorrow. Logan'll take good care of you now you're on the mend."

My recovery is slow but, May, besides setting off explosions of wild flowers on every nook, rock and cranny, brings Deb for a visit. Billy takes us on a wild flower trip down to Spring Pass, Freshwater Bay, Mammalilliculla and Karlukwees, and many of the little islands in Beware Passage. On his favourite island, Goat Island, one lone tree stands and two different kinds of chocolate lily grow amongst the rocks. This is the only place I've noted two variations of the species, though my flower books denote at least four, possibly five variations. Blooming abundantly amongst the lilies are orange and yellow columbine and rare pink thrift in two small clumps. Some islands have large swaths of blue-eyed Mary, which are violet and blue, very tiny flowers. Wild flowers touch me in a different way than those I cultivate. They're so tough, need no fertilizer, in fact they often shrivel right up when transplanted into the domestic garden. Gardening guru Brian Minter, who guests on a CBC gardening tips radio show, says repeatedly that you must stress flowers to make them bloom, and this certainly is true of the flowers on the windswept rocks in Knight Inlet. They are deluged with rain, dried right out in blazing sun, or—the worst—subjected to weeks of grey cloud with no rain. Tough, yes, but lovely and delicate. Most are faintly fragrant and, I'm certain, interlocked for survival in myriad ways with the birds and mammals of these sea-girt islands.

Fishing Again

*They that sail on the sea tell of the danger thereof,
and we hear it with our ears, we marvel thereat.*

Ecclesiástes XLIII 26

YES, INDEED, I AM GOING OUT FISHING AGAIN in spite of my last dreadful experience. I'm already gone. I'm lucky, because competition for this job as Billy's deckhand is fierce. One disappointed young man grumbled in disgust that "old lady Maximchuk" got the job again. I'm forty-three.

Fishing begins with the usual mad day in Port Hardy taking care of business. I ship some paintings to my gallery in White Rock, and Billy finds a fellow to install the recently repaired autopilot. At the Seafoods dock, we idle the boat up beside the narrow walkway below the ice machine, waiting our turn. Hurry up and wait: the mantra of the coast. When the boat ahead of us pulls away, Billy powers *Ocean Dawn* in close under the chute. I leap over the side to secure the tie-up lines. We scramble to lift the heavy blue hatch cover and tilt it on its side on the deck. Then Billy climbs down into the belly of the boat and the fellows on the dock above manoeuvre the long white chute so it hangs over the opening. Billy grabs it just before they yell, "Let 'er go." An avalanche of small ice chunks roars down the chute as Billy directs the flow of ice into the side chambers. We'll use this ice to bury the salmon in as soon as they are dressed and washed. In the best of all possible worlds the hold will be filled with neatly arrayed ranks of almost frozen salmon in the next ten days.

Our first evening's anchorage is Hope Island. Immediately I'm caught in the spell of this mysterious and magic island. We go for a leisurely row around a narrow gut and beach the dinghy at the old village site. I wander alone with my sketchbook at twilight. The beach is composed of one- to two-inch dark, smooth, oval stones that slide against each other, making walking difficult. The stones are an enlarged version of the shape of clay platelets in suspension in water, the structure that makes clay plastic. Another pattern to ponder in the larger scheme of universal design. I collect a bag of stones to take home to arrange somewhere in my garden. A few years back I took home a wonderful brick-red rock from Lauder Island in the Charlottes, about two inches deep, ten by twelve with perpendicular squared sides. If Billy had let me, I would have brought home enough of them to pave a patio. Now, that one piece serves as the doorstep to my fenced garden. I have some small shells, too, so I'm thinking I'll make a small "fairy" town with the Hope Island rocks under the billowing 'Rose des Peintres'.

While waiting for some action on the gear, I snooze in the sun. Photo Theda Miller.

Hope Island's original name is Xumdaspe. It's the site of another deserted First Nations village. The anchorage is protected from weather, and yet the view from the headland by the curving beach is expansive. Crumbling away to salal and moss in an overgrown thicket are the skeletons of a couple of old houses, and on the grassy expanse by the beach fragrant narcissus bloom. Hope Island has a melancholy, evocative air; if I listen hard enough I catch traces of a melody just beyond my range of hearing. I long to stay for a while and paint, however, we're on a fishing trip so on we must go. Someday I'll reconnect to this haunting place.

Our first day of serious travelling we run in fog all the way past Cape Caution, Calvert Island, to anchor in Swanson Bay, the site of the first pulp mill in British Columbia. A giant brick chimney rears up, and great tall posts rammed into the sea bottom are all that is left of what was once a mammoth dock. Hard to visualize this thickly forested bay as a townsite for five hundred people, a Fisheries station and a regular steamer stop. It's so still and gloomy. Next day we're on to Graham Reach, Fraser Reach... these long channels with steep sides make for a safe passage but they're monotonous. After a long droning run we arrive in Prince Rupert and once again my brother Frank joins me for a good dinner and visit.

A change of pace as we make our way from Rupert the next morning to the top end of Graham Island. The weather switches up from gloomy fog to pelagic nightmare. I stow the kettle and teapot in the sink, clear the countertop and the table of dishes and salt and pepper shakers. Crib board and cards are stashed in the drawers. An enraged sea god sends a screaming wind through the rigging and hurls it in all directions. It scoops up prodigious hunks of sea water and shatters them over *Ocean Dawn*. Colossal foaming waves rupture into smoking froth as the tempest rips their tops off. The drawer under the table flies open and slams shut as we roll hard from one side to the other. Finally it bursts open so forcefully the contents explode onto the floor.

"Leave it," says Bill. "No point in trying to pick it up now." The music tapes dive off their shelf on the back wall and join the pile on the floor.

Braced in the wheelhouse door I take pictures when the starboard gunwale disappears under green water boiling over the side. I'm fully appreciating scuppers at this moment. A small photograph won't effectively portray the unleashed elemental energies, but I can't resist trying to get a good shot. It's better than flopping about the wheelhouse. The mountainous sea surpasses itself at Rose Spit, and I shoot two photos of a boat we pass: one of the boat on the crest of the swell, almost bounding off the water and a second with just the tip of the mast showing.

Mid-afternoon, we drop the anchor behind Striae Island and fall into the bunks. Billy gets his happy, "I'm in my little bunk" smile on his face and begins to snore within ten seconds. I am rattled in my bones and lie awake waiting for the pumping adrenaline to recede. Soon the cradle-like rocking of the boat performs its soothing magic, and I too fall into sleep. Later we spend a long time tidying things up in the wheelhouse, then take a look at the fishing gear. What a mess. It takes hours to untangle all the leader lines, flashers and hooks and to make neat coils of the fishing lines.

Opening day finally. July 1 brings perfect fishing conditions: a shell pink and yellow sunrise as we set the gear, followed by a cloudy grey sky, a spit of rain and a little chop on the sea surface. The sea is whipped cream on lime green jello, so green variations of hoochies work well in the morning. In the afternoon the silver spoons are more effective. Billy is particular about keeping the spoons shiny. I wipe them with Billy's special liquid, Stay-Brite "hydrotone." We're delighted with our day's catch of forty-eight chinook and sixteen coho, though all day we battle slimy stinging jellyfish that get hung up on the gurdy wires. The red jelly sprays out in burning glops as we wind up the wire to bring in the fish. The constant cleaning of the gear and the irritation of jellyfish on skin doesn't do much for the skipper's temper. Early in the day I put on my rain gear and donned gloves and chrome-yellow wristers to protect my "lily-white hands" but the skipper is much tougher and can't be bothered to cover up. Boy, is he sorry. The fisherman's cure for jellyfish stings, a liberal application of canned milk, doesn't help. Neither does baking soda or peeing on his hands.

The second day of fishing is awful, fewer salmon, more jellyfish, and the third day even worse. No fish, and a lot of complaining by the skippers to each other on their secret channel. Fish or run? By day four our

Billy is happy when the wind is from the west, his favourite for ripping around in his boat.

daily catch has deteriorated to a grand total of six. Billy is so dispirited we pack it in early, anchor in our old spot by Cape Naden and watch a pretty sunset. We discuss the bad rumours abounding: the lack of salmon anywhere, the terrible price, our catch and the too-small allocation of the total amount of salmon the trollers, gillnetters and seine boats are allowed to catch. Plan A, to fish the top end of the Charlottes and make our fishing fortune, is a complete bust. Conclusion? We'll head for the Oval Bank and try our luck there.

The scene at the Oval Bank is equally bleak. One large chinook salmon and nine coho are not enough to keep us here. Plan B, also a bust.

"So much for Plan A and Plan B," says Billy. "I'll have to work on Plan C."

We anchor for the night in a mosquito-ridden bay near McDonald Island and get the hell out of there as early as possible in the dawn light.

The place names here are ominous, enough to strike fear into the heart of any able yet superstitious mariner: Terror Point, Devastation Channel, Anger Island. Even the usually thrilling sound of wolves howling strikes a mournful note. What trials and tribulations afflicted Captain Vancouver and his crew here? For us, poor fishing keeps us moving. Billy catches a couple of reports of good fishing at Topknot on the west coast of Vancouver Island. He contemplates setting a heading directly for Cape Scott instead of swinging close by Cape Sutil; the weather looks good for it.

Departing McDonald Island we set our course. Plan C: head for Cape Scott, destination Topknot. On this wonderful run, I truly have the sense of being a sailor surging "over the bounding main," gliding smoothly over long, sapphire swells, into the western sea. I wash out my nightie and some t-shirts and hang the laundry on the lines under the boom. The clothes snap and dance in the sunny breeze. A quick sketch in my book: what a terrific painting this'll make. I love the look of laundry for a painting anyway. It's one of my favourite subjects and something that attracts my eye whether it's hanging here or hanging off the balconies of southern France.

The setting sun burns into our eyes as we run towards it. Finally the swollen orange ball slips behind the long arc of the horizon, and dusky amethyst twilight envelops us. The splendour of the sunset is encored when the aurora borealis lights up the sky and is reflected on the smooth sea we traverse.

Endless hours of running bring us by midnight to Hansen Lagoon, around the corner from Cape Scott. We set the hook, collapse into the bunks and are up again at 3:30 am. Three hours of sleep is not enough to energize a body for a long fishing day. However, we are buoyed by our catch of nineteen springs off Topknot, a tremendous improvement over zero, zero, one, six and ten in the previous five days. Hours in the cockpit trying different lures and hoochies keeps us awake as the boat rises and falls in a somnolent swell. Finally I can't take it anymore and lie down on the deck for a snooze. Every once in a while, the gear jerks and there's a fish on.

A couple of days go by like this. It's peaceful. We don't talk much, just work the gear.

One morning Billy is all squirmy in the cockpit, hitching up his rain gear, adjusting it repeatedly.

"What's your problem, got ants in your pants?" I inquire as I bring in the mainline. He doesn't reply, just reaches inside his rain pants and tugs.

"What the hell are you doing?" I ask again. Abruptly he leaps out of the cockpit, scurries into the wheelhouse, reappears seconds later wielding a big knife.

Holy shit! I think. He's lost it completely. Back to the cockpit, Billy sticks the knife in his pants, sawing it up and down under the rubber rain gear. He withdraws the knife, lays it on the deck and reaches in again. A couple of tugs and out comes his boxer shorts, cut completely down the side seams. He flings them into the air, and they sail away behind us.

"Goddam shorts got no elastic, and they keep falling down," he mutters. I laugh all afternoon. Days later I'm still laughing.

Another day of fishing the big springs, still sunny with a long slow swell. We haul in eleven. The next day the sky has a brassy yellow-grey lustre, and the sea is flat calm. A ring circles the sun as we head out to the fishing grounds. Off to starboard I spot a large round object.

"Pass me the binoculars, would you?" I ask, peering out the window.

"What do you see?"

"A *big* glass Japanese fishing float. Billy, it's really big. Let's go get it."

"It's probably just a plastic one," he says. "You don't get big glass ones like that anymore."

"No, I'm sure it's glass. At least let's go take a look," I plead.

Billy huffs his breath out but turns the wheel. I'm jubilant as we pull alongside the turquoise beauty. How to get it into the boat is the problem. Our first idea is to stick the pike pole through a plastic garbage bag and scoop it up. No joy. The pretty treasure bobs gently by the boat while we discuss its capture. Finally Billy says to me, "You hold my legs and I'll lean over the side and grab it, okay?"

"I guess," I say dubiously. Visions of how I'll get him back if I drop him into the chuck flash through my mind. What'll I tell the Coast Guard when I call in a "man overboard" Mayday? What'll I tell Yvonne P. if I drop him and can't get him back? What'll I tell *anyone* if I drop him and can't get him back?

"You're not gonna drop me," says Billy, impatiently, reading my mind. "Let's do it so we can get fishing." I hold onto his knees as he hangs over the side and grabs the big glass ball. He heaves himself up again as I anchor his feet. We argue about who should get the prize and I win, because a) I spotted it, b) he already has forty glass balls, and c) I didn't drop him.

Again we bring in eleven big springs. The calm air feels like it's holding its breath. It reminds of when my children were babies and were about to scream: the long indrawn breath and the pause before the explosive wail. The sea lies like yellowed parchment etched with the calligraphic marks of small zephyrs and bird trackways.

"Kind of strange light, isn't it?" I comment as we put the gear in the bucket.

"Yup. Time to pack it in," says Billy. "The weather's turning bad. We'd better go deliver."

Although we didn't make buckets of money this trip, fishing with Billy is always an amazing adventure. I've experienced more of our country's epic scenery, broadened my horizons, acquired a big glass Japanese fishing float. I've got a new memory to give me a giggle, as well: Billy's boxer shorts flapping off the stern to join the gulls.

Eating Gilford Island

My garden is slow work, pursued with love and I do not deny, I am proud of it.

—Lila Monet

SEPTEMBER IS THE BOUNTIFUL PEAK of the year in the garden. Mistakes are forgotten, undone tasks forgiven. All that effort results in fabulous dinners we call "eating Gilford Island," a phrase coined by Ron Turner. Every night we eat prawns, crab, salmon or halibut dishes with huge salads of cherry tomatoes, lettuce greens, peas, beets and their greens, carrots, a cucumber (!) from my mini-greenhouse, round white potatoes snatched from the beaks of the voracious Steller's jays... well, almost snatched from their beaks—I sure have to work hard for my share. Dinner often ends with the pièce de résistance, raspberry/huckleberry pie.

Herbs bloom amongst the vegetables and flowers, providing healthy seasoning for every dish and flavourful stuffing in the winter turkeys to come. Dill sends up feathery fronds. Masses of oregano cover new territory each year. Savory, thyme, rosemary, sage, catnip and the sweet substitute stevia all wend their way through the flowers. Pillowy peonies hang heavy-headed, roses are so fragrant you can smell them down Cramer Pass when the wind is from the east, and tall stalks of hollyhocks and delphiniums bloom in a glorious crescendo of colour. From August into October, I divide my day between painting flowers—huge voluptuous bouquets or individual studies—say, of the nearly black iris or white lily, harvesting and preserving food, and nailing up siding, window trims, soffits and fascia boards.

I drill holes in the soffits and staple fine mesh over the holes to keep out bugs. The holes are for ventilation, air flow up over the insulation in the ceilings. Turns out gutters only come in brown or white, so I'm painting all the pieces turquoise to match the roof. I'd no idea how many little pieces are required to put up an eavestrough. Besides the long gutters and downspouts, there are corners, straps to hook the pieces onto the house, and small baskets to install above the drainpipes. We need three forty-four-foot-long gutters. I rough sand all these little and big pieces before I paint them. I commandeer Logan's help with this, and he's not happy about it, although he does an excellent and willing job of squeezing joint compound down all the trim seams where the siding meets the corners of the house. The smart thing to do is arrange our tasks so he does the caulking with his strong hands, and I do the gutters. Yup, it's easier than fighting.

Albert flies to town a couple of times with the prawns he ships live and entrusts Logan with the task of running *John* home. Through the summer both the kids had deckhand opportunities with Albert on the

John, the prawn boat at the dock.

prawns. Logan went with Billy on the salmon, too. Everybody gets a chance to make the big bucks and it's all over by September.

Theda left early in the summer after her prawning stint, with no immediate plans to return. She's taken a course in massage and has signed up for voice lessons with a coach beginning in October. One sunny September day my girl comes home again. For a long time Theda has wanted her friend Alison to come to Echo Bay and the day came when it just worked out. When the two of them arrived at the dispatch office of the float plane company in Port McNeill to see about getting on the afternoon sched, magically, there was Albert in the office, paying his prawn shipping bill prior to running *John* home. He had one stop to make first: a quick trip to Sointula to pick up a six-week-old Abyssinian kitten.

"*Sea Rose, Sea Rose, John.*" I hear his radio call.

"Go zero six, Al," I answer.

"Be there in ten minutes," he says with a lilt in his voice.

"Boy," I turn to Logan, who is helping me chop vegetables for salad. "He sure sounds cheery, doesn't he?"

John sweeps into the dock, and as I reach for the tie-up line, Theda bursts out of the cabin hollering "Surprise!" Tears of joy spurt from my eyes. Out comes Alison with a happy smile. Albert's next. A small triangular black face with yellow eyes peeps out of the cradle of his arms. What a homecoming! Albert names the new member of our family Bee-Gee, short for Brown Girl. Logan thinks it should be Black Girl, I'm thinking Beasty Girl or Blessed Gift, depending on her mood. We open the front door for her to meet Buddy the St. Bernard, and the tiny critter jumps on his head, then down to his paws, and turns around as if to say, "There, *who's* the boss?" Buddy's good with that. He lowers his massive head, acknowledging her obvious superiority, and sniffs her. She sniffs back. Looks like a lifelong friendship.

I've been getting those soffits up under the roof of the top floor. Access is out the upstairs bedroom window onto the sloping roof, where I carefully measure overhead the distance from rafter to rafter. I climb back in, saw the board to length, set in a few nails to start, manhandle it out the window, then follow it out. Holding the board in place overhead while bending backwards and cursing, I hammer the nails in upwards.

Alison takes over sawing the boards to the length of my measurement calls, and passes them out the window. Theda holds up one end while I whack in three nails; I pass her the hammer, and she nails in the second end. My aching arms are thankful. My neck and back and legs are thankful. In less than a third of the time I expected to complete the job, we're done.

Bears are the wildlife of the early fall this year. We've seen many mother/cub groups the last few weeks. A mature sow with two cubs and another with three forage on the low tide foreshore almost daily. The Mama Bear ambles along turning over small boulders, and I hear the popcorn crunch as she and the cubs scoop pawsful of scrabbling crabs and cram them in their mouths. They gorge on the salal berries glowing purple, thick and ripe outside the garden gate.

Floating in the fog between asleep and awake one morning, I hear mewling, grunting noises. Unremitting whining finally penetrates my dreams. I sit up and look out the window, and there's the two-cub mama inside the fenced garden compound, one cub in there with her. The second cub is stuck up a tree, unable to descend and loudly crying the blues. In the spring I'd enclosed a larger garden area with ten-foot fence units I tied to the few skinny hemlock trees left standing. The bears had climbed up one of these trees on the outside of the fence, swiveled around it and slid down—except for the second cub, who could not figure it out. Big Mama has the lid off the compost box and is rooting around in it while the cub with her is tearing up my potato patch.

What to do, what to do?

"Wake up, Albert, there's bears in the garden."

I call to Logan and the girls, too, and we watch the bears being bears for a while. Finally my Hercules gets his gun and sneaks over to the garden, opens the gate stealthily, returns to the porch and yells loudly, throws a couple rocks. Happily the bears get the message and skedaddle,

though the little one stuck up the tree doesn't know if he's coming or going. He's squealing, panicky; Big Mama's barking emphatically. At last he figures out how to release his grip on the bark and half falls, half humps himself down the tree he's clinging to and the bear family lopes off into the woods. They'll get busy down in the streams now, just as we humans do in the fall, both species focussed on salmon.

Most of our community, as members of the hatchery organization, have been capturing coho brood stock from Scott Cove Creek. Nine years we've been helping with this effort. I was elected secretary-treasurer at the annual general meeting. I'm learning the routines and issues and politics (!) involved. This year we must inoculate the salmon against furunculosis, a disease that, although it's endemic to the wild fish, has proliferated out of control since the arrival of fish farms in the late 1980s. Doug Knierim, once the hatchery manager and now builder and owner of Kwatsi Bay Marina, shows our current manager, Claudia Maas, and me how to insert the drug-filled needle just behind the adipose fin, where there is a small, pocket-like space. Billy holds each fish in a wooden trough and guesstimates its weight while Claudia prepares the dose. Billy's touch induces sleep in the salmon; they lie calm under his hands, and I inject the drug as efficiently and painlessly as possible. Some would argue that fish can't feel pain, but I believe from watching them in various situations that they do. Somebody will prove it someday, I'm certain.

I am feeling pain this fall, though, as my second child packs up and leaves. Longing for more adventure and to manage his own life, Logan decides it is time for him to head for the city. His departure leaves me stricken. I spend the better part of a week mostly in bed, until Claudia calls me one cold October day, needing a ride from her float house in Viner to the Scott Cove hatchery. I spend the day at the hatchery, helping her with the egg-take and it draws me out of my misery.

Coho are returning well into fall, but finally slow down. By Christmas all the females have been stripped of their eggs and the fertilized eggs have been placed carefully in the trays of flowing creek water. We barely give Christmas its due before the new year celebrations are over and January nearly spent.

Research is underway around various issues in the Broughton. Alex Morton has been spearheading resistance to the fish farms in our area. In spite of our hopes that they would draw new residents to Echo Bay, we are discovering that a few new residents are not worth the apparent negative effects on wildlife. Piercing underwater noises designed to prevent seals from attempting to get at the net-caged Atlantic salmon seem to be the cause of a marked decrease in orcas traversing the waters. Alex has a lot on her plate, though, with a new man in her life, Eric Nelson, and their new baby, Clio. One day she comes to me with an adventuresome idea.

"I need help with a, um, dirty job," she says.

"What's that?" I ask.

"I've got to get some sea lion shit samples for DFO," she says.

"I suppose you are the boat driver and I am the shit collector," I say, raising my eyebrows.

"Please?" she says.

On a windless grey day in February we run to the rocky haul-out at the end of Fife Sound in her boat *Blackfish Sound* while neighbours Ron and Ann come along in *Kvitsoy* to look after Clio. The sea lion excrement is for Fisheries and Oceans Canada to examine, presumably to ascertain what, and how much of what, sea lions eat and whether it offers clues to the state of their health. I'm suited up in rain gear, rubber gloves and gumboots. A low swell from Queen Charlotte Strait surges gently as Alex nudges her boat up close to the sea lion rock. I swing over the side on the lift of the swell, and she hands me a large scoop and half a dozen resealable plastic bags.

"See if you can get a few different piles, for colour, consistency or texture..." She backs her boat off and I'm alone, except for thirty or forty gigantic creatures out of sight on the other side of the rock. My knees are trembling as I climb the stinking slippery slope. The roars, moans and snorts of the three-quarter-ton sea lions a few feet beyond the crest of stone thunder over my heartbeat. My pulse pounds in my ears as I look around, trying to fulfill the requirements of the task. Alex backs her boat

203

farther from the rock. Panicked, I yell, "Don't go away!" She smiles and waves. I hurry to scoop a variety of poop into the bags. The stink nearly brings me to my knees, my eyes tearing. I hold my breath as long as I can while I do the dirty deed, then madly wave at Alex to come pick me up when the bags are filled.

"Yuck, gross, that was so disgusting," I cry as I leap into her boat. She backs off the rock. Ron brings *Kvitsoy* up close and fastens his towline to the bow of *Blackfish Sound*.

"You got it! *All right*, bags of sea lion shit, wow!" He and Alex are laughing as I take my stinking rain gear off and leave it in the stern.

"Very funny," I mutter. But it *is* funny, and I laugh too, cuddling Clio while we travel in comfort down Fife Sound. I feel like I've put in an eight-hour day as adrenaline slowly dissipates.

We have criteria out here—for those who can cut it—as mainlanders. And one of these is that you must be deeply interested in shit, as when, for example, you are walking by the river or down a logging road and you come across some bear scat, even old scat that mushrooms are growing out of. If you stop and poke at it with a stick to see what the bear has been eating, whether berries or a seagull, we regard this as a mark of character, distinguishing those who are *real mainlanders* from those who simply don't have what it takes. I've never heard what was discovered in the sea lion scats I so fearlessly gathered, but that poop expedition alone should provide me with a lifetime of mainlander credibility.

The planet turns and with it comes spring. April is blustery. Like inebriated pugilists, clouds collide in big piles, roil around until they shamble drunkenly into each other all over again, delivering soft, slow-motion punches. Theda is here, Al offered her the prawn deckhand job again. I hope she's tough enough; he's grumpy from lack of sleep, and demanding. They're up at 5:00 am each morning and away, working a fourteen-hour-day pulling the gear and sorting, coming home exhausted at dusk or not at all if they're too far from home. Fishing is amazing, though, and so far it looks like the perfect (wonderful) storm. There are tons of prawns, the price is good, the boat is working well with no breakdowns—touch wood—and the crew, except for needing some sleep, is in good health.

The season turns out to be so good, in fact, that Albert and I make plans, at long last, for a trip to Europe next March. But before we go, there are a few things we must tackle and the main challenge is the completion of the dreaded drain field for the septic tank.

We want to do this job properly to code, as we do everything. Our main objective is for the plumbing to be functional, trouble-free and environmentally acceptable. We cannot just order up a truckload of the right size gravel and wait for it to pull up into the driveway. The terrain slopes so we've terraced it with stone walls. I'm using "we" rather loosely here; it's Albert, my Hercules, who muscles the massive rocks out of the soil, although I help when he needs me to hold a board to support the jack in position under a rock. With a mechanical Gilchrist jack and a hydraulic jack, a crowbar and a variety of planks he inches out formidable half-ton boulders once embedded in the slope and stacks them into a retaining wall. He constructs a septic tank out of 4 x 6 beams and a lily pond to sit behind the rock wall above the septic field. The field is situated in the lower part of the garden, into which I barrowed thousands of loads of soil a few years ago and it consists of three fifty-foot trenches for the sewage pipes to sit on.

Each trench must be filled with several inches of small stones so the water can filter through into the soil. Hundreds of buckets of rocks are gathered from our creek bed. Logan decides to take the skiff to various rocky beaches nearby where his rock-gathering goes much faster. He returns in just over an hour with four or five bucketsful.

Completing the drain field, the rock wall and the septic tank occupies Albert, entirely, and Logan and me, less so, from mid-summer to the end of the year. When Theda comes at Christmas, all four of us collect the final stones from the creek bed. On December 31 Albert and Logan pile in the last buckets of rocks in the third row of the drain field, cover them with cardboard and shovel soil over top. Billy comes over to help take down scaffolding from the east side of the house. The year ends with a triumphant round of self-congratulatory applause for the completion of the third wall of siding and a Very Important Project, the waste disposal field.

Canoes to Kingcome

ALBERT HAS HAD A VERY FRUSTRATING WAIT for the finalization of his purchase of a shrimp fishing boat, *Miss Jenny*. Because he believes there is too much gear in the water, too many fishers of prawns for the stocks to support, and too much aggression and friction between skippers, he's decided to sell his prawn licence and switch to a more solitary fishery: shrimp species such as coon stripe and side stripe, pink and humpback. He makes a good dollar from the prawn licence, and finally buys *Miss Jenny*. He also uses some of the money to buy a brand new outboard motor for me. It's a Yamaha fifty-horse four-stroke, so I no longer have to mix oil into the gas. The new motor is less polluting, wonderfully quiet and fuel-efficient.

Learning to fish shrimp isn't easy. Albert was an accomplished and conscientious prawn fisher, and the prawns are still reasonably plentiful. Shrimp fishing is a whole new ball game. He has a new boat to become familiar with, a new style of fishing, new techniques for managing and selling the catch and he'll have to fish much farther from home. I'm a little apprehensive on his behalf, but he is optimistic and sets off eagerly on fishing trips.

Before he goes anywhere, he puts *Miss Jenny* up on Billy's ways to scrape and paint the bottom. Billy's boat shed is big, arch-shaped, wide and high enough to encompass his own fishing boat without taking off the trolling poles. He'd just built this shed when we moved here in 1986. The first "neighbour assistance" project I participated in was nailing down shakes. There've been a lot of boats up on Billy's ways over the years. I put *Sea Rose* up twice a year, usually April and November, as Billy advised me to years ago, for maintenance as well as problems that crop up. I'm certain the regular maintenance keeps unanticipated problems to a minimum.

A train track runs from the low tide zone right up into his shed. On the boat shed floor at the top of the track sits Billy's sixty-year-old Wakasha winch motor. The large wooden "cradle" he built, a flat rectangular grid with two long and five short cross beams, is set on train wheels and attached to a cable wrapped round the Skagit winch drum.

It's time for my spring maintenance, and the steering cable Billy gave me has packed it in; the wheel is almost too stiff to turn. Today, when the tide is half flood, I head over in *Sea Rose*. Billy has already released the

Albert's new shrimp boat *Miss Jenny* on the cradle of Billy's boat ways.

cable that holds the cradle up in the shed, and there's just enough water over it for me to settle my boat gently over two sets of cross beams, one under the bow and the other under the stern. I strain over the side of my boat to tie a line to the uprights on the left of the cradle.

Billy comes hot-footing it over to the boat shed when he sees me coming and cranks over the putt motor. Sometimes things don't go smoothly, and a blue streak of curse fire shoots out until the putt motor fires up. This time the motor starts right up so there's no cursing. When Billy throws it into gear, the cradle jerks, then slowly rolls up the track. I hold on tight to the uprights to keep *Sea Rose* aligned with the supporting beams until she settles on them as we move up out of the water. The stern has to sit over the last beam so that the motor on the transom, the back end wall of the boat, is fully supported when out of the water. Another minute or two of chugging and we're under the shelter of the boat shed. I scramble out and tie the line from the towing ring over the beam ahead of the bow. The likelihood of *Sea Rose* slipping off the beam is low to non-existent but I tie the safety line anyway. I take no chances with my precious vessel.

There are two plugs in the transom of *Sea Rose*. One drains the inside of the deck area, and I pull it out first. Not much water there since I have a good pump Albert installed to pump out rainwater. The other plug sits at the centre bottom of the transom, and when I pull it out a gush of water pours forth. There's a tiny air leak somewhere in the fibreglass I put on the new floor, and rainwater slowly seeps into the hull. Billy and I've tried to find and patch the leak, but to no avail. The leak is annoying but not dangerous. It just gives the motor more weight to push, when there are thirty or forty gallons of water in the hull, and me more incentive to put my boat up for its twice annual check-up and cleaning.

Next job is to scrape the barnacles and mussels off the motor and its attachment parts and the bottom edge of the transom. Barnacles there can slow me down five to eight knots or more.

The most important task is to drain the oil from the leg of the engine and make sure there is no sea water leaking in. I picked up a new container of leg oil on our last trip to town so I am ready. If the oil is whitish it means it's mixed with water, not a good thing. This time, the oil is dirty but not whitish and Billy and I drain it out into a can. We pump the thick clear leg oil into the small hole designed for the job. There's a lower screw and an upper screw on the leg. The trick is to squeeze the oil into the lower hole with a manual pump and watch for it to ooze out of the upper hole. I quickly snug in the tiny rubber washer, follow it with the screw and tighten everything without making too much of a mess. The rubber washers are often beat up or worn out, but I finally had the forethought to buy four or five at once. Sometimes we've had to poke around Billy's workshop or Albert's bits and pieces trying to find a good one. Once, Billy and I ran into Shoal Harbour and ransacked three derelict motors perched on a rotten float, before we found a usable rubber washer. No more scrounging now that I have a little stash.

Next I scrape the bottom. This is my least favourite job but it has to be done. All the barnacles must go in order to travel speedily through the ocean. I lie on my back, reaching up to scrape away the barnacles that have attached themselves to the hull in the last six months. Billy helps me take off the old steering cable and install the new one. I replace the plugs in the hull, make sure all my tools are in the boat and Billy's are back on the work counter. I untie the safety line I'd tied over the beam, climb into the boat, untie the lines to the uprights and lay them ready for quick release when the boat rolls down the railroad track.

"All set?" Billy yells. I give him a thumbs-up yes, he releases the cable and whoosh—a slow whoosh—down we slide, my boat and I into the salt chuck with a soft rush and a gurgle. I let go the lines to the cradle uprights, we float off the cradle and are waterborne again.

A press of the hydraulic button lowers the motor into running position. I fire it up and take off out of Proctors Bay like a bat out of hell. I love how quick Sea Rose gets up on the step and skims like a bird across the surface after her session on the ways. I love my boat, it is freedom and independence and every good thing.

It's a fast, short arc to my own dock, and while I run I see in the sky long skeins of northbound geese, lengthy symmetrical Vs marking flight patterns in the high blue. Almost time to go ling cod fishing again. I set

First Nations paddlers
en route to Kingcome.

some spring bedding plants into the garden, and there's the yellow iris I rescued last year poking up tender green stalks. I'm thrilled it survived its transport from Cox Island to safe haven in my garden. Flowers? Don't know, hope so.

The days lengthen and stretch up to the summer solstice, then begin to shrink again. Albert fishes, taking Ted as deckhand; Billy and I fish; Theda goes to sea as well, tuna fishing with Billy and his grandson Glen. Tuna can be found sixty to a hundred miles out to sea where the warm North Pacific current sweeps in close to the BC coastline. This is way too far to run for an anchorage at night, and she found it uncomfortable simply climbing into her bunk way out at sea, but eventually she got used to it. The vast array of marine life was a special treat for the crew.

Deb comes for her annual visit and she and I run to Port McNeill to try out my wonderful new Yamaha fifty-horse four-stroke motor. On our way home, just past the White Cliff Rocks at the Merry-Go-Round—where the trollers once lined up to take a turn circling the small salmon-rich area—we spot a huge boil of finning dogfish. We sit quiet in the boat amongst the bubbling, twisting mass of fish for a while. Just when I'm suggesting to Deb there might be some orca around as well, a sudden blow and the great tall fin of a male killer whale startles us both. It's only the one, but Deb and I are thrilled with our wildlife encounter. That night Theda makes a call home, relayed through Coast Guard Radio, from the fishing grounds. I was excited to tell her about our wildlife adventure.

"We saw hundreds of dogfish on the surface at the Merry-Go-Round," I tell her, knowing this tidbit will interest Billy.

After a three-second delay, she says, "We saw a sunfish and a giant sea turtle!"

My next offering, "Then we saw a killer whale right there beside us."

Theda squeals, "We saw a blue shark and five sperm whales!" Clearly my little wildlife sighting is nothing compared to five sperm whales. The variety of marine creatures they saw was truly extraordinary. The warm current brings with it a vast array of prey and predators.

Deb is my gyproc angel this week. She happens to be a pro at mudding

Tuna girl, Theda. Photo Deborah Putman.

and sanding since she worked at renovating houses earlier in her life. I'm glad to be learning from her. It will save me a lot of fumbling around. It's a dusty, seemingly endless way to finish walls. In spite of the long hours spent running up and down ladders, we have plenty of painting time during the long sunny days before she leaves.

On the only rainy, gloomy day of July, I pull up at home with the mail, tie my boat to the dock and shut the motor off. There is a letter in the mail, from Canada Post Corporation, Pacific Division. In one neat, undated, typed line, the letter informs me that my item of mail was on a float plane that recently crashed and sank in the inlet at Blind Channel, BC. They advised me that this incident was beyond the control of Canada Post and regretted any inconvenience caused by this occurrence.

From afar I hear rhythmic chanting. Against the shore of Baker Island I spy an old gillnet boat puddling along and two or three canoes filled with paddlers. Jump back into the boat, fire it up and run over to see what's happening. The beautiful canoes have high, carved prows with bold First Nations motifs painted on them. They are filled with crews of mostly young First Nations people, chanting and paddling, moving swiftly along the shore. I motor up and ask if I can take some pictures. They nod and smile so I run up ahead of them, take shots from all angles. They are paddling to Kingcome, part of the revival of First Nations skills and traditions. I ask one group if I can ride in the boat with them. After a short discussion I get the go-ahead, so I tie my boat alongside the gillnetter and climb into the bow of the canoe. I lean back against its sloping sides, facing the paddling people, and through it I feel and hear how the canoe cleaves the water. The paddlers aren't wearing a lot, in spite of the drizzle, and I watch the smooth play of muscle under gleaming brown skin as they swing, dip, and pull the paddles in rhythmic unison. I concentrate hard to make mental pictures. My skin prickles with the rush of a great painting image about a significant event.

On the second day of September, I hear on channel 16, the Coast Guard station, that *Miss Jenny* has broken down near Cape Caution. I'll learn later that Albert went down into the engine room and was overcome with fumes. Ted was deckhanding, and he called the Coast Guard when Al collapsed on the deck. The fast Zodiac from Port Hardy was dispatched with oxygen to take him in to the hospital. The paramedics had him off the boat, into the Zodiac, into the ambulance waiting at the dock and then off to the hospital, in jig time. Ted brought the boat into Port Hardy, and both men came home safe and sound, with some shrimp as well: a big bonus.

Fall harvesting flows swiftly towards an important moment in the seasons, the solstice, when the days begin to slowly stretch. We host our annual community sit-down dinner on Boxing Day, inviting everyone in the community, and hoping that stubborn grudges might melt away in the warmth of breaking bread together, and all that Christmas symbolizes. February brings, as usual, a freeze-up and two weeks of frigid sunshine. Northerly outflows from the mainland inlets blow the mist and rain away, and a mass of iceberg air sits immovably over the sea. The first clear night that the temperature is dropping, and the stars shimmering with extra radiant scintillation, we fill the bathtub to the brim with water, and keep the tap trickling a thin stream through the night. This keeps us in running water until either the tank empties out, or the waterline freezes solid. We've found we can manage over a week with thirty gallons of bathtub water.

Reliably, the southeast wind reasserts itself in March, melting all in its path with weeks of wind-driven rain and the daffodils herald spring once again.

215

In Search of the Single Delight

He who is born with a silver spoon in his mouth
is generally considered a fortunate person, but his
good fortune is small compared to that of the happy
mortal who enters this world with a passion for
flowers in his soul.

—Celia Thaxter *An Island Garden*

O MAY, DELICIOUS MAY, the sheer *bliss* of each succeeding day. A little ditty from my college days goes round and round in my head. "Hooray, hooray, it's the first of May, outdoor f___g begins today." I overflow with joy and am periodically struck with a "fall down on your knees" feeling of awe and gratitude. I want to roll in the mud, fluff my feathers in a dust bath like the grouse mama, spin in dizzy circles like the cloud of small bugs.

I'm in intense gardening mode, creating gorgeous soil from a mix of compost, peat moss, kelp, lime, and crumbly soil from the land. I love to fill up the big red plastic boxes Al used to ship prawns in, then stir and mix until all the separate textures become one rich, dark, loamy mass. Hundreds of healthy worms populate the soil now. I recall a day many years ago when Billy came up the ramp packing a dirty tin can. I laughed with pleasure when he revealed his gift, worms from their garden. All my worms are descendants of Billy's worms. I offer them the best accommodations I can, but some fall prey to robins.

So many of my garden residents, like immigrants through the ages, arrived by ship from elsewhere. As I do my morning slug patrol, checking the new rose buds and under the little baby lettuces, I'm reminded of everyone who has touched my life through the garden. It has become a memory map of intimate connections with people who've enriched my life in ways both big and small. Here's a healthy-looking lilac bush that has yet to flower in six years. I took it as a cutting from Yvonne Scott's garden in Shoal Harbour. She told me that the bush originally came from Walla Walla, Washington, over fifty years ago. This is a garden of tough love though, and if Walla Walla doesn't bloom soon she'll get turfed. There's also a lilac that does flower, purchased with birthday money from my parents.

All along the edges of the flower and vegetable beds dance the paired blue and pink blooms of pulmonaria, aka "A Sailor and his Girl." These gay flowers, framed with silvery spotted leaves, all spring from two little plants found in my friend Peggy's garden. The feminine pink flowers

The columbines given to me by Mrs. Clayton of Port Hardy are hardy growers in my expanding coastal garden.

make me think of her; she too likes to have a fellow to dance with. Deb gave me the red Japanese maple tree, 'Bloodgood,' for my fortieth birthday and I moved it a couple of times before I found the right place for it beside the lily pond. It won't be moved again in my lifetime unless it is to be felled. This tree is often under attack from the yellow-bellied sapsucker and suffers from the rings of small holes drilled into the bark. Nevertheless, it produces a bountiful array of glorious red leaves. In the lily pond, the green knobs of the unopened lilies float gently on the surface beside the wide round leaves the red-legged frogs love. These were given to me by Carol Puff, the lady who came around to do the census several years ago. When she divided her waterlilies afterwards, she thought of me and sent them out for my pond. Like floating dance skirts or a divan for Thumbelina, the pink flowers hint at much more than they reveal. In different moods, and in different light they beg to be painted, and like Monet, I rush to get the brushes.

A wedding gift from Joanie and her husband, Phil, is another elegant Japanese maple. Its peach-coloured leaves are the last to surrender to the autumn winds and after a blow lie all over the yard like fallen stars. Nearby, two sugar maples Irene and Dave Myers gave me have grown so tall they cast a cool shadow over the raspberries, and the walnut tree Albert's brother Bill gave us grows higher up the slope. In another stump hole, we planted a western maple that Albert dug up in Liz Humphreys' yard in Campbell River. Of the four we brought home, two have withstood the terrible wrenching of the move and transplant. I need to decide very soon, yesterday, in fact, if this is its permanent position or if the larger one needs a better spot; clearly it's going to be a big tree. I love my maple trees. And the sturdy white pine and long-needled shore pine I dug up along the Eve River while driving the up-island highway a few years ago: where the hell am I going to plant them? I walk around a long time trying to decide on the best place to plant everything. Buddy the St. Bernard has become the oak tree we planted over him to honour his memory.

Columbines are everywhere. The original seed given to me by Mrs. Clayton from Port Hardy years ago has bloomed, multiplied. Every year new versions appear. Originally they were all pink, with three or four frilly layers of petal petticoats. I surmise that each year the thrown seed recedes to different parents as the hybridization unravels. Now the columbines bloom sky blue and midnight blue, light pink, dark rose, a Tyrian purple, a single-petalled purple and yellow, and pure white. Two plants came up this year that most closely resemble the wild columbine; pure-hued, outward-sweeping orange petals with a protruding central yellow shaft.

I do not neglect the wild flowers in my garden frenzy. We've identified many interesting plants on our land as we've worked to shape the house and garden. A flowering serviceberry has thrust its way up from the centre of the mauve rhododendron, and a stink-currant shrub flourishes at the edge of the lily pond. Not a pretty name, but the prolific leaves provide cool cover for the fish in the pond. Over by the creek grows a blue huckleberry, and the red huckleberries are everywhere, expanding in the sunshine, and producing pounds of berries for our favourite, raspberry/huckleberry pie. The volunteer foxgloves spring up in great abundance year after year. I transplanted the ancestor plants from Yvonne Proctor's yard years ago. They surprise me all over the garden and easily withstand transplanting both spring and fall, a great boon when the yard was unfenced since the deer do not eat them due to the digitalis content. Yellow monkey face flowers raise their cheerful smiles in the oddest places. A little bit of crud between some planks on the dock supports the sweet little yellow face and I nod to it every day as I pass on my way to the boat. In the shade near the creek, tiarella, or foamflower, raise long slim stems hanging with bell-shaped florets. I saved a copper bush from annihilation by secateurs during the clearing, and—the most delightful prize of all—I came upon two ground cones, one yellow, one pink, pushing their way up through the duff side by side. The Cox Island *Iris pseudacorus* sends up tall candelabra-like stalks topped with bright yellow blooms.

I awake with the sun, thinking about the garden beds to be turned, the blueberries Greg and Sandy brought in need of planting, the seedlings to be bedded in the hospitable earth. I'm inspired by Celia Thaxter, an author and lighthouse keeper on Appledore Island, off New Hampshire, like me, gardener of a windswept rock. I learned of her through the sun-sparkled watercolours of Childe Hassam, illustrator of Thaxter's book, *An Island Garden*. From Celia I learned to start seedlings in half

eggshells so there is no need to disturb the tiny roots when transplanting them into the garden. Yesterday though, I abandoned the cultivated
garden and went in search of the single delight.

The single delight is the most delicate of wild flowers. It rivals the calypso orchid in its shyness and unwillingness to be disturbed. My flower
book says it can bloom right into August, although my experience here is
that May is the month. After that the blooms are more elusive. Into the
cool dark forest I go, not too far from home, treading very lightly so as
not to squash any. Once my eyes adjust to the verdant gloom, I wander
about, sweeping my gaze from side to side, and there, illuminated by a
sunbeam, a single greenish-white flower rises tenderly from the mossy
duff. Nearby another one, and over there, another. I fall to my knees to
examine more closely these delicate wood nymphs. A long stem rises
from a corolla of serrated leaves nestled in soil replete with rotting bark.
Each flower bends gracefully, spreading five lightly frilled petals. From
the centre protrudes a long green pistil, like an upside-down castle turret.
Delicate golden stamens surround the central array. So enchanting are
these small woodland flowers I simply lie down beside one, cradle my
head in my arms and contemplate.

For sure these will be in the next painting of the wildflower documen-
tation series I've done for Billy over the years. I've an ongoing list, along
with reference drawings and photos. The painting will include the single
delight and the rosy twinflower, which grow in a healthy little clump
right beside Billy's lumber loading ramp below his mill. Ground cone,
too, I think, which erupts from the earth in succulent creamy yellow or
pink pinecone shapes. I haven't yet decided what the centre image will
be, possibly Pocket Inlet or one of the wildflower islands around here.
An old First Nations carved cedar halibut float lies nestled under the
foliage on one of the islands; that could work as a centrepiece for a painting, too. If only there weren't so many other wonderful and distracting
subjects to paint! I could be happy if limited only to the wild flowers as
subjects.

Beginnings and Endings

Including proven formulae for baits, scents and
expert methods of making sets.

—V.E. Lynch, *Trails to Successful Trapping*, 1935

IT'S TRULY A HOTBED OF CONSTRUCTION in this neck of the woods. Billy
has spent the spring building a museum to house his growing collection
of "junk." For years people were invited into Billy and Yvonne's house
to traipse up the stairs to see his collection of First Nations artifacts and
historical logging, fishing, trapping and household items. The light up
there is poor and the number of visitors is increasing every summer so
he constructed the museum with red cedar boards he'd milled. There is
a walkway of salvaged planks leading to the steps up to the front door,
over which hangs the sign he made, using pink fishing lures nailed to a
board to spell out the words, "Billy's Museum." Billy placed four windows down each side wall, and built display stands that are positioned
to create alcoves for the various categories of items. Once every item is
in place in the museum I make descriptive information cards. Shelves of
bottles of every description, and from every culture that left their garbage
here, glow in the light from the large windows. There are opium bottles,
Chinese and Caucasian whiskey bottles, food, medicinal and Avon bottles. One section holds Billy's collection of traps and a 1909 copy·of *Wolf
and Coyote Trapping* he received from Matt Rose. Another section show-
cases old-time fishing gear, including the metal pieces, wooden molds
and the round-headed, cylinder-shaped hammer the old-timers would
use to make lures. A precious matchbook from Proctor's Fish Camp
sits on the windowsill, the only one left from the business his father,

Yvonne Proctor cuts the ribbon to officially open "Billy's Museum."

then his mother ran through Billy's childhood. Glass-covered cases display diverse artifacts such as trading beads from the early explorers, stone slave-killers made and used by the early First Nations people, paint mixing and sharpening stones, bird points, larger arrowheads of chert, chalcedony and quartz. One of my favourites is a black stone bear spear Billy found on the beach at Charles Creek when he was a kid.

Among the artifacts is a smoothly chiselled, green jade knife that surfaced while he was digging in the garden at Freshwater Bay with his mom when he was five years old. This special piece ignited Billy's life-long interest in the treasures to be found in the earth and on the beaches. Making the information cards opens my eyes to the history of this place. Billy's knowledge of his home territory is astounding in its breadth, encompassing natural history as well as human history. If he doesn't know something, he looks it up in one of his tremendous collection of reference books.

July 1, 1999, is opening day for Billy's Museum, and a small crowd gathers on the grass at the foot of the steps. With big shears Yvonne cuts the ribbon draped across the door, and it's official: Billy's Museum is open for visitors.

Immediately, boating visitors beat a path to his door. Freed from their hesitation at invading Yvonne's household space, they come in droves, leaving behind money and appreciation. Billy donates all the money to our hatchery organization. He decides the next building will be a gift shop, good news for me, for sure.

The museum building is a relief for Yvonne, who is beginning to have more trouble breathing and tires easily. Billy doesn't want to leave her to look after the museum on her own, and decides not to go away fishing for salmon. We go "sport" fishing several times, since it's a good year for pinks. We limit out on them, and on coho, along with a couple of big spring salmon. Albert and I have the smoker going and the pressure canner burbling away on the stove throughout the summer.

Billy's collection includes everything from Chinese opium bottles to these colourful glass resistors.

Near summer's end, Billy decides he's going to have another go at tuna fishing.

"How soon can you be ready?" He pulls up in his speedboat and surprises me with the query. Last year's deckhands, Theda and Billy's grandson Glen, are unavailable and the tourists visiting the museum have slowed down to a trickle. Yvonne says she can deal with that lot.

"I've got to can my last batch of smoked salmon, bring the hatchery paperwork up to date and get the last of the red cedar paneling installed in the fern bedroom. I can be ready in two days; is that soon enough?"

"Yup. Don't forget your boots." He roars off. I only forgot my boots once, but he never lets me forget it.

On September 2, we leave in the dawn's early light, 6:00 am. It's a far cry from the 3:30 am rising time of high summer fishing. The deck lifts and sways under my feet; my body remembers the familiar dance of the west-coast troller. Alive with anticipation, I compile a grocery list for the Port Hardy stop as the sun rises on Queen Charlotte Strait. The famil iarity of long hours running on the way to the fishing grounds comforts me. I feared I might never go to sea again. This sudden tuna trip may be my last fishing trip, and my senses are on full alert. I don't want to miss a thing. Up through Goletas Channel, past Wiser Island and across the Bar, we run west past Cape Sutil towards Cape Scott, then beyond Cape Scott, seeking "tuna water," the true blue water of the North Pacific current that carries the tuna in its warm embrace. Seventy miles out to sea Billy shuts down the engine, and we float, feeling small. Like Theda said, it takes some getting used to, just bobbing around like a cork, attached to neither a dock nor a mooring buoy, not even the bottom through the anchor. I make dinner as the sun sets in a red blaze of fisherman's delight far across the vast Pacific. Tired, but I'm reluctant to climb in the bunk.

"What if a big freighter comes by in the night and runs into us?" I ask Billy.

"We're way out of the shipping lanes," he assures me, "and I'll turn on the strobe light on the top of the mast. Don't worry. We didn't see a soul last year."

"I'm holding you personally responsible if we get run down in the night," I tell him.

It doesn't take me long to fall asleep but slumber is fitful, and I'm glad to get up and get to work. The morning is grey and gloomy in spite of yesterday's red sky, and Billy sets to getting the gear in the water. The tuna rig is completely different once again. There are ten long lines running back out behind the boat, made of 300-pound test perlon. The longest line hangs off the tip of each spread trolling pole and is twenty-two fathoms long—one fathom equals six feet—with no weight on the end. The tuna jig and barbless double hook skip along the surface. The second line is seventeen fathoms long, weighted with three chain links so it drags just under the surface. The third line is fourteen fathoms and weighted with five or six chain links to sit a little deeper in the water. The line closest to the boat is only three fathoms long and carries a three-pound lead weight. Each line has a "pull-in" line we can grab hold of to bring it closer to the cockpit. A short line hangs off each gurdy post and another off the boom. The whole works looks like a delicate spider web against the sky, but for most of the day we spiders catch no flies. We troll around on a restless grey sea under an oppressive cloud cover through which the sun tries to peek from time to time.

We gaze around constantly, looking to see what there is to see. Billy shakes his head repeatedly.

"I can't get over it. There's nothing here. Where the hell are all the critters?"

Finally an albatross keeps us company for a while, dipping and gliding on its invisible cushion of air, maintaining its precise distance from the water at all times. We listen to the marine weather; it doesn't sound good.

"Solander Island, wind southeast 45 and gusting to 54, pressure 998.5 millibars and falling. Sartine Island, wind southeast 42 and gusting to 50. Pressure 997 and falling." The forecast is for the southeast to shift to southwest storm-force winds, not good weather when you're sixty miles out at sea.

Late in the afternoon there is a bit of action on the gear. We bring in every line for three tuna. They are beautiful, streamlined and sleek with a perfect narrow trench along the spine into which their delicately pleated dorsal fins neatly fold, and slim tail stocks before the flare of their elegantly pointed fins. The sea roughens as we work, and we are careful with our footing.

The waves are shadowed and dark on one side, lighter grey on the other. Amongst the shadows I suddenly spot several narrow, finless black sausage shapes leaping along.

"Hey, Billy, we've got company."

"Finally," he says. "Northern right whale dolphins. I thought we weren't going to see anything this trip. I was hoping for a sunfish or a turtle or a blue shark, something... anything."

The dolphin crowd increases until there are a couple hundred leaping alongside *Ocean Dawn*. Their long black backs beg for a fin; they look incomplete. The much larger right whale (so-called by the whalers because among the many whale species to choose from, it was the "right"

one, the valuable one, to catch) also has no dorsal fin, hence the name of these dolphins. I'm glad to see these creatures, new to me, since they do not inhabit our home waters.

"One more night," Billy says, "then I think we better head for shelter." The fisherman's gamble, stay and fish or run for cover, isn't a hard decision to make today. Only three tuna is not promising; there is no lure of an illusory fishing fortune influencing us to risk bad weather. Our last restless night at sea is short. Billy fires up the motor before daybreak, we hang out the gear, and run east towards Vancouver Island. Rain slashes the windows and drums on the roof. Around noon Billy decides to pull in the gear and make time for Solander Island. One more tuna is added to our pile. We are mostly silent as he concentrates on steering through the sloppy seas until the charcoal smudge of land shows through the gloom. Solander looks desolate, threatening, and we carry on for the north side

Billy repairing the broken rigging in Goose Bay near Hansen Lagoon.

of Brooks Peninsula, hoping to find shelter there from the steepening swell. Brooks isn't much better. White surf-horses gallop in long lines; near shore they rear up and leap over black rocks. We could go in close and anchor for the night, but four more hours running with the sea on our stern quarter will bring us to the security of the mooring buoys of Sea Otter Cove.

"What d'ya think?" says Billy. It doesn't matter what I think, but I like it that he asks.

"Sea Otter's got my vote," I reply.

It's a tired crew that bunks down in Sea Otter Cove, but I awake to Captain Billy banging around the galley making pancakes at 5:00 am. "Jeez, Billy, we could sleep one extra hour when we're weathered in, couldn't we?"

Billy writing what would become part of our book *Full Moon, Flood Tide* published by Harbour Publishing in 2003.

"Gawd no," he says. "We're going to row down the cove here and walk out to Lowrie Bay."

"Okay, but not until seven o'clock, alright? I want to update my notes first. And shouldn't it be daylight when we're walking in the woods?"

Billy grudgingly agrees and cleans up the breakfast dishes after we eat. He works on his notes while I work on mine. It's quiet in the cabin, with just the soft sound of the pump that brings diesel to the stove and the hissing of the kettle. Outside, the rigging whistles and rattles, keeping time with the stormy bluster. Just after 7:00 am, we pull on our boots, lower the dinghy over the side and climb in. The air is moist and gloomy, and the treetops whip back and forth, but it's not raining and the sea calms the farther into the cove we row. I lean back in the stern as Billy rows, deeply inhaling a feeling of enormous well-being along with the sweet sea air.

"Ah, this is the life, breakfast served, dishes done, and now I can gaze around with queenly delight as my loyal servant rows…"

I do a "queen wave" at the crows we pass. Billy snorts. When we beach the rowboat, there's a little buck with six-inch horns protruding from his head at the edge of the shore. He's been slipping kelp through his mouth, slurping off the salt, I guess. He's unafraid as we walk slowly towards him. Billy croons to the handsome guy as he does to the deer at home.

"Wish I had an apple," he laments. "I bet he'd eat it out of my hand."

Plunging into the woods we head towards the open coast. Treetops sway high above our heads and branches crack loose and drift to the forest floor. The closer we get to the beach, the wilder the wind blows. It's only a short walk before the long stretch of Lowrie Bay opens before us. On the beach, Billy and I, as usual, turn away from each other: he heads north and I south. Even though we get along so well, there's nothing like a little solitude to be the cure, and the prevention, against feeling crowded and cramped. The surf rolls in, and gulls fly in the face of the gale. I'm thinking about the many ships that have run aground on this unforgiving coastline when I come upon a life-saving cabin, tidy and self-contained with a small supply of firewood, a candle and a bunk with a blanket. I'm always drawn to off-the-beaten-path hideaways, and this one is perfect. I fantasize about spending the night, but of course I don't want Billy to have to come searching for me, so I retrace my footprints in the sand.

Back at the boat I put together lunch for us. After he tidies up, Billy says, "Let's walk around the island at the entrance. The wind's died down a bit." This expedition turns out to be a bit gruelling. The island is not big, but there are steep rocky places that billy-goat Billy leaps across. I don't feel so daring. I make it across the worst gaps with his helping hand, and as we round the island there is a little black bear foraging at the tide's edge. We stroll right by him, and I'm glad that I brought my camera, even though it is cumbersome around my neck. My feet are burning in my boots. I'm not used to walking on such stony terrain and gumboots offer no support. Billy gallops ahead full throttle. Go ahead, I flap my hand at him when he turns back to look for me.

It's almost dark by the time we regain our floating haven. I'm done, burnt out, but throw together dinner, play a couple of hands of crib, and go to bed. Billy grins at me from under his sleeping bag.

"I just love my little bunk," he says, for the zillionth time.

"Hold that pose," I say. "I gotta get a picture of you in your little bunk."

"Make it quick," he says. "I'm fading fast." He does, and I do too.

Monday morning: the sun shines, the surf boils, but there are no teeth in it. Billy puts on the weather channel, and comments that we haven't heard another boat on the radio for three days. He's trying to decide whether to fish or head for home. We un-moor from the buoy, and head out of Sea Otter. I wave goodbye to the sea otters. They look up as we go by and keep cracking urchin shells on their chests. They don't wave back. We set our course to the west, then northwest. The sea is rough and Billy puts the stabilizers in the water. An hour en route and the stabilizer line breaks.

"Dammit, that does it, we're going home." Billy is reading the signs, and this is the final one. Discretion is the better part of valour, and no

boats around means no help should it be needed. We roll into Goose Bay at the mouth of Hansen Lagoon, and Billy climbs the rigging to repair the stabilizer line. I burn the bacon while keeping an eye on him—not that watching could prevent him from falling. Stabilizer line repaired, burnt bacon and perfectly scrambled eggs eaten, we carry on around Cape Scott and east towards the rising sun.

"'Six days on the boat and I'm gonna make it home tonight" jingles through my head. We do, and it is indeed the last time I go to sea with Billy. His fishing trips grow more infrequent as Yvonne's health deteriorates. Often when he goes to town or elsewhere, I eat lunch with her and visit for a while. When Billy does finally fish again, his grandsons, my kids and other young people wanting a sea-going experience are all eager candidates for the deckhand job. My fishing days are over but I'll cherish my sea-going memories forever. These eight years fishing with Billy have been extraordinary, one of the very best seasons of my life.

My Inspiration

We are all the eyes and ears of the earth; and we
think the world's thoughts.

—Lyall Watson, *Gifts of Unknown Things*

THE BEGINNING OF EACH NEW DAY is my quiet time, but often the day just takes over sooner than I might like. Something is always happening. A neighbour needs a hand or to borrow something, or the boomstick has come loose, on and on. I noticed from the start when I moved here that life is like this—hurry up and wait. I make a plan, and by 9:00 am my plan has vanished like an unweighted prawn trap caught in the tide. I just try to stay with the outline as the details get coloured in by unfolding events. A day that turns out as planned is rare, although town trip days with Billy generally stay on schedule.

The beginning of each new year is full of promise. I'm thrilled when money arrives on the first mail day after the Christmas holidays. January is the slowest month of the year for painting sales, and I try to make sure I have a little money left over from pre-Christmas earnings to get me through to February. Things always pick up around Valentine's Day.

The money in the mail today is a $600 cheque from the Museum of Northern Affairs for the sale of the Boat Bluff Lighthouse painting. I'd sent that to them along with one of the lighthouse-keeper at Pulteney Point polishing the lens. The paintings were displayed in a group show at the museum to raise awareness about the government's decision to de-staff several BC lighthouses. De-staffing lighthouses is a bad idea from a mariner's point of view. Frequently the keeper of a lighthouse is the only

other living soul for hundreds of miles around. I've listened to many conversations between Billy and the lightkeeper at Cape Scott and Cape St. James at all hours of the night. There's an area near Cape St. James where you can't pick up any Coast Guard weather station and so have no idea what to expect without a chat with the Cape St. James keeper.

BC lighthouses, like lighthouses worldwide, are of immeasurable importance to the safety of mariners through the lightkeeper's long-range weather information, local knowledge of wind and tide, and courage and expertise in the saving of countless lives. From my own experience, I believe their supreme value is in knowing, when you venture out into the boundless expanse of the sea, that out there in the vast unknown, there are humans eager for your arrival, eager to chat through the dark hours as you approach an unfamiliar shore. Humans on these lonely outposts are a bright spot of light in a black void. Due to technology, though, the sad day is coming when there will no longer be those welcoming voices from the lights.

My world wish is that all people could experience such idyllic joy as I am privileged to. It's Friday the thirteenth, thus disproving (again) the old adage of bad luck. All is flawless here in my Burdwood campsite. A perfect afternoon has slipped into a perfect apricot evening. A pot of potatoes flavoured with wild onions from the rock nearby simmers over a comfortable fire. Solitude sweetens my every moment. The natural beauty of this place can't help but bring ease to a stressed psyche. Many hands have made this an excellent campsite. Kayakers, boat travellers, painters: hundreds, maybe thousands of people have camped here over the years. Everyone who comes here must surely carry away a little bit of this tranquil beauty, a precious memory drawn out from time to time and savoured.

This place is a perfect and practical manifestation of the spirit or soul energy shaping everything. An upended log round softened with a cushion is the perfect spot to tend my dinner or paint. Looking through a green sweep of cedar branches, the view north towards Mount Read begins with a curve of white shell beach. Tenderly lapping the shore is the most delicate silken peridot-green sea, deepening to blue-green as it recedes into the distance. Way out there, the dark teal colour is stitched through horizontally with pale blue marks, a cyan blue, a pure, distilled blue, the sky's reflection.

In the tent I store painting supplies, my journal, one of Elizabeth Peters' Egyptian mysteries, clothing for all weathers, food and bedding. I gather a pile of firewood, small red cedar pieces for a hot cook-fire and larger hemlock chunks that will burn slow and bright. After I eat, I wash all the dishes and place everything tidily in the tent.

As I prepare for bed a soft wind soughs through the trees. It increases as I burrow into my sleeping bag, from a sigh to breathy billows. Darkness complete falls and I lie in drifting sleeplessness. In that dreamy state I see luminous shapes, like old-fashioned magic lantern shapes, on the wall of the tent. Through the mesh window opening, the night sky brightens, so I crawl out of the tent to take a look.

On the southern horizon, a golden not quite half-moon sails swiftly up from behind the distant hills; the fat crescent is encircled by a gauzy mist of light. Intensely black patterns of islands and trees are etched against the sky, gold spangles tossing upon the crinkled black sea: my all-time favourite image. As the moon sails higher the wind falls silent. In the sleeping bag again, I descend fast into a deep sleep.

Morning. I awake to perfect stillness, shrouded silence. When the first bird call pierces the thick quiet, the sweet trill of the varied thrush, I stretch and unzip the sleeping bag and the tent flap to grey pillows of fog. I fire up a little cooking flame from the coals for coffee and an egg. As the sun begins its work on the fog, birds call and respond. The friendly neighbourhood squirrel runs down the fir tree and chatters at me; I toss it a bit of toast. It's wonderful to be consciously happy for a few minutes, even a few hours. To be happy for days on end is almost unbearable. Ridiculous to feel like crying, but tears of joy well up in my eyes and sting my nose. I laugh out loud and startle a fox sparrow. My soul melts into the river of soul, the *all that is* that surrounds and encompasses me.

A darling little bird sings in many voices this morning. I watch it for several minutes. It has an impressive repertoire of calls, precisely mimick-

ing a chattering chipmunk, a squeaking mouse, a full-throated robin and a song sparrow. The squirrel sidles closer. I hesitate to scare it, but it's time to set up for painting now. Squirrel will just have to get used to me.

In the dappled sunlight I squirt juicy blobs of burnt sienna and French ultramarine blue, raw sienna and cobalt violet on my white palette. Beside the palette are pencils, the water jar, flexible sable brushes. I sit. Ready. In the crotch of a fir tree a backlit spider web hangs high. The spider web is bedewed with moisture beads that gleam like diamonds. I tape heavy rag paper to the drawing board, open the bottle of masking fluid to articulate the water drops hanging from the web. I begin.

Late in the afternoon, a cheeky breeze blows off the last tendrils of fog and along with it the bugs. So warm I stroll around like Robinson Crusoe, just me in my skin. I had a wonderful time painting but next time, I'll bring a lawn chair; the cushion on a stump just does not cut it. I'll bring a TV tray to set the drawing board on; it's too uncomfortable to hold on my knees for a lengthy painting session. I've wrestled a couple of log rounds under a big plank to make a counter/table for dining and painting, although it's a bit low. The water jars are stowed under the shade of the salal. I'm all ready for another day.

The wind is from the south and east again on my second night, fragrant but fiercer, packing a bite. The music of the trees bending, dancing, clapping is louder, with a faintly ominous resonance. The surf against the east-facing beach plays a solid percussion, a rhythm in sync with the rise and fall of the wind. Sharp snaps and creaky rubbing noises punctuate the beat as the ranks of treetops comb the wind. The last rays of the setting sun stain the hills in Viner Sound a wine-dark purple. This wind pulls with it a thick fog, dragging puffy duvets of cloud like a bedcover up over the hills. The noise is loud, insistent.

I hear the outboard motor long before my speedboat buzzes into view. Albert has timed his arrival with the rising of the tide and his departure for just after the high slack. The wind/tide conditions are much too turbulent for us to contemplate retiring to the tent together. Instead, I cook and eat my dinner while we visit. Dusk approaches, and he clasps me to his manly chest before motoring off home.

Lovely to visit with my dear husband, but I'm off to bed now. I am in need of a thicker foam mattress. I am sure Emily Carr had a good bed in Elephant, her camping van, surrounded by all her animals.

Crows sound the alarm next morning, yet I cannot see what alarms them. All day I listen to their conversation, translating and deciphering crow code. I practise crow language, enunciating with appropriate nuances, and try to write a crow dictionary. There may not be many more entries.

Un uh, un uh, un uh ~ (emphasis on un) a cautionary communication.

No fair, no fair, no fair ~ (emphasis on fair) the crow is annoyed.

It's mine, it's mine, it's mine ~ another variation of annoyance with a slight change in tonal inflection.

Give it back, give it back, give it back ~ the crow is furious.

When I was young, my mother was always pointing out birds to me. I was interested but not fascinated. Now I'm fascinated. I'm out running around in my speedboat with my daughter. The voice coaching she began years ago has developed into a lifetime calling, and she wants me to take pictures of her for the cover of her first CD.

"Theda, look! There's a pair of common loons! They're pretty rare here."

"Someday I'll be interested in birds, Mommy," she says patting my knee. It's true that bird-watching, the most popular hobby in the world, is mostly a hobby of older folks. When I hear about a Citizen Science Project seeking people to identify and count water birds up and down the British Columbia coast, for the purpose of quantifying and tracking population trends, I know right away this is something I could do. Billy is interested, too, so now, like three hundred or so other bird lovers, we go out and count birds on the shoreline the second Sunday of every month.

Billy picks me up in his hard-working blue speedboat. I climb in over the dog lines and stamping hammer, settle in my seat. I'm ready

Off to camp in the Burdwood Group in my loaded rowboat. Photo Albert Munro.

with a yellow, "rite-in-the-rain" notebook and a sharp pencil in hand. Billy has a couple of chocolate bars lying on the dash. We leave my dock and run northwest towards the Burdwood Group. Right away there are red-throated loons, murrelets and murres, red-necked grebes, guillemots and gulls. My counting notation is four bar marks, a cross for the fifth. Close to the seal haul-out on the south side of Denham Island, there are usually a number of common mergansers, surf scoters and more grebes. We know where to find the eagles now, and which nests are active. Our area from the Burdwood Group into Viner Sound estuary supports an average of ten resident eagles, a number that is slowly increasing as newly hatched young mature and build their own nests. Inside the lagoon-like protected centre of the islands we see pairs of harlequin ducks, the male so beautiful. All he needs is a bowler hat to top off his natty outfit. The female, dun brown yet dignified knows *he* is so gaily arrayed simply to attract *her* attention and interest. We've discov-

The Burdwood Group offers a vast array of subjects to paint and sketch. I camp and observe and I am blissfully happy. Photo Albert Munro.

ered the small rocks where the black turnstones chortle and flutter in large groups, nibbling at the mussels and barnacles of the low tide zone, skippety-hopping, running in short bursts, taking flight as one creature, decorative black-and-white bars stitching herring-bone patterns in the sky as they wheel and turn, belly-side, back-side, belly-side. Often we can turn the motor off and drift up close without spooking them. A charming busy species, unlike the combative crows and Steller's jays. In among the turnstones, the surf birds are almost indistinguishable until we sit quietly and notice greyer birds with yellow legs in the mix, sometimes only one or two, sometimes as many as half the group.

Large flocks of buffleheads—we call them butterballs—puddle around the narrows near the Japanese garden island. The males look like small sailboats from a distance, low white hull, black neck and white head as the sail. The females, muted browns and greys like the "harlies," are

almost invisible against the shore. Often they can only be distinguished by the faint light that underlines them on the water as they paddle after the boys.

We circumnavigate the entire group of islands, peeking into the small bays to check for intensely mated pairs of hooded mergansers, or "hoodies," marking off each bird we count in my yellow notebook. Leaving the Burdwood Group where it faces up Tribune Channel, we head for Penn Island to see if the eagle is home, scanning for the western grebes that float with the tide upon the open sea. The flock fluctuates between two hundred and nine hundred, an extraordinary number of birds. Often their elegant white-throated necks are curled in a sleeping arc, but up comes the heads and the bright red eyes to search for the source of the disturbance, us. Billy cruises alongside the spread-out group and I count in tens, moving an imaginary dividing bar to separate each group of ten. I've practised this enough to believe I'm making a reasonably accurate count.

From Penn Island we aim for the shore of King Point, turning to run along the north side of Viner Sound. One heron lives on our beat, and it usually takes off with a squawk. Just past Old Gus, as Billy calls the bird, a precipitous cliff face is the right place for guillemot nesting. Often we see several bobbing below the nest opening, watch their brilliant red legs when they dive or do "running on water." One nesting site is notable for the distinctive white guano streak below it.

It's not difficult to identify uniquely patterned birds like harlequin ducks and hooded mergansers. The tough ones are the gulls. I know now when I see fifty or sixty bright white gulls perched on the stark branches of a dead fir tree that they're mew gulls. The smallest gulls on our beat, the appealing Bonaparte's gulls, wear a solid black hood in summer and are almost always seen in a group, bobbing for tiny wriggling creatures or perched on small chunks caught in an eddy. Further into Viner we see large flocks of Barrow's goldeneyes, one or two kingfishers, the odd raven pair gliding high. In Viner we've been thrilled to spot a soaring osprey, vultures and a sharp-shinned hawk. In October, hundreds of great bald eagles feast on the chum salmon run. In January and February, the winter flocks of trumpeter swans reside at the river mouth, because the lakes higher up the slopes of the valley freeze up. This flock is slowly increasing as well; we've seen up to five grey goslings in a group of eleven. Keeping the swans company in the tall grasses are flocks of tiny savannah sparrows, Canada geese that burst into flight with great honking calls, widgeons, mallards and once in a while a teal or two.

Running out to count birds on purpose once a month often brings other surprises. We rarely see wolves, but once we watched a swimming wolf make it to shore and climb out. Bears ramble around Viner estuary from spring to autumn. Always there are seals, of course, and sometimes porpoises, dolphins, whales—killer and humpback, minke and grey. Frequently we surprise an otter or a mink, although never a raccoon anymore. Occasionally a curious sea lion will approach as we slow. In the mud flats of Viner at low water, we hang over the side of the boat to watch for flounder slipping off with a little puff of mud. Crabs crawl, often swimming surprisingly swiftly in two feet of water. The bushy shoreline, low water, tall trees of the forest and the sky beyond are so full of rich life forms. For those who love to discover the hidden treasures and secret delights of anywhere wild, and maybe some places not so wild, a bird count is only the opening gateway.

Rediscovering Clay

IN MY PREVIOUS LIFE IN WHITE ROCK, I WAS A POTTER as well as a painter. A cumbersome kick-wheel sat by the refrigerator, and when I messed up a pot, I threw the sorry lump against the fridge, scraping up the wet clay to be recycled at the end of each session. The kids and I had to move three times in four months once, and I could not manage the herculean task of repeatedly moving a pile of kiln bricks, my heavy kick-wheel, fifty-pound boxes of clay, buckets of glaze and glaze materials. I'd also made a shift to watercolour painting and it was so portable. I could take my watercolour gear out on the boat when I went to visit Albert. So I sold the works, except for the gram scales, knowing they would cost more to replace if I should ever pot again.

Now, after years of building our house and garden, learning the secrets of my new world and painting them, I awake from dreams of clay. It's not as if I don't have enough to do, yet I feel drawn again to the tactile pleasure of shaping slick clay, putting it through the fire and cradling in my hand a beautiful new object from which I can eat or drink or use to hold earrings, oranges or soap. I love the marriage of art and function.

I buy a kick-wheel and an electric kiln from a Vancouver Island potter, never thinking about how much electricity it might require. Luckily, the kiln draws eleven-and-a-half kilowatts, and the generator, old as it is, puts out thirteen. Albert wires in a double breaker and a switch to divert the entire output of the generator to run the kiln.

"Where can we set up the pottery studio?" I ask Albert. Every space in our house is allocated for some function but many have yet to be realized. After a day or two, he has a plan.

"What about the main floor bathroom-to-be?" Currently, the working bathroom is on the first floor in the "woodworking" half, where piles of lumber are drying and the planer and other house-building tools live. We still reside in the future painting studio on the same floor.

The bathroom-to-be becomes a temporary pottery studio. Just after New Year's 1999, Albert and Billy, with a lot of grunting, pack my heavy new potter's wheel up the stairs. It sits beside the seven-foot window where the bathtub will someday reside. Two counters with storage shelves run along two walls. It's a happy place to pot; I love gazing out on my garden from this high vantage point. After only two throwing sessions my body recovers its remembered skills. My fingers fall naturally into the configurations used to centre, pull and shape the clay. Like riding a bicycle, I guess. You never forget.

Albert by the high fire kiln he built. Soon our days are filled with making clay creations.

I'm astonished at the thrill my clay dreams bring to the whole community. Immediately I have two students, and more follow. Billy's younger daughter, Patty, who has tried her hand at an assortment of artistic endeavours, comes over for throwing lessons. During lesson one, I realize we need to arrange her short-fingered hands differently from the way mine work to accomplish the same goals. She practises with such passion that within a few weeks she is throwing pots good enough to test glazes on. Pat Steernberg, who also comes as a student, hand-builds bearded wizards and two-dimensional plaques portraying grizzled old-time pioneer characters. All these items go into the kiln and reward their creators with further inspiration.

Now my already full days include finding time to throw and trim, glaze and fire pots, but it's no hardship. I love potting, and I'm satisfied with the delayed gratification. Immediately pottery aficionados begin buying the pots and I use the money to buy more clay and diesel to run the generator. It's expensive getting pottery supplies out to Echo Bay, though, so one day Albert, Patty and I go on a hunt with Billy for sources of local clay. Substantial deposits of iron-rich clay can be found along the banks of Shoal Harbour Creek, on Dixon Island and in Broughton Lagoon. I test some of it, but due to the high iron content it has a low melting temperature, and I can't use it for making the style of tableware I prefer. I discover that some local clays serve as beautiful glaze colourants, and I make some dishes with a combination of Alder Island clay and high-fire stoneware. It takes a lot of experimenting to find the melting temperature of raw wild clay and a body of glazes that "fit" the clay and mature at the same temperature.

More students show up to play with clay. Almost every day through the spring and early summer, someone is messing around in the studio with me. Near the end of June, I take clay and tools to Echo Bay School for a project. It gives me such joy to see the kids' art spirit light up. Yvonne P. likes the results of the firings but is mostly glad to see her daughter happy. Patty makes up her mind to get her own wheel and builds an addition onto the front of her house for a pottery studio.

Albert asks me to teach him how to pot, too, fulfilling a dream from his younger days. He is an amazing potter, it turns out, and a terrific technician. He builds a big propane-fired kiln, relocates the pottery studio to the downstairs "shop" space and finishes the bathroom as a bathroom. My own work is energized by his interest and the different work he does. It's no wonder that, worldwide, community pottery studios are a nexus of energy, activity and production. I'm seeing it happen right here at home.

November is a big production month for potters aiming for the Christmas market. We throw, fire and glaze over a hundred and fifty pots through the fall. Albert, night owl that he is, fires the load through the night and comes to bed at dawn, as I'm getting up.

November is also birthday month for me and my kids, and often it's been a month for moving. The move this year is only from the downstairs painting studio-to-be to the upstairs living room/ kitchen. Last spring I'd mentioned to my Hercules that I desperately needed a kitchen by my fiftieth birthday, and he has striven to manifest that for me. Creating it is a complicated process (isn't everything?), but at long last, after many months of back-breaking labour, the upstairs kitchen and living room are real.

We planed seemingly endless piles of yellow cedar lumber first, for the ceiling, which extends down the hallway. Each board is routered twice; tongue on one side and groove on the other. We did most of this work together as it made the job simpler. I carried each completed board upstairs to one of the empty guest bedrooms, set them on sawhorses and rubbed on two coats of Varathane. Albert installed the ceiling over a three-week period while I was away. It's much easier with me gone since he can work at night. Together we nailed up the four-foot-high yellow cedar wainscot panelling and for the finale, Albert nailed down the fir floor. These boards are three inches wide, half the width of the ceiling and floorboards, therefore, twice the labour.

Albert made a beautiful large U-shaped counter out of two-inch-thick yellow cedar planks. He built it in three sections, gluing and dowelling the pieces together. It is not quite complete, so the pieces are sitting in their proper places but not secured.

I have the mad idea that I need to have a big house party for my fiftieth birthday. My children and several friends from away come. The Sointula Winterfest, our big Christmas pottery sale, falls on the weekend of November 17, the date of my birthday, so the party is the following weekend. Albert runs *Miss Jenny* to Port McNeill the day before, to pick up my guests. At home, with the help of neighbours Carol and Jerry, I sweep, wipe, install bits of trim, make up beds and do a million other little final jobs.

On the Saturday, all my guests pitch in to create the rooms. Theda vacuums everywhere. Logan's been doing carpentry work with his dad on construction sites, and he hangs the kitchen door to the side deck. Music plays as Marcel, Deb and I hang paintings. An altar of symbolic objects is set in the space where the stove will go. The men, with many expletives, pack my old red velvet couch and chair up the stairs from the studio into the new living room. The pièce de résistance is the yew-wood dining table that Billy made for us ten years ago as a wedding gift. Logan and Billy bring it over from the Proctors' in Billy's speedboat. It's heavy and too big to fit through the door, so they remove the legs to carry it in. Setting the table upside down on the kitchen floor, the men bolt on the legs again, turn it right side up and withdraw the protective blanket. I'm intensely happy, laughter and tears close to the surface. The table is beautiful, and it represents so much TLC. Billy has artfully used a contoured outside piece of yew for the long edges and the colours flow from the blond tones of the sapwood to the deeper reddish notes of the heartwood.

These rooms are not complete. There's still much to be done including sanding and varnishing the fir floor Albert laid, and installing the ceramic tiles I bought years ago in the kitchen. However, having a kitchen makes me euphoric. We're over the hump, past some indefinable halfway point in the construction.

For so long this house was only a dream, the blending of what I love about European and west-coast architecture. I'm so familiar with every element of its creation. Vividly I recall Logan and me, making the first cuts into the salal with garden loppers and snippers to begin the clearing. The chainsaw I purchased when Al moved out brought a whole new dimension to my clearing capability. I bucked up a lot of wood with that little saw. Using it reminds me of the days when Harley and Steven Snowdon and Don Cameron were taking down the big timber and leaving me the small stuff for firewood. At times I see their figures materialize in the mist that wraps the hillside.

I'm familiar with the many species of trees, and bushy shrubs, the colour and texture of the soil, the drainage and water flow characteristics. I know where the moon rises and sets, and all these elements are incorporated into the house design.

And now, I've got a house with two studios, light-filled and cozy bedrooms, a golden kitchen, and a living room with, as Ted calls it, a Kitsilano floor, and best of all, a loving husband creating it all with me. Happy fiftieth.

Being Mother Nature

*Nature I loved; and next to Nature art, I warmed
my hands before the fire of life.*

—Walter Landor

THIS IS MY YEAR TO TRY EVERYTHING I can to get my art out into the
world. Applications I'd sent in response to Calls for Entry last fall have
resulted in much intense painting effort through January and February.
I was happy with my acceptance to the Brant Wildlife Festival in Quali-
cum, in March, and my thrilling but ironic first prize win—for a photograph. Delighted, too, with my subsequent acceptance into Vancouver's
"Artropolis" show. It's easy out here in my wilderness life to get discon-
nected from the rest of the world, but at heart, I do want my work to be
seen and appreciated.

Prawn fishing for Albert rolls around once again. Although he no longer owns his own boat, he can still make the most of this good earning
opportunity by deckhanding for another skipper. No headaches and you
still get a paycheque. Out my studio window now, I see the *Thunder Bay*,
Larry Duggan's prawn-fishing boat. Albert is out there, under the canopy, sorting prawns by size and packing them in precise rows in labelled
boxes. Larry is steering a zigzag course, and Brian, the other deckhand,
flings traps quickly, one after the other over the stern, as they set the gear.
They are doing well and the price is good this year, but I fear the season
will be cut short, as it has been each of the last three years.

It's complicated to have a perspective on twenty years of a fishery. I'd

246

almost prefer to be in ignorant bliss than to comprehend our own part in the reduction of stocks. We follow the rules, but simply being a fisher, trying to make a living from the sea, along with everyone else who wants the same thing, still makes us complicit in decreasing the abundance of prawns. I remember when Albert had fifty traps, and we were happy if he averaged fifty pounds a day. It was the fisherman's dream, an apparently unlimited, self-renewing supply. Then came the years when there were dozens of boats fishing this area, laden with eight or nine hundred traps apiece. It doesn't take too long after that to notice the supply is limited.

Boating season follows prawn season and art-loving visitors seek out the studio for lessons and tours. The roses and lilies thrive in summer's heat but the wild flowers bloom and are spent quickly. I bravely planted tomatoes outdoors, instead of in the greenhouse, and it looks like the gamble is paying off; they are beginning to blush tomato red. Three days of hard rain follow eleven days of sunshine. The heavy-headed dahlias got knocked over by both the warm-weather westerlies and the southeast wind, but they'll regain their erect posture with support from some garden stakes.

When the wind and rain finally let up, Albert and I head for Port McNeill in *Miss Jenny* on a shopping trip. Al finally has some time to lay the tiles for the kitchen floor, but the grout I bought four years ago has hardened into solid lumps, so we must buy some more. I try not to think about how long it is taking to get every little thing done on this house.

A black streak on the water at the horizon's edge signals a rain squall coming our way.

"Get ready to roll," says Al, watching the squall boil towards us. He's already turning the wheel into the oncoming wind. It smacks the windows hard, and the rigging hums.

We are taking a few hard rolls coming across Queen Charlotte Strait and over Egeria Shoal. The tide rips are mesmerizing: great, glossy, spinning boils that suggest disappearing whale backs from a distance. When you're on top of them, the rips appear as a series of giant green glass plates slowly revolving on the surface. *Miss Jenny* shudders and swings

in one direction, then the other. The ocean is at work on the boat's hull but she is a sturdy vessel with a calm and competent skipper at the wheel. Some charts take a dive off the counter, and I wait for a smoother moment to retrieve and store them. I think about how I would paint the rips and how it might look underneath the surface, imagining watery tornados that flare at the surface.

Second Sunday of September, gloomy; Billy and I do the monthly bird count. A heavy cloud cover almost as wet as rain softens and obscures the tops of islands. We see thirty-five harlequin ducks in the Burdwood Group, and in Viner Sound we come upon a pair of common loons. Bill shuts the motor off and we're treated to a five-minute concert of ululating loon calls. My guess is it's the male calling. He stays between us and his mate, and his song echoes back from the steep treed slopes of the sound, the quintessential song of the Canadian wilderness. We also observe a crow chasing a kingfisher back and forth across the water. Bill figures the crows harass the kingfishers to find their nests and get at the eggs.

The winter months sweep me up in an express train wave and toss me into a cold February. I come to my studio in the early-morning dark and watch the sky brighten to full daylight. Morning sun dyes the hills a deep burgundy rose. A cold breeze sends a little cat's paw rush of ripples across the water. Treetops scribe slow arcs onto a parchment sky. If there was snow on Mount Stevens it would be a bright gleaming pink; however, this year for the first time ever, the mountain is stone cold bare, devoid of the tiniest scrap of snow. It looks colder this way, the peak rising barren and uncloaked to the icy cerulean of the sky. I don't have to bail out my speedboat, which must be done when it rains a lot, but I do cover the motor and the gearshift with old clothing and blankets. That makes it an awful lot easier to start the boat. If I don't throw a blanket over the motor on a cold night, the steering freezes up and must be thawed with a kettleful of boiling water.

So what happened the next night was this: a gentle percussion on the roof, a tentative delicate tapping that after a while swelled into a full-bodied rain. The rain was brief but it meant that the iron fist of cold had loosened its grip. A warmer mass of air from the southeast slipped over us in the night. I melted into sleep and awoke later when the plump globe of full moon, like a Victorian street lamp, beamed into our room. Its fallen twin floated, a pearl in black water. I watched for a while painting it in my mind. Watercolour? Mm, or maybe chalk pastel on dark grey paper. Soft streaks of charcoal cloud shifted across the face of the moon as it slid down behind the island. Almost dawn; I slept.

Sure enough, it's much warmer today. I don't mind a week or two of solid freeze-up, but despite the compensation of bright sunshine, the biting cold, the frozen water line and the constant stuffing of firewood into the heater gets old fast. I'm ready for the warmth of a rainy southeast. A small miracle this year: our water never ran dry. As usual when the temperature dropped, I filled the tub, and the tap has been open and running day and night for ten days. Although it isn't a big creek, the water originates on the property, so the supply cannot be jeopardized by logging. The line from the tank to the house is short and if it does freeze solid, it's not difficult to thaw it. Albert simply undoes the hose clamp at the base of the tank and drags the whole length of hose down the dock and into the ocean. The core of ice melts quickly, and as he drags the hose from the water, out pop little dowels of ice.

While Albert deals with the water line, a clear painting day awaits me, and I get early into the studio. I have a strong idea in my mind's eye. I've wanted to work with some of the Knight Inlet, Glacier Bay imagery for a while, but I'm more a painter of sea than of mountains. I surprise myself by painting a bold, strongly composed, canvas of the mountains at the head of the inlet and their reflections in the milky green waters in just over four hours. I'm not trying to paint with a great deal of speed; however, I'm determined not to fiddle the thing to death. "Painterly" is my mantra these days. I want to paint in such a way that Emily Carr or Lawren Harris or Tom Thomson would be proud of me. All my life I've admired those artists, and I see the same thing in their work: a transcendent quality, a "fall down on your knees" kind of feeling emanating from the canvas. I have that feeling so often in my life, especially here, and I hope it comes through in the paintings.

My number one fan, Albert, thinks it a wonderful painting. When Billy comes over with a chunk of halibut for us late in the afternoon, he pronounces it "excellent." High praise!

"I've walked right there many times, climbed up the glacier hunting for mountain goats," he says, pointing to a spot in the painting. "One time, I saw giant bear tracks, grizzly tracks, all around the edges of a crevasse. I looked way down into the crevasse, deep blue ice all the way down, and there at the bottom was the carcass of a mountain goat." Billy's story adds a new dimension to my work. I love it even more.

I invite the substitute teacher at the school over for dinner. He has no transportation so I run over to Echo Bay to collect him. It's a little awkward in the kitchen right now because—at last—Albert is laying the kitchen floor. He is painstaking and meticulous. We laid all the tiles out in the pattern we wanted first, and now over half the floor is set. They're very nice ceramic tiles, inspired by visions of old stone-walled homes in southern France, but I don't think I'll choose them for any other floors. All that mixing and mudding with caustic cement is too much to put Albert through. We can find other floor treatments that won't be as punishing. He's already been ten days at the job.

He mixes up enough cement for six tiles, spreads it to the correct thickness and then presses in each tile, levelling as he goes. He does another batch of six, and another. He lays out several rows of tile in the centre of the room, leaving enough space around the perimeter for us to get at the sink, stove and counters. The tiles must sit undisturbed for a couple of days before they can be walked upon, so Albert arranges a barrier of milk crates and 2 x 4's around them. The table Billy made us gets moved around accordingly.

Slowly the house has metamorphosed to be mostly complete. We've had plastic windows for a long time, but they are slowly being replaced with glass. After years of looking at plastic-covered windows that create a permanent fog, it shocks me to look out the window and see the garden and the sea beyond. When I'm in the bathroom I open the window and lean out to inhale garden perfume, a delicious odour of heated earth, salty sea wrack from the low tide foreshore, green growing things. One element I will miss about the plastic windows is that sound carries extremely well through them. We've often heard clearly the bell-tone howling of wolves or the guttural growls of sea lions splashing about. Some nights I've heard the hooting call of two different owls. There are pygmy owls here, western screech owls, great horned, barn and saw-whet owls. It sure sounded like a dialogue, the two owls communicating. Or maybe not. Maybe they were just two lonely voices in the wilderness saying, "I'm here."

Certainly eagles communicate with each other, and ravens are positively amorous. Down on the foreshore a pair sits face to face, bill rubbing bill, making soft gutteral noises for over twenty minutes. Definitely kissing. There aren't a lot of salmon around these days, and the eagles are supplementing their diet with birds. What a lot of energy they expend, flying with their great wingspan after agile gulls. I was down on my knees poking about in the garden a few days ago and looked up to see an eagle with a strange white triangular shape clutched in its talons, a gull. I've also seen an eagle hovering over and dive-bombing a female hooded merganser. The poor thing was exhausted, paddling around trying to evade the big bird's aerial attacks. When I approached her in my boat, instead of flying away in a burst of "running on water" she considered me the lesser of two evils and stayed near. I hung about for five or ten minutes until the eagle flew off. I know I'm interfering with nature, the law of the survival of the fittest, but I'm "nature" too.

Sometimes we forget that we are not separate from nature. At the end of the last school year, our teacher, Rena Sweeney, asked some adults to participate in the "Predator, Prey" game the kids play. Clio's father, Eric, got to be "Disease," and Rena assigned me the role of "Mother Nature." It's an active game with a lot of running and screaming as the kids play the different roles of predator and prey in the natural food chain. Rena assigns them each an animal identity. Running through the woods by the school, their job is to find stashes of "chips" or "vouchers" that signify food, water, disease, death, etc. I, Mother Nature, possessed the power to heal or not, to give or take life. The "prey" kids ran to me to save themselves from a "predator." I reminded them that Mother Nature doesn't necessarily always save a life, but they looked so skeptical at this news, I gave that up and just saved everybody who sought me out. So much more fun than having organized races or sports days. The kids are all different ages anyway, so races don't work well, except for team events like wheelbarrow races.

Mother Nature decides to mess with us now, giving Albert a little nudge just for the heck of it. The kitchen floor is proving to be a tough go and he takes a break from it for a day or two. Our friend Ron Turner, whom we haven't seen for months, radios and I invite him for dinner.

Ron brings his new girlfriend, Kathleen Cooper, a nurse, with him. Kathleen tells me she is apprehensive about travelling in small boats so the voyage to Echo Bay is a big effort for her. She enjoys it, though, as long as the weather stays pleasant. Albert doesn't eat much and is quiet during dinner, although there's nothing unusual about that especially, when there are three expert talkers in the room. Replete with dinner and good conversation, Ron and Kathleen putz off to tie up at the dock in Echo Bay.

In the night Albert awakes, sits up.

"I can't breathe," he says, putting his hand on his chest.

"Do you want me to go get Kathleen?"

"Yes," he says. Something is truly wrong. He'd never have disturbed her for any trivial reason. I leap out of bed, throw on my clothes and rush to my boat. It's velvet black, surprisingly warm. Sheet lightning embroiders the northwards horizon and a stiff breeze raises little slapping waves. No time to find a hat, the wind lifts the hair off my face. It smells resinous, like fir pitch and warm land. I can't go fast; I can barely see the darkness of the landmass to starboard as I head for the point to Echo Bay.

I secure my boat beside *Kvitsoy*, bound in the doorway.

"Kathleen, wake up, I need you." Immediately she swings her legs over the side of the bunk in the galley, pulls on her clothes and stands, ready to go. Ron grunts, waking more slowly, and I brief him quickly.

"I'll fire up *Kvitsoy* and see you in a few minutes," he mutters. Kathleen climbs into my speedboat. I hand her a life jacket and pull away from the dock. I run fast this time, as if guided by an unseen light.

Once we get home, Kathleen sends me in search of Aspirin for Albert, who looks wan and grey. After a couple of hours, he falls asleep.

"I'm pretty sure he's had a heart attack, Yvonne. You should go to bed now, he's okay. We'll go to Port McNeill in the morning." When Kathleen hugs me, my eyes fill with hot tears.

In the morning Al's colour is pink again, and he claims, "I'm fine, I feel fine."

"I've already spoken to Dr. Yeomans, and he's expecting you," insists Kathleen. Glowering, Albert fires up *Miss Jenny*. The four of us go to Port McNeill, with Albert repeating all the way how fine he is.

At the hospital the doctor says he must stay the night under observation. Kathleen offers me a bed. The next day Ron and I run *Miss Jenny* home, since Albert's hospital stay has now extended to several days. Late at night he is flown by jet to Victoria, and on his birthday, February 20, he has two stents installed in his heart to widen a congenital narrowing. Three weeks later, a lot of people help to get him home, and the recovery begins. A heart attack is always a shock, not only to the one who has it but also to the one who loves the one who has it. I'm impressed and grateful for the level of care he received and the swiftness with which it happened. I'll forever be thankful to Kathleen, without whose courage and competency I might no longer have my sweetheart.

For sure, there'll be no more ceramic tile floors.

Memorial For Sharon

A SWIFT SPRING AND SUMMER PASS, September glows, yet winter looms behind the golden leaves. The garden demands all my attention, and between harvesting the herbs and vegetables, fishing, smoking and canning I am going dawn 'til dusk. When I do sit for five minutes these days, I find myself missing the comfort of older women. Often I take Catherine Nelson, Eric's mother, out to puddle around in my boat or over to have tea with Yvonne Proctor. The two of them take turns telling stories. I love listening and laugh so hard. Women have a different slant on things. Many of Catherine's and Yvonne's stories revolve around domestic things, small events that have significance in their lives or their children's lives. Usually the funniest, the most ridiculous involve things their husbands did, or tried to do, that went wrong. Yvonne's favourite, "He doesn't understand everything he knows," covers either husbandly or neighbourly screw-ups, and her cooking critique, "She couldn't parboil shit for a Chicago bum," is devastating.

Men's stories are mostly about other men, their working life, or hunting, motors or fishing. That's also true for painters. There aren't many male artists who have chosen a simple domestic scene as a subject, or mothers and children. There are few painters, period, who have chosen mothers and children as subject matter. Mary Cassatt springs to mind, of course. Painting women and children was thought to be sentimental and not an "important" subject; it's still that way. Yet the mother/child bond is arguably the most significant bond any human being forms with another, and possibly the connection that most deeply informs and shapes our lives, for good or ill. Worthwhile, weighty subject matter to me, and more compelling than paintings of dead hares, partridges, or a string of fish.

I've been looking through my photographs of people, thinking about painting a series of portraits. I notice many friends who have enriched my life, many no longer with us. I unearth a few good photographs of my friend Sharon Rogers from early fishing trips with Albert. The best one is just Sharon, with her beautiful gap-toothed smile, wearing a t-shirt with "Big Blue" emblazoned on the front. That's what Chris had called her, in acknowledgment of her integrity and personality. It was also her personal radio call sign.

Broken by the loss of Sharon and their son, Matthew, Chris disappeared, surfacing only briefly once or twice over the years. When I ran into Deborah Murray in the produce section of the grocery store a couple of months ago, she told me she and Craig had a plaque made several years ago to commemorate Sharon. Every year since, Deborah said, they'd talk about having a service and attaching the plaque to the rock at the entrance to Turnbull Cove. And every year, the opportunity slipped away because the service has to be in September and summer is the busy season. Deb told me they'd finally connected with the *Coastal Messenger*, the Christian mission boat that visits everyone on the coast at least once a year. Roy Getman, fondly known as "Uncle Roy," agrees to conduct a service and a date is set.

I've worried over the years about Dustin and Miranda, Sharon's children from her first marriage. Periodically I'd get an update from Theda or Logan. Dustyn has a tile and flooring business in White Rock near Logan's home. So now I get his cell phone number from Theda, call to tell him there is going to be a memorial service for his mother and brother Matthew, finally, after what? Is it fourteen years? Can you make it to Port McNeill, I ask. He can, and Miranda, too, and both of their partners.

Sunday, September 26, dawns golden and sunny. Brightness spills from the sky. Theda is with us. As we rush around preparing to depart,

255

memories of our times in Turnbull Cove and Nepah Lagoon crowd in. It was to Turnbull Cove in 1985 that Albert suggested I bring the kids with me, to visit him on the boat. Easter break we'd flown in to Turnbull Cove on the Orca Air Beaver to stay with him. We'd spent many happy days with Sharon, Chris and Matt, and attended the Murrays' Easter party at Nimmo Bay.

Sharon and Chris had a float house in those days, two trailers joined together sitting on a big log float, the whole thing set up in the shelter of Turnbull Cove. On the large front deck Sharon had pots and planters and a wide array of flowers, vegetables and herbs. She was so proud of her little float garden and supportive of my efforts when we got our own float house trailer from Hopetown in 1987. Sharon was always so welcoming, she'd want to know what books I was reading and have some to exchange. We did crossword puzzles together while we cooked, and she taught me how to make "boat bread" in a small pressure cooker. She filled me in, in a gentle way, on coastal protocols such as not using a lot of expensive propane to heat water that can be heated on a woodstove. She kept me up to date on the affairs of other people in the neighbourhood and did so in the nicest way. When disharmony raised its ugly head, she took pains to let me know that it was all good between her and me.

Sharon is one of those people who spring to mind whenever I go around my garden, and a garden tour was part of our visiting ritual. It was in her garden boxes I first saw monkey face flowers, with their buttery blooms. All over my garden now, they spring forth freely and enjoy the additional nourishment they don't get on a barren rock.

The memorial service is moving, tearful, joyful. It feels like the closing of a circle, this return to Turnbull Cove to see Deborah and Craig, to see Miranda and Dustyn and to reminisce about their brother Matthew and mother Sharon, and to remember how funny and generous and loyal she was.

Inside the quiet of Turnbull Cove, *Coastal Messenger* is anchored with Henry and Julie Speck's boat, *Gwa' was Provider*, and Murray's boat, *The Dance*, rafted on each side. We bring *Miss Jenny* alongside *The Dance*.

The company gathers and Roy ferries us to the shore in three trips. He and his crew have already bolted and glued the plaque to the rock, so we wander about for a few minutes while Roy brings chairs for Henry and Julie. Roy conducts the service eloquently, reminding us of the circumstances of Sharon's death, of Matthew and the pilot, Syl. We'll never know exactly what happened, only that it was foggy, and the plane disappeared. On the rock where we perch, remembering, the sun shines warm. The sea ripples, bouncing dizzying reflections off the water. I think about Sharon and where life takes us and how quickly and brutally those we love can be wrenched from our embrace.

Georgia and Clifton Murray sing with great emotion and beauty a song they'd prepared. Theda sings, too, creating in the moment a heartfelt song of remembrance for Sharon. Some of us tell stories. We laugh and cry and hug a lot. I hope Sharon knows somehow that her children came through okay.

Sharon's children and friends gather to remember her. Roy Getman (far right on rock) from *Coastal Messenger* listens, with the others, to Henry Speck's (left) memories of Sharon.

We part, with more hugs all around. Such warmth in the heart lingers a while and it colours the rest of our day. Just being there was, as Billy calls it, a trip down memory lane.

We leave Turnbull Cove and take *Miss Jenny* back to the entrance to Nepah Lagoon. The lagoon is a place Al fished for many years, and our best visit with him before we moved here was spent in the hot stillness of this long narrow body of water. Inside the waters of the lagoon, the sea is warm in the summer. Once they overcame their initial fear, Theda and Logan swam several times a day, jumping off the side of the boat repeatedly, or off the rigging. They swam, as did I, in three hundred feet of water and when they told their friends in White Rock, no one believed them.

A tidal narrows has a dramatic flow sequence. Nepah's only entrance is long and narrow. When the lagoon is full of water and the tide is ebbing, a torrent pours forth into Kenneth Passage. It's a waterfall that starts small but swiftly increases in height as the tide drops. When the tide turns from ebb to flood, the water level outside the lagoon rises, decreasing the height of the waterfall, until the water outside the lagoon is the same level as the water inside. This is the best moment to scoot in. While the tide continues to rise past the point of level water outside the lagoon, inside the entrance, a maelstrom of furiously seething water boils around with nowhere to go. The waterfall now begins to grow as the rising tide fills the lagoon. The configuration of rocks on the bottom combined with an in-flooding tide can create seven- or eight-foot-high standing waves. I've never seen it like that but Al has; he scared the liver out of himself and Ted after an impulsive decision to come back home to make peace with me after an angry departure. He pointed the bow of *John* into the standing waves, put the throttle down and they were airborne a couple of times as they bounced their way up and out of the lagoon.

Yvonne Proctor told us her family was living in a float house here when she was born. The entrance was unnavigable when her mother went into labour, and the doctor was not able to get in to deliver her.

Now, the lagoon has almost filled to an even water level inside and out. Al, judging the moment to be just right this afternoon, puts the "pedal to the metal." We motor through the narrows over boulders as big as houses, and through the Roaring Hole Rapids (there's a clue). Whew! Albert is red-faced with the fierce focus required to keep the boat on course. Theda and I can hardly keep from jumping up and down, squealing about the size of the boulders visible below us.

The current slackens, masses of kelp undulate in lazy amber ribbons towards the inner lagoon, and then, whoosh, we are in. We drift slowly. The kelp stills, settles, but ever so subtly the waters begin to shift direction. The amber ribbons circle leisurely, then lengthen in the pull of the turning tide, stretching out as the current changes direction and the waters begin to pour out. When the tide turns fully to outflow, we go with it, effortlessly sweeping out of the narrows with the pressing current. Albert turns the bow towards home.

I've already completed one of what I plan as a series: depictions of the ancient rock paintings that stain the stone cliffs of this area. I'm fascinated by their mysterious iconography. I like the concept of making a painting of a painting and becoming part of the vast continuum of time. Our route homewards takes us past several of these rock paintings. The first one is in Kenneth Passage. The steep sides of these shores descend hundreds of feet, so it is easy to pull in close alongside what we call the "Monkey Face" image for me to shoot photos.

All along the north shore of Penphrase Passage we travel, as close to the cliffside as the bottom permits. In this fashion we locate several paintings that are obscured by foliage. There are certain similarities to the painting sites and once I note these, it becomes easier to make an educated guess as to where they might be found. We watch for these characteristics: a sloped wall of white or light-coloured rock that leans slightly out at the top, and a ledge below the wall, for good footing and access at high tide. In this way, motoring along in the golden autumn sunshine, we end our memorial-for-Sharon day, but never our memories of her.

Yvonne P.'s Legacy

SCENE THROUGH A WIDE WINDOW: Vancouver Island mountains behind the lights of a small town and a harbour. It's the view from First Street in Sointula, near Rough Bay. I'm on a painting getaway as Albert struggles to complete our hot water heating system, another house project that is running true to the maxim "However long you think it will take, double it and add thirty." I'm snugged into a spacious B & B room that Dani Tribe and Lionel Lewis have added on to their home on the waterfront. So this month Dani is my angel.

Many of the old boathouses and ways that so distinctly epitomize Sointula's Finnish pioneer heritage are crumpling into piles of shattered sticks. Wonderful painting material is everywhere. My first few days here, I walk around in a sensation cloud, processing how to paint the calligraphy of colours that coalesce into nameable forms. In spite of a bit of rain, I take the easel and canvas to Bere Point to paint plein air. I'm half-done sketching in the basics when the wind blows the canvas off the easel. Back at the B & B, like a bird in its nest, I paint from my window overlooking the waterfront.

To get my blood going, I walk up the road to Choyce's, where Joyce Corbett displays my work in her shop by the ferry dock. I walk to the Co-op to buy snacks and wine, to the library to read or do e-mail, stop at the Living Oceans office for a brief visit with Oonagh or Thea or Lori Anderson. Walking to such services and social warmth is a big change from my home routines where nothing is simple to access. I'm sad to hear from Lori that Kayak Bill has died, alone and ill up the coast on the Goose Islands. Lori shows me an hour-long video made by Bill's old climbing buddies from Alberta. It consists of footage of him climbing various mountains and rock faces as well as some film that Bill shot of others climbing. There's a bit from a video he wanted to produce and star in, about a guy who found the soullessness of the city unbearable and went to wilderness as a remedy—which, of course, was the path Bill took in his own life. Tears overflow as Lori and I watch. It's been many years since my magical three-day visit with him and I feel dislocated, watching the living man laughing, talking and gesturing on film. I'm sad I didn't know in time to attend Bill's memorial service and thankful to Lori for the opportunity to remember him this way.

The last few days in Sointula I paint on the beach every afternoon. Even the wind hibernates in the February cold, and days of freezing sunshine offers perfect painting conditions. The tide shifts to low in the afternoon as the sun sets, saturating the shoreline with a patina of antique gold. The timeworn boat sheds and busy Tarkanen Marina stand graceful and dignified in the lambent glow. My painting kit is simple: a 10" x 14" sheet of watercolour paper taped onto a drawing board, two brushes and my "jewel box" palette, warm vibrant reds and yellows that glow when placed beside cool blues. Everything I need fits in an old suitcase and it's easy to find a log or large rock to perch upon. For one boat-shed painting, I find a good view beside a herring skiff and drag several feet of heavy bowline out into a coil to cushion me. The urge to paint pulses down my arm to my fingertips. Every day I feel more confident about expressing the essence of these old buildings by the sea. Juicy violet, sweet rose and vibrant gold melt into a wet area; I love how they light up those blues.

The end of a beautiful month is imminent. Albert has triumphed over the heating system and noticed that he misses me. I want to visit Yvonne P., who is not well, and the garden needs me desperately. Daffodils stunted by the overarching branches of the 'Nova Zembla' rhododendron are begging to be moved, and primroses sit in small pots longing to be rooted. I need to prepare for the voracious flocks of golden-crowned

sparrows that will mow down the greening shoots of peas and other baby plants. Our next house project is to lay a plywood floor over the diagonal sheathing in both the painting and the pottery studios. That'll require a huge amount of packing, shifting and moving of plywood and furniture. I'm eager to get at it. Once all the baseboard heating elements are in we can retire the indoor heater and activate the outdoor boiler. Clean heat!

I'm over to see Yvonne P. and Billy when I get home. Yvonne looks a bit smaller, is having more trouble breathing. She nods out sitting at the table, just has a little snooze for a few minutes. On town trips I wait with her while she stops to rest, hands on her knees, gasping. Finally, after a short stint in Port McNeill Hospital, the word is out, she's not getting enough oxygen. The solution is an oxygen machine, which requires electricity to pump the life-giving gas into Yvonne's lungs night and day. Billy puts in an expensive solar panel and battery bank so the generator doesn't have to run 24/7. The doctor gives her six months to live but she holds on for over two and a half years.

I visit Yvonne regularly for a cup of tea or a glass of sherry, and once a week I shampoo and condition her cloud of fine white hair and set it in pin curls. This is a tiring business for her, and I try to make it as painless as possible. Although she's weakened by lungs damaged by years of working in a paper bag factory as a young woman, Yvonne has more breath than ever for her lightning wit. One day, she's sitting back in the big rocker Billy bought her, after a hair wash and curl. I tell her how I heard on the CBC that we use 40 per cent more energy when we're using our brain to think than we do when we're simply working. Billy comes in the door, hungry after a long morning's work, and I say to Yvonne, "Oh, here's Billy now. You better give him a big lunch to keep his brain working." Quicker than a heron after a fish, she strikes, "Ha. There's not enough food in the whole house for that." We crack up and the rest of the lunch hour goes by in much the same vein as we remind Billy to stop laughing and eat up: he needs to get his brain working.

Yvonne didn't make it to her seventy-fifth birthday on November 14. On November 6, Billy took us all to Port McNeill on *Ocean Dawn* to see her at the hospital and say goodbye. Shortly thereafter, Joanie phoned Billy to tell him Yvonne had slipped away in the night. A month later, Bill Mackay brings the *Naiad Explorer* out to Echo Bay to transport the entire community, as one in our sadness and sense of loss, to Port McNeill for Yvonne's well-attended memorial service.

I miss Yvonne. No one has ever made me laugh so hard and so often. She was a match for Billy in her generosity with food, support and money. Yvonne, like Billy, purchased several paintings from me in the beginning hard years, as gifts for her daughters or for herself. She bought dozens of money orders to send off to charitable organizations, thus supporting both the charities and the local post office. She's the one who quietly provided the coffee, milk and sugar for the big do's at the community hall.

There's an empty place at the Proctors' table, and sadness in my heart.

Epilogue

I HAVE SPENT TWENTY-SIX YEARS HERE on the north shore of Gilford Island. Some things have stayed the same, a lot more has changed, most noticeably, populations of inhabitants—two- and four-legged, winged and finned.

Cougars are a clear and present danger these days. Five or six years ago, a big male cougar attacked and killed one of Bruce McMorrans two dogs. Bruce's home is cozied in the forest, beautiful, well tended yet woodsy, plenty of cover for a creeping cat, unfortunately. His son Solomon had just returned from the biffy as the dogs began screaming below the house. The cougar hung around its kill long enough for the game warden to make it out from Port McNeill. After he shot the cougar, he told Bruce and his wife, Josée, there can be up to seven females in the territory of one male. Two more cougars were killed near Bruce's place over the next two years. Billy has seen the big tawny cats dozens of times on his property. There's not much cover at his place, but the cougars are attracted by the chickens and the deer hanging around, munching on fallen apples and the leaves of the cottonwood trees.

Our own fenced yard has been invaded on several occasions. Albert was sitting down by the back door one day, and looked up to see a tail disappear into the woodshed. Wondering whose dog it was, Al got up, looked into the woodshed and then peered under the house. An

unusually dark cat face turned to look back at him. The creature saun-
tered out from under the other side of the house and left by the garden
gate I'd forgotten to close. The incident gave me shivers; less than half
an hour before I'd been down on my knees weeding in the garden plot.
Fair game. This cat was interesting for its extremely dark coat. Billy saw
a chocolate-coloured cougar on Broughton Island once as well, so we
know they are not all yellow-brown in colour.

A short-lived half-inch snowfall in April 2011 revealed cougar tracks
all over our yard. Heading out the door to take my mail to Echo Bay, I
skidded to a halt before I even got off the front steps. Albert and I traced
the passage of two cats all through our garden, a mom and a young one.
We followed the tracks around the yard from where the two had entered
through a loose picket, walked by the raspberry patch, and along the
front path to the bottom of the studio steps. They had retraced their
path back to the dock, jumped down onto the foreshore rocks, trod the
sharpest ridge of the rocks for seventy-five feet, then slipped away into
the forest. It was the same pair, we surmised, that we'd heard yeowling
on the rock below the house one cold night in February. Al had shot the
gun over their heads and the last I saw of them, then, was a straight-up
yard-long tail above two running legs lit up in the flashlight beam.

"*Ocean Dawn, Sea Rose.*" I radioed Billy.

"Zero six," he answered.

"There's cougar tracks in the snow all over our yard," I told him,
"two sets, a big one and a small one. They headed for Shoal Harbour."

"Holy Christ," he said. "I'll go look around and get back to you."

Later he called to tell me he had found the same set of two and a third
larger set of tracks at his place.

These cougars need a lot to eat. There are no charming but disgust-
ingly messy river otter families playing on my dock on foggy mornings
anymore, a solitary mink hunts near our dock and I haven't seen a raccoon in two years. The wolves that used to serenade us soulfully don't
howl much on the island anymore. The expanding cougar population
may have driven them out to other smaller islands.

DRAWN TO SEA

It's a lot of predatory cats to be worried about, and we are. We breathed easy when there were no resident cougars on Gilford Island, but now we know there are several. Their presence has changed things for us. Instead of feeling safe and secure when I land on a small island these days, I'm always on the alert.

Bird species and populations are showing marked differences as well. You get interesting results when you keep accurate records of birds on a regular basis. Last year I noticed some birds out front of the house that looked like common mergansers but weren't. I went for the bird book and identified them as red-breasted mergansers, a bird so uncommon here that I'd only seen one once. Winter of 2011, there were over a dozen puddling about in our bay for weeks. Hundreds of rhinocerous auklets have appeared over the last five years. Billy saw the first half-dozen on his log salvage run one morning, and the population has expanded rapidly. These auklets are feeding on a great influx of sand lance, and at dusk can be seen flying off down Cramer Pass, with six or eight shiny fish hanging out of their bills. They are bearing the fish to their young on the Storm Islands, forty miles away. Oyster-catchers occupy territory closer to the open ocean, but last winter I counted twenty-seven, an extraordinary number, on the rock near Steep Island.

While some bird species are increasing in number, or shifting their territory to follow food sources, others are declining. The bluff where hundreds of guillemots once bred is far quieter these days. Hundreds of Barrow's goldeneye used to arrive in the late fall and spend the winter entertaining me with their antics.

The salmon we've worked so hard to enhance and protect are still at risk. Increased logging on the inner slopes and steep sides of the Viner River valley has continued to degrade the river as habitat for spawning chum and pink salmon. Salmon farms in the area threaten ocean-growing fry with death by sea lice. Our community efforts to restore numerous creeks to their former vitality has had mixed results. We never know whether the numbers will be next to none, as in 2010, or inexplicably high, like the 10,000 returning chum counted in Viner River in 2008, but at least we have had some big-run years again. Due to budget cutbacks,

Fisheries and Oceans Canada contracts Mainland Enhancement of Salmonoid Species Society to do the work once done by Fisheries officers: counting the returning spawning salmon in the fall of the year. M.E.S.S.S. no longer grows chum and coho to enhance the stocks, hoping our years of effort and the healing over of logging scars will blossom into increasingly healthy returns of salmon in the Broughton Archipelago. With only a small population here now, it's proving difficult to find volunteers to take on enhancement activities. It's hard to think it might have been all for nothing, but at least we tried.

As for the question lying unanswered in my mind for so many years, researcher Victoria Braithwaite in her recent book, *Do Fish Feel Pain?*, recounts studies by scientists showing that fish do in fact feel pain, and furthermore appear to have cognitive abilities also seen in lions, dolphins, hawks and chimpanzees. I'm not surprised by their findings; it was only a matter of time. The real mystery is why it's taken humans so long to ask the question.

The effects of climate change on BC's five species of wild salmon are of consuming interest to most British Columbians. A slight rise in the temperature of BC's streams and rivers due to global warming may be having a negative impact on returning salmon. Researchers have discovered that the handsome blue Chilko River salmon travel through a wider temperature variation than other salmon do. The temperature of the glacier-fed streams they migrate home to is much colder than the Pacific Ocean where they spend most of their lives. Their genes are better adapted for these extreme conditions, and researchers are hoping what they learn about these "super salmon" can be used to help other salmon adapt to increasing temperatures. Billy wonders if the Wakeman River salmon may be similar to the Chilko River salmon, since they, too, travel through the warm waters of the mainland inlets and up into glacier-fed lakes to spawn.

Other populations also ebb and flow. Jackie Hildering of the Marine Education and Research Society has been tracking humpback whale populations. She reports fourteen individuals were identified in 2004. This number increased by the summer of 2011 to a high of sixty-five

individuals in the Blackfish/ Broughton Archipelago area. These whales show remarkable "site fidelity," returning each year and staying the full feeding season. We see them frequently out in front of our house, and on a town trip with Billy one day in September, we counted fourteen (fourteen!) at the White Cliff Rocks. An exploding population of a giant marine mammal is a notable turnaround from the days of the whaling industry.

Killer whale populations are shaky, since often the first-born babies don't survive long. Studies are underway to try to understand the causes. Thousands of Pacific white-sided dolphins are seen all year round in the Broughton Archipelago, and they are wonderful to watch, but they are targeting the wavering stocks of local-run salmon. Groups of anywhere from twenty-five to several hundred dolphins herd schools of pink or coho into small bays and then consume them rapidly. If there were plenty of salmon, this would be fine, but currently a run of only 300 to 400 might spawn in Shoal Harbour Creek or Scott Cove, and they can be wiped out in an hour. It's hard to watch a phalanx of leaping dolphins charge into our bay and see pink salmon bound for Bond Sound or Knight Inlet springing out of the water ahead of them, hiding under the float to survive. Most of them don't.

The human population has declined steadily over the years. When we moved here in 1986, our family of four brought the year-round resident total from thirty-two to thirty-six. The total went up to almost fifty for a few years when Claudia Maas and Pierre Alarie moved in, and Bill and Hiromi Ford, along with a few other families for short periods. When we arrived, Theda and Logan were children number twelve and thirteen at the school, but enrollment declined from there. The school board kept our school open for just five children for years, trying hard to accommodate the unique and expensive needs of a school in a water-access only community. The inevitable closure happened when the last group of children was ready for high school and Hannah and Chris Bennett's two new ones, Robin and Stephen, were still pre-schoolers.

Currently only eight or nine people reside year round in or near Echo Bay. Another half-dozen spend at least half the year here. All the babies whose births I celebrated with a homemade quilt have grown up and gone away: Marieke Knierim, the first to graduate and begin university studies; her brother, Russell; Clio Nelson; Lucas Maas-Alarie; Anna, Beth and Billy Ford. Robin and Stephen Bennett brighten our community, but they are only here part of the year. Four-year-old Salix moved in next door with her parents recently, but whether they stay in the community only time will tell. The lack of a school is significant, although Salix's mother, Zephyr, was herself home-schooled. Salix's cheerful father, Cody, a welcome member of the community, is the only male under forty-five, and he's ready to help with anything.

At seventy-eight, Billy, the last of the old-timers, is going strong. He's one of the lucky ones who, through good genetic fortune combined with healthy living (no booze or drugs and lots of pork fat), has no major health problems. A ten-year supply of firewood packs his woodshed, and a constant stream of three to four thousand visitors, most of them seniors themselves, arrives at his museum each year, between April and October. As always, Billy is more than ready to help those who are helping themselves. He's still the go-to guy for moving houses on or off the land, providing boomsticks, building a float or doing a salvage job of a sunken vessel. He roars out in his speedboat every morning, rain or shine, to see what he can see in the way of salvageable logs. He's especially eager when it rains, since the potential for a big slide is heightened. I see him from my window every morning as I write or paint, ripping out of his bay, headed for Tribune. As usual, I send a shot of gratitude his way. Thanks, Billy. Thanks for everything.

Almost my entire adult life has been spent in this place, a wild place, marked by humans past and present, and their attempts to wrest a living from the substance of the earth. Our three-storey house has risen where once blowdowns and salal ruled. It's always going to be a battle as the salal and salmonberry relentlessly struggle to regain their territory. Our house is not yet finished. Economics, heart attacks, and increasing issues of age have caused the vision of completion to dance on ahead of us. It could happen one day, but it might not.

I move through our home, feeling under my feet the springy warmth

of the fir floor Albert painstakingly laid, and open the French doors to the sundeck. The view is fabulous—a million-dollar view, says Billy—and I often sleep out on the deck under the night sky, particularly during the August rain of stars. When I walk in the garden with Albert, I smell the roses, gather blueberries, pick a cucumber for dinner, and promise, "tomorrow" to potted plants begging to be earthed. The studio space invites me in to paint, write, or cut and paste collage images. I don't look up at the unfinished ceiling. It'll get done. Instead, I work with the photographic material and drawings from my coastal journeys. Hope Island, Xumdaspe, never let me go. When I came upon photographs of ancestor poles taken from Hope Island in 1956 and set up at the Museum of Anthropology at UBC, I knew they were the elements needed to complete the image. I placed them in the sky above the treetops and over the bay. The ancestor figures are not cheerful or lighthearted, they sombrely gaze

Sea Rose makes the islands and inlets so accessible to me, it is my vehicle to independence, my ticket to ride, the sole significant factor that enables me to really "live" fully in the Broughton Archipelago.

out at the world, standing on or holding human skulls; one holds a tiny naked man. We're all part of the endless ladder of life, born of our ancestors, born of the sea and the sky.

Eight fishing seasons of crushing eggshells turned into a lifelong habit. They biodegrade in the garden faster that way, although I'm not convinced the wind witches are deterred. I still love to rip around in my boat, tie off to some kelp and paint. In recent years we've hosted young travellers, WWOOFers—members of World Wide Opportunities on Organic Farms—who've helped us with the weeding and the firewood pile. They are such a blessing. Making it across the strait to doctors and dentists is, as always, weather dependent, and emergencies can be fatal. We've had our share of emergency trips but have been lucky so far and survived them all.

The double-edged sword, the half-full, half-empty glass, the paradox of everything is ever present. Living in wilderness has taught me to stop complaining. It's a wonderful life: so what if my ambitions have exceeded my grasp. That's how it goes. Living here has taught me to pay attention to the messages, both external and internal, and to trust myself. In nature's solitude I've sought my own wisdom, my own voice and inspiration as one being among many, each with our gift to offer. When the world and the affairs of humans look dark, as they do so often, when optimism and gratitude flag, I gather the painting gear, jump in the boat and point the bow into the wind. I seek to stir up the creativity colouring every aspect of my being. Creativity is in the mind, yes, and in the breath and the eye. It springs forth in the body's kinetic energy. It is rooted in the soul and in our senses.

Art can be put to many uses, expressed in as many ways as there are people. While using art for social comment, for revolution or change, is often necessary, I choose not to be the bearer of bad news. My message is of the magnificent splendor of creation, the healing available to be found in wilderness. This world is the place we get to *live* in and *be conscious* of. I can't get over it. I don't *want* to get over it. I live to be excited, thrilled, knocked off my pins by another magical natural event that glorifies my soul. I want that for everyone.

Acknowledgements

THANK YOU, MOM, for nurturing my awareness of the beauties of nature, opening the door to the library of everything, and buying me artist quality paints when I was fourteen years old.

Thanks to you, Billy Proctor, for so many unforgettable expeditions both near and far away. The world would be a better place if everyone was a neighbour like you.

Theda and Logan, you two were the best birthday gifts a woman could have. Thank you for being mine, and coming on the adventure.

Special thanks, Paula Wild, for your magically timely writer's workshop ad and all your encouragement. Your advice to find a "writing buddy" really raised the bar when I found one, thank you, Nikki Van Schyndel. You're the best! And thanks to you, Vici Johnstone, for turning a bunch of words into a book, and having so much faith in me.